CHILDREN WHO HAVE LIVED BEFORE

TRUTZ HARDO

Children
Who Have
Lived Before

Reincarnation Today

FOREWORD
BY ELISABETH KÜBLER-ROSS, M.D., D.D.

RIDER

LONDON · SYDNEY · AUCKLAND · JOHANNESBURG

First published in Germany in 2000
by Verlag Die Silberschnur GmbH, Güllesheim
under the title *Reinkarnation Aktuell.*
First published in the United Kingdom
by the C.W. Daniel Company Limited.
This edition published in 2005 by Rider,
an imprint of Ebury Publishing, Random House,
20 Vauxhall Bridge Road, London SW1V 2SA

www.randomhouse.co.uk

Addresses for companies within The Random House Group Limited can be found at:
www.randomhouse.co.uk/offices.htm

The Random House Group Limited Reg. No. 954009

The publisher and author are grateful to Praegar Publishers, Westport, Connecticut, USA, for permission to quote extensively from their publication *Where Reincarnation and Biology Intersect* by Ian Stevenson, M.D.

Translated from the German by Bridget Jenkin and Ulla Schmid
Index compiled by Ann Griffiths

Designed by Ward Partnership, Saffron Walden

A CIP catalogue record for this book is available from the British Library

ISBN 9781844132980

Penguin Random House is committed to a sustainable future for our business, our readers and our planet. This book is made from Forest Stewardship Council® certified paper.

Printed and bound in Great Britain by Clays Ltd, Elcograf S.p.A.

Contents

Foreword

Elisabeth Kübler-Ross

At the end of my life I get to know that Professor Ian Stevenson proved reincarnation to be a fact. I am very delighted that at the end of the second millennium this truth is finally scientifically proven. For I am very much convinced that we will have a better world in the third millennium if mankind integrates reincarnation including the karmic law in its thinking and acting. Most probably I am not going to live that long to see this happening but I will follow up from another realm of existence what's happening on earth and I will be happy about the changes in mankind's thinking.

For me the belief in reincarnation and in the Law of Karma is for a long time already a matter of course. I am delighted to read in this book by Trutz Hardo that he presents the reader convincing evidence on reincarnation that will even give the toughest sceptic much to think about. I hope that finally many readers will learn about the truth of reincarnation and thus integrate this truth in their thinking and acting for their own benefit and for the benefit of all mankind.

Introduction

In this book you will find 33 case histories from children who remember their past lives. In most of these cases these memories are confirmed by people who knew the person the child claims to have been, and who are still alive when the reborn child remembers the past life in question. The events surrounding the actual recognition of and reunion with past relations are often very moving. In most cases these children are accepted as being the reincarnation of a deceased family member, relative, neighbour or friend, purely on the grounds of their conclusive statements. Most cases of past-life memories occur in countries or among peoples or races that believe in reincarnation. This is closely connected with the fact that parents from these cultures tend to listen to what their children are saying, and help them make contact with the people from their past. Often it is through coincidences that these connections are made possible.

Professor Stevenson discovered many cases of children remembering their past lives. He found these mainly among the following nations and peoples: the Igbo in

Nigeria, the Druses in Lebanon, the Allevites in Turkey, the Indians, the Burmese, the Thai, the Ceylonese, the Brazilians, the West Canadian Indians, and even in the so-called Western countries such as Europe and America. Of course, cases of past-life memories are not limited to those countries. There are cases all over the world, especially among races of shamanic tradition, that is to say races that have not been entirely brainwashed with any type of Christian or Islamic religion. I am referring to the numerous Indian tribes, Eskimos, and especially the Africans, most of which managed not to renounce their ancient traditional beliefs in reincarnation completely, despite islamisation and christianisation. There has been a definite upward trend in the belief in reincarnation in Western countries among those born in the last 40 years. This is due on one hand to the fact that books keep appearing that deal with the subject in a very convincing way; for another, that the generalised search for new values makes people flock to talks and seminars where the lecturers take the existence of reincarnation for granted, in most cases due to 'hands-on' experience of their own gained through meditation or induced regression. Neo-Buddhism has gained a large following especially in the United States, and the effect of the widespread worship of the Dalai Lama, a living example of a man reborn, is becoming more and more noticeable even in the West. Yet all this spread of interest in reincarnation is mainly based on belief or, as many would claim, on an 'inner knowing'.

For the first time in the history of mankind, reincarnation has finally been scientifically proven through the research into this subject – particularly the investigative efforts of Professor Ian Stevenson. Among other examples, this book presents you with a good number of cases researched by Stevenson which offer no other conclusive explanation than that of reincarnation.

This book will make it clear to you that many children know about past lives and are able to give conclusive information about those lives. In many cases this data will now have to be accepted as cogent scientific evidence, even by the world of academia, thanks to the results of Professor Stevenson's research and those of his numerous assistants. The c. 225 cases presented in his extensive work *Reincarnation and Biology* (of which a condensed and richly illustrated version is available entitled *Where Reincarnation and Biology Intersect* – a must-read for anyone publicly speaking about the subject of reincarnation lest he should lost his credibility) are examples of children remembering their past lives. They were all born with birthmarks or even birth deformities, which had no genetic or pre-natal cause. The children's claims are subjected to scientific examination and where children have explicitly named people or places relating to past lives it has frequently been possible to trace them. The result of this is that all (or nearly all) their statements are found to be correct. Stevenson calls these 'solved cases'. These cases account for the most important evidence of reincarnation.

Stevenson gives the following reasons for predominantly dealing with cases of children remember their past lives rather than those of adults.

1 Due to their age children are closer to their previous earth life and therefore find it easier to remember it.
2 Children's minds are not as yet full of knowledge of the past, since they have heard little or nothing about these things and have certainly not read about them either. (Another factor: television was not widely available in Third World countries until the 1980s and can therefore be ruled out as a possible source of information.)
3 Children are not afraid to be ridiculed or seen as stupid.
4 Adults may get real past-life memories mixed up or distorted over a period of time, especially due to wishful thinking.
5 Science cannot reject childish statements as being lies or as having been invented.

For these reasons it is more 'scientific' to work with children, since their statements are closer to the truth. The great pioneer Elisabeth Kübler-Ross M.D. knew this and frankly admitted that children had been her real teachers. Children who remember past lives normally begin to speak about them as soon as they can talk. Their statements are usually about people, things or experiences from their past lives. After the age of four their inner memories gradually seem to dry up and by the time they are nine years old there is hardly an original memory left. What they remember after that is simply what others have said about what they used to say in the past. Even so there are some amazing exceptions such as Joan Grant and Daskalos from Cyprus, who continued to remember their past lives throughout their entire lives.

It is out of the mouth of babes that we have been blessed with the great and eternal truth of reincarnation. Is it not ironical that the world of academe and all the book learning in the West proved incapable of doing the same? The fact that this eternal truth and primordial lore has now been proven by children and once more made available to us, should make us feel extremely humble. It seems that we humans will not attain eternal truths through grandiose, pompous philosophising. Instead, we must acknowledge now that what the children have knowingly declared is much closer to the truth than what the cleverest people, be they theologians, philosophers or even scientists, have dared to come up with. Therefore it is not the intellect that is the measure of all things, but rather knowledge conveyed with innocence and simplicity.

In this book the indisputable proof comes from the mouths of children. Their truth states that there is life after death and that the human soul is reincarnated on earth again and again. The scientists have sought the truth outside, rooting it in the delusions of existence and were thus unable to truly find the path that leads inside.

Sigmund Freud, that most renowned of all researchers into the human soul, for all his 'depth psychology' did not actually penetrate into these inner truths; nor did his colleague, Carl Gustav Jung, do more than just set foot on the threshold.

This book does not 'merely' aim to prove reincarnation through the mouths of children, but endeavours to convey some of the realisations and ideas arising out of those findings. This will include answers to questions such as: how do we behave towards children who speak of their past lives? or: how can we deal with children suffering from a phobia as a result of a past-life trauma? As well as this I have added many comments in order to give those readers open to a broadened spiritual understanding further leads. I have written these comments in italics so that those of you who already know of these things, or are not interested in these remarks, can continue to read about the cases in this book without further delay.

1

Children from all over the world remember past lives

YOU ARE NOT MY REAL MUMMY

The belief in reincarnation existed before the arrival of Christianity in Germany, as in most of the European countries, but has only gradually begun to conquer the European minds in the course of the last centuries. The Germanic people were among those who believed in life after death and repeated lives on Earth. Yet with the spread of Christianity, whose guardians officially banned the concept of reincarnation in the year 553 AD (and even threatened to excommunicate all followers of this belief), the belief in reincarnation became a private matter to be kept extremely secret lest one should fall into the hands of the Inquisition (this Roman Catholic tribunal for the discovery and punishment of heresy viewed any deviance from the Church's dogmas as the devil's work to be categorically combated).

Since the age of enlightenment the belief in reincarnation spread extremely swiftly, especially among those who took a critical view of the Church. An increasing number of German poets including Lessing, Herder, Goethe and Schiller and later right into the 20th century the poets Morgenstern, Werfel, Hesse and many others professed their belief in reincarnation. Even so, public opinion has remained divided by two strictly speaking conflicting views on life. One is the scientific world-view, which denies everything that is not measurable or verifiable any claim to reality whatsoever. The other is the Christian doctrine, deeply rooted in the minds of the people to this day which claims that each soul has only a single life on earth.

These two pillars of 20th-century thinking have become increasingly unstable, since the number of truth seekers adopting belief in reincarnation has been growing continuously. In my estimation, by the end of the 20th century approximately 30 per cent of the German population were convinced of the truth of reincarnation. Another 30 per cent will not deny the possibility of repeated lives on earth. And with the wealth of evidence now available, especially through the works of Professor Stevenson, the latter are certain to become equally dedicated followers of reincarnation by the beginning of the 21st century.

I have not as yet seen any tangible evidence in Germany of a child's statements about a past life having been demonstrably proven, as has been particularly the case in many Asian countries for example. In the past we have not given enough significance to children's statements referring to what could possibly be past lives, mostly dismissing them as wild imaginings of childish minds. With the spread of the idea of reincarnation we will become more sensitive to children's hints concerning past lives they have experienced. Some parents will even encourage their children to tell them more. They will take notes and may even wish to prove the truth of these statements.

Edith, a woman from Berlin who came to me in order to train as a regression therapist, told me the following: initially she had great difficulties with her youngest son Peter. He completely rejected her as his mother, resisting her and being a very difficult child for her to deal with. He flatly refused to be touched by her and when she tried to breastfeed him as a baby he turned his head away. He did not want to drink from her breast unless his hunger was greater than his dislike of her. He provoked her intentionally over a long period of time by not using the potty and wetting his nappy or his bed. When sitting on his potty at the age of two he said to her, 'You have not always been my mummy. I don't love you.' His mother felt very hurt by this.

Instead of being shocked and feeling hurt she could have used this as an opportunity to get closer to the cause of his rejection. When children make these kinds of statements about past lives we should always remember that as they get older these memories are likely to fade. It then becomes more and more difficult to retrieve correct information about their past lives.

Six months later Peter said to her, 'I want to go to my real parents.' Edith believed in past lives and had become used to the fact that her son was remembering a past life and could not accept her as his present mother. She asked him, 'What are your real parents called?' 'My daddy's called Herbert and my mummy Rosalind and you are my wicked auntie.' Edith, unlike many other parents, I suppose, did not punish her son with harsh words of violence for such 'naughty behaviour'. Instead she lovingly explained to him that he was in a different life now, and that she was not his wicked auntie any longer, but his new mummy who loved him very much. As time went by the child's memories of his past life faded, and with them his memories of his wicked aunt. He has now totally accepted Edith as his mother and has told her, 'I love you, Mummy.'

We as adults can learn much if we listen to our children, which is to say, to take them seriously and not ridicule them, which incidentally is very hurtful to a child. A great deal will be said about that in this book. Carol Bowman, who became convinced of the truth in reincarnation through the past-life statements made by her own two children said, 'When small children share their memories with us, they teach us grown-ups something that we have forgotten, namely that life does not end with death.'[1] We will look at her story in greater detail later.

I AM YOUR SISTER, SILVIA

The Swiss healer Peter Singer and I have been friends for some time. I have never met another person in Europe who could see people's auras so clearly and could detect foci of disease or infection with the naked eye. He has run seminars for many years now in which he teaches the participants how to use energies for their own as well as other people's benefit. To demonstrate these energies, he will sometimes ask his participants to stand in front of their chairs while he goes into the room next door. He is then able to leave his body in that room and reappear invisibly to his audience. In this invisible state he is able to gently push the participants into their chairs.

Peter was a friend of the famous German pop singer, Roy Black. They had made an arrangement that the one who died first would give the other a sign as proof that he continues to live on invisibly. On the fifth anniversary of Roy Black's death, Peter woke up, looked at the electric bedside clock, which displayed the days of the week and the month, and suddenly realised, 'Hey Roy, it's the anniversary of your death today, and I still haven't heard a peep from you.' Suddenly he heard a great crash coming from the corridor. Peter jumped out of bed, rushed outside and discovered that the huge framed Alpine landscape had fallen from its nail onto the floor. Yet the nail was still in the wall. How could this have been possible?

One day when we were discussing reincarnation, he told me the following story. In 1990 he was still working in his practice in Goldach in the Saint-Gall canton. One of his clients had talked about her clairvoyant daughter and had told him among other things that she was able to read letters from a distance with the back of the letter facing her. Peter Singer really wanted to get to know this girl. The woman then brought her nine-year-old daughter, Ines, with her on her next visit. Ines watched while Peter was treating her mother. Turning to Peter the girl suddenly said, 'I know you from the past, Peter.' Her mother was shocked and tried to silence her by saying, 'Don't talk to Mr Singer like that. How dare you?'

'But I know him,' she replied. And turning to Peter she continued, 'You were once my brother. I was your sister Silvia.' Her mother reacted in a shocked manner saying, 'Now please stop it!' Her daughter continued, 'I was your sister in your present life, but I died when I was very young. Now I have come back and have a different mother.' Even though Peter had only been three years old at the time, he could well remember his sister Silvia who had died at the age of four and a half. He encouraged her to tell him more about their life together. Ines continued by saying, 'We used to live in the Appenzell canton. That is where I died.' Peter went to the room next door and fetched a photograph and showed it to her face down. 'Your mother tells me that you can read letters with the back facing you. Are you also able to see who is on this picture?' Without thinking Ines answered, 'My mother and my father from the past. They are our parents.' 'What else can you see?' 'Mummy is wearing a white blouse. They are both holding hands.' Everything she said was correct. 'What else do you know about our mother?' 'Mummy joined me some time after my death.' Peter's mother had died in 1978, 20 years after Ines. Then she added, 'We also had an older brother.' She also knew his name. 'I didn't know my other brothers and sisters because they were born later.'

Ines' mother had meanwhile been following their conversation with bated breath. Once more she was speechless about the things her daughter had come up with. Peter encouraged the nine-year-old to describe their parents' house. Everything she said was correct. When asked after their father's profession she said, 'He had a fabric shop. But he also owned a outdoor swimming pool, which was in a valley.' Even this was all correct. Her father really did own a public swimming pool at that time, which provided him with a second income. Peter could no longer doubt the truth of the statements this girl was making. Even so he continued to ask questions, all of which she was able to answer as best she could based on facts from her memories. She also described exactly what happened immediately after her death. 'I saw myself floating above my body. Our mother had suffered a nervous breakdown and I tried to comfort her by telling her, "Mummy you need not fear anything, I am always with you. I will bring many customers into your shop." '

After this Ines often visited her brother from the past and sometimes took part in his seminars. By now she had acquired the gift of automatic writing and was able to channel messages from the invisible world directly to those participating in his seminars. Peter has kept many pages of her communications. For instance, in one of these sessions a deceased craftsman asked Ines to forward his dictated message to his widow. This she did and to her great amazement the message had been written in the handwriting of her deceased husband. Peter once took one of these letters and showed it to a famous graphologist, who said that this handwriting belonged to a very down-to-earth man, possibly a craftsman. Whenever Ines was on a school trip or on holiday with her parents she would send Peter a postcard, which usually began with the words, 'Hello big brother!'

Ines had become well-known in local circles and all sorts of people came to see her, who either wished to contact their deceased relatives and friends, or hoped to gain answers to a variety of problems via her channelled communications. When she was 14 she said to her mother, 'Mum, I am soon going to have a bad accident. A motorbike will hit me on my way back from school and I will be badly hurt. But you need not worry about me because I'm not going to die, even if the doctors tell you that I will not survive.' A few weeks later this accident really happened. Ines was in a coma for a long time and the doctors didn't think she would make it, but as predicted she really did regain consciousness and made a full recovery. Yet something in her had changed. All her psychic abilities had gone.

I asked Peter, who had not been in contact with Ines for some time, to give me her telephone number so that I could find out more about the events that took place in Peter's practice years ago. Peter wanted to ring her himself first, in order to introduce me. He talked to her in person on the telephone and she asked him to tell me to please refrain from calling her, for she was not interested in going back over 'that past business'. She told him that she felt she had been pushed into being a medium and that her psychic abilities had brought her unwanted attention, which was why she now wished to distance herself from it all. Peter said the following about Ines before her accident, 'There was no doubt about the truth of the statements she made at that time.' Yet a critic could claim that maybe she had never been Peter's sister and that she could have tapped into his thoughts due to her psychic powers. At this point we could argue that Peter had not been thinking about the swimming pool when asking her about his father's profession. She had also told him things which he himself could not remember and which he was only able to confirm by talking to his older brother.

THE GIRL WHO PRESENTED THE PRESIDENT
WITH A BUNCH OF FLOWERS IN HER PAST LIFE

In Scandinavia I had difficulties finding children who could remember their past lives. In Sweden, Babro Karlén wrote an autobiography[2] in which she states that even as a young child she knew that she had lived in Holland and had kept a diary at that time. One day she and her parents had suddenly been taken away by soldiers. These memories were spontaneous long before she had heard anything about Anne Frank. When her parents finally took the young teenager on a trip to Amsterdam to visit the Anne Frank museum the girl recognised everything. She even noticed that her pictures of famous actors were no longer pinned up above her bed. An employee of the museum explained to her that they had temporarily been taken down. At the age of 12, Babro already was a famous Swedish writer whose critics were amazed at her grown-up style of writing.

I am always very sceptical when someone tells me that he or she was a famous person from the past. This soon gets put to the test when I lead the person into regression and find out that they were not Marie-Antoinette, Cleopatra, Napoleon or whoever they claimed to have been. This is why I asked Babro Karlén's publisher to give me her telephone number or her address, so that I could try to arrange to visit her in Göteborg. I wanted to conduct a regression, which might shed some light on whether she had really been Anne Frank. The publisher did not think it a good idea, however, to contact her about this matter.

We do have a report from Copenhagen of a girl who can remember a past life. Her name is Luna Marconi whose parents are Italian. One day the three-year-old told her parents, 'I want to go home.' When asked where her home was she told them that it was in the Philippines. Her parents were very surprised that she knew of this country, since they had never told her about it and could not think how she could have come by this name. Several days later she again expressed a wish to go home. She said that her name was Maria Espina, that her father owned a restaurant and that her house was on Highway 54 not far from the Church of Christ. When asked more about her alleged past life in the Philippines, she said that she often loved to eat bocan. She also described various festivals and ceremonies in great detail. Sometimes she would start to dance whilst humming a tune that was completely unfamiliar to her parents. These were all things that the little girl could not have learnt from her parents. One day she talked about President Diosdado Macapagal visiting her village, who had apparently been a very tall man. In honour of this special occasion she had worn new shoes and was chosen to present the president with a bunch of red flowers.

Then a most surprising thing happened. Having heard of the little girl's claims, some newspaper reporters travelled to the Philippines. They found a sweet made of coconut called bocan. They even found the Church of Christ on Highway 54. Not far from the Church was a restaurant belonging to Yves Espina and his wife. They really did have a daughter named Maria who had died of a fever at the age of 12. They also confirmed that Luna had been bought a new pair of shoes after they had been told that she was to present the president (who was indeed tall) with flowers.[3]

WHY AM I A BOY THIS TIME?

Numerous investigations into reincarnation have been carried out in England over the years, often using television programmes to back them up. You may remember Dr Bloxham, or, more recently, seeing television reports about Jenny Cockell who was the woman who found her children from a past life in Ireland.[4] (Her children are of course several years older than she is in her present life.) The following story is based on a case taken from Peter and Mary Harrison's book, *Life Before Birth*.[5]

By the time Nicola was five years old she had convinced her mother, Mrs Kathleen Wheater, in numerous ways that she had lived in Yorkshire as a boy in her past life, and had been run down by a train over 80 years ago. It all began with a wooden dog on wheels, which Nicola had been given for her second birthday. She was overjoyed with this present and said, 'I'm going to call him Muff.'

When asked why she had chosen this particular name she said, 'I'm calling him Muff because that was the name of my dog which I used to have.' Her mother laughed at her childish fantasy, knowing full well that they had never owned a dog by that name. She often overheard Nicola scolding her dog for not being able to remember things from the past. All this seemed to arouse little suspicion in her mother, until one day Nicola asked her, 'Mummy, why am I not a boy like I used to be?' It was only then that her mother asked her what she meant by that. Her little daughter replied, 'My mummy used to be called Mrs Benson. I was her little boy and I played with Muff.' Mrs Wheater could not think why on earth her daughter should use that particular name, since the name Benson had never been mentioned in her house and she could not think of anyone with that name in her village.

From now on Mrs Wheater accepted the possibility that her daughter could well be telling her about a previous incarnation. She bought a special book in which she made a note of everything her daughter mentioned that could possibly refer to her past life. Even though Nicola could not remember her own name from the past, she was able to remember her mother's first name as well as the surname Benson. When asked about her father's occupation she said that he worked for the railway and that he was in charge of inspecting the rails. She also remembered that the Bensons had lived in Haworth. She talked in meticulous detail about the clothes her parents used to wear, but her favourite subject of conversation continued to be about her dog, Muff, and the games they used to play. She also remembered a boy who had been her playmate. The three of them had roamed the countryside together. Their mothers had warned them about the dangers of playing on the train lines. One day it happened that the boy was hit by a train and died shortly after in hospital. Then Nicola said to her mother, 'But I couldn't have died, because I came to you, and now you are my new mummy.' Whenever Nicola was questioned about her statements, she was consistent in what she said.

Mrs Wheater had now become curious and wanted to know for certain how many of her daughter's statements were true. One day she decided to take her daughter on a trip by car to Haworth in Yorkshire, the place where Nicola claimed to have lived in her past life. As they approached the small town Nicola began to recognise the area and talked about all the places where she and Muff had gone for walks. When they were in Haworth she gave her mother directions on how to reach her 'other' home. Finally they arrived at an old terraced house, which was one of four and looked just as Nicola had previously described it. It was also true that there were fields behind these houses. When Mrs Wheater went to the house to enquire whether they had heard of a family by the name of Benson who may have lived there, no one seemed to know. Then she asked where the church registry office for births, christenings and deaths was. When she had found it she asked to be allowed to check the register of christenings. Even here the man in charge assured her that to his knowledge no family with this name now lived or had ever lived in this town. Even so Mrs Wheater insisted on seeing the register of christenings herself. No matter how far back she looked, the name Benson did not appear, but just as she had decided to give up and go home, she suddenly discovered an entry made on the 25th July 1875: John Henry Benson, born as the son of Thomas Benson (a railway employee). So her daughter's former Christian name had to be John.

Some time later Mrs Wheater was allowed to consult another document in the library dating back to the year 1881, a census statistic. A census had to be taken every ten years by law and had to include all living family members. Mrs Wheater discovered that the family Benson had indeed lived in the house her daughter had directed her to in Haworth. She was certain of this, since the name of the road and the house number were the same as in the address Nicola had taken them to. In the list both the Christian and surname, including the age of every family member was listed, but the name John Henry was missing. If he had really been born in 1875 and had died five years later, according to Nicola's statements, then he would not have been included in these statistics.

Yet Mrs Wheater added a further twist to her story. One day, when the family was watching a film on television there was a scene in which a train hit someone. At this point Nicola let out a bloodcurdling scream. She threw herself on the floor, wildly throwing her arms around while crying and gasping for air. They thought she was having a fit. But then she kept screaming, 'The train! The train!' She only calmed down when the television was turned off.

Critics in the know might argue that Nicola was possessed by an earthbound spirit who used to be John Henry and now influenced her by imprinting his own experiences on the girl or whispering them into her ear. But those who are even more knowledgeable will be aware that only real past experiences of a horrific nature, such as being hit by a train, could spark off such convulsive reactions in a person who had indeed such experiences stored in his or her emotional body. Experiencing something similar in the present can then reactivate these memories and the accompanying emotions. So there is no doubt that Nicola's experience was a real-life flashback to a past life. Later in the book I shall return to this subject in a separate section dealing with reactions triggered by similar experiences. Such reactivated emotions are among the most powerful evidence of actual experiences of people's past lives and serve to illustrate the truth of reincarnation.

MY MOTHER LIVES IN CHARLES CITY

The number of people in the USA believing in reincarnation is probably a little higher than in Western Europe.

People in the States have repeatedly been able to see talk shows on television presenting the theme of reincarnation, and practically all the famous research scientists as well as reincarnation and regression experts have made repeated appearances on national television. Even though the Christian fundamentalists appear to continue to grow in numbers, the followers of reincarnation seem to be increasing in numbers at an even higher rate. Much seems to be indicating that in the first half of the 21st century the majority of Americans will become followers of reincarnation. This is particularly likely since Professor Ian Stevenson from the University of Virginia has more or less proven the existence of reincarnation once and for all. In America there is a whole string of documented cases of children and particularly adults remembering their past lives, whose statements have been followed up and confirmed. From the huge wealth of cases available, I finally chose the case of Romy Crees for this chapter.[6]

Romy is the daughter of Barry and Bonnie Crees and lives in the State of Iowa in Des Moines where she was born. The little girl often talked about having been a boy whose name was Joe Williams. As time went by her parents discovered more and more about the life of Joe. At first they believed their daughter's statements to be nothing but wild fantasies of a child's imagination. She claimed to have lived in Charles City. It was possible that she had picked up the name of this town from the television since it is about 250 kilometres from Des Moines. She also claimed to have been married to a woman called Sheila and that they had had three children. Her parents were not a bit worried about any of this. Some time later she talked about her previous mother having been called Louise Williams, and that he (Joe) grew up in her house, which had red tiles on the roof. One day he had caused a fire there and his mother had burnt her hand while trying to extinguish it. His mother had also injured her leg on this occasion and Romy showed her parents the exact place where the painful injury had been.

She begged her parents to take her to Charles City, because she wanted to visit her mother to tell her that everything was all right. Her parents did not quite know what to make of all this. Whenever they were out in the streets with Romy and a motorbike zoomed past, she would have panic attacks. She had often told them about the motorbike accident in which Joe and Sheila had died. Sheila had been his passenger. When Romy continued to beg her parents to go to Charles City so that she could show them everything, especially her mother Louise, all these strange things now seemed important enough to comply with Romy's request. But how were they to go about it?

They had heard of a professor from California who apparently followed up cases of children remembering their past lives. They came to an agreement with the Indian professor, Hemendra Banerjee, who came to Des Moines in the winter of 1981 with his wife and two

Swedish journalists from the magazine *Allers*, to investigate the case of Romy Crees. Where research into reincarnation was concerned this was an 'ideal' case they were dealing with, in which a research scientist takes over a case that is not seen as 'solved' by those involved. If on the contrary a client sees the case as 'closed', they they can only rely on the reports of others in the hope that all the statements have been conveyed correctly.

After Professor Banerjee had listened carefully to everything Romy and her parents had to say, they all got into the car to drive to Charles City. When they approached the city, Romy became more and more excited and climbed into the front seat. When they arrived in the town she said, 'We must buy some flowers for Mother Williams. She likes blue flowers best. We must not use the front door but must go around the corner to the back door.' They bought a bunch of blue flowers like Romy had asked for. They also checked the telephone book and were overjoyed to find the name Louise Williams as well as her full address. Romy had no trouble showing them the way to her house.

Finally, accompanied by the two reporters, they arrived at the house previously described by their daughter, which was in a suburb of Charles City. It was a white bungalow but it did not have red tiles like Romy had talked about. To their amazement there really was a note on the door saying, 'Please use back door'. When they knocked on the back door an elderly woman opened it. She was resting on a crutch and was wearing a bandage on her right leg.

They asked her whether she was Mrs Louise Williams, to which she replied, 'Yes.' 'Did you have a son named Joe?' She answered, 'Yes.' They then asked whether it was convenient to talk with her. Mrs Williams told them that this was not possible right now since she had to keep an important doctor's appointment. She would be pleased to see them afterwards in about an hours time. Romy was very disappointed since she had envisaged her first meeting with her past mother to be completely different. She had also not had a chance to give her the blue flowers yet and her eyes filled with tears.

An hour later the group of seven once more knocked on Mrs Williams' door. She had been expecting them and invited them in. At last Romy was able to give her the blue flowers. Mrs Williams was overjoyed and said that she had not had a bunch of flowers like this since her son Joe had given her some a long time ago. They told her who Romy was and that she remembered her past life as her son Joe. Mrs Williams was speechless as she listened to what they had to say.

She must have felt like someone being visited by aliens who knew everything about her past. She confirmed everything she was told and kept asking, 'Where does she know all this from?' She could not understand how a little girl could know everything about her and her deceased son. She did not know anybody in Des Moines who could have told Romy anything about her. When asked why Romy had described her house with red tiles, she said that some years ago a terrible tornado had caused a lot of damage in Charles City and had damaged the roof so badly that it had had to be replaced. In doing so they had used different tiles. They told her that Romy remembered having to use the back door of the house. Mrs Williams explained that Joe had helped her build the house and had suggested that they keep the front door locked in winter.

Even though Mrs Williams did not believe in reincarnation and found a lot of things unbelievable, she felt very drawn to Romy. They both went into the room next door and when they returned they were holding hands. Mrs Williams held a framed photograph in one hand and said, beaming, 'She recognised them all!' She then showed the photograph to the others present, telling them that it had been taken at the last Christmas celebration before Sheila and Joe's death. Mrs Williams told them again and again that Romy had named them all correctly when they were in the other room.

During their conversation, Mrs Williams was able to confirm many of the things that Romy had told her parents in Des Moines. Her son had really died with Sheila in a motorbike accident in 1975 and they had had three children. Even the names of their relatives Romy had mentioned at home were correct. Mrs Williams also confirmed the fire Romy had talked about in which she had burnt her hand.

Neither Mrs Williams nor Romy's parents were prepared to believe in reincarnation. They were too heavily steeped in the dogmas of their church to be able to accept the possibility of Joe having been reborn as Romy. Everything described here remains an unexplained mystery for the three of them. Yet Mrs Crees tells us that one thing is certain, 'I am convinced that my daughter is not lying.'

From this example we can see how difficult it is for some people to let go of their old beliefs and thought patterns. Contrary to the three mentioned above, many others would immediately have accepted reincarnation as the truth. Perhaps the idea of reincarnation will continue to germinate in the minds of Mrs Williams and Romy's parents, who may just need a little more time to allow the belief in reincarnation to take root within themselves.

I MISS MY GRANDMA ALICE SO MUCH

A mother from Louisiana told Carol Bowman the following story. A couple by the name of Pirosko had three children. Their middle child was a girl by the name of Courtney. When she was three years old she was sitting at the table in the kitchen scribbling on a piece of paper while her mother was busy preparing some food. Suddenly the little girl was overheard saying, 'I miss my grandma Alice so much.' 'Who is Grandma Alice?' asked her mother. 'Grandma Alice is my grandma.' 'But you already have two grandmas and neither of them are called Alice.' The little girl now gave her mother a very knowing look and said, 'I know that. Grandma Alice was my grandma before I was Courtney.' Mrs Pirosko, as she told Carol, felt shivers running down her spine. When she asked her daughter about Grandma Alice, she was told that Courtney had lived with her grandma and grandpa after her parents had died. Her grandmother had always loved her and used to play board games with her, always allowing her to win because she was little. Courtney giggled whilst telling her mother about this. She seemed to be able to remember her past life very clearly.

All the time she was telling her mother about her past life, she continued scribbling on the paper in front of her.

This kind of incessant scribbling is a typical giveaway for the fact that Courtney was in a kind of half-trance whilst telling her story. In this state it is easy to reach your subconscious in which all past experiences are stored, be they from this life or a past life.

Mrs Pirosko added that while Courtney was tapping into all those memories and chatting away to herself she had sat perfectly still, which was completely unlike her. The three-year-old continued to talk. Her grandmother had died when she had been 16 years old. Then she sighed and said, 'I miss my grandma Alice so much.' Her mother answered, 'I am glad that you are with me now.' Then Courtney said something that alarmed Mrs Pirosko. 'I know that you love me. That is why I chose you.' Apparently Grandma Alice had recommended her to Courtney as her new mother on earth.

In the afterlife we choose our parents before each new incarnation. We are happy to allow wise beings to recommend certain parents to us, who will provide the best circumstances for whatever we wish to learn in the school of life.

Whenever Mrs Pirosko heard her daughter talking about her past life she came out in goose bumps. She just didn't know how to deal with this whole business, because something like reincarnation was beyond her imagination. Therefore she always tried to distract her daughter as soon as she started talking about it, or she would suggest to her that she should tell her about it another time.

Two years later she found herself reading Carol Bowman's book.[7] In this most informative book, the author describes how at first she did not believe in reincarnation, but became convinced of it through her own children's statements, which you will read about in the course of this book. After having gained greater understanding of these things by reading Carol Bowman's book, she has learnt to feel at ease when listening to Courtney's descriptions of her life with Grandma Alice. Her daughter continued to tell her many things about her past life. She talked about there having been hills where she lived and trees that lost their leaves before the start of the very cold winter. Winters had been very cold, not warm like in Louisiana.

One day when all of Mrs Pirosko's children were in the bath, Courtney told them that there had been no bath at Grandma Alice's and that they'd had to use a very primitive outside toilet. Only later her grandfather had bought a toilet bowl from town and had installed it in the house. From where could this five-year-old have got all this information?

Six months before this incident, while looking at baby photographs, her little brother asked his oldest sister, Aubrey, where he had been when this photo was taken. When she told him that he had been in heaven at that time waiting to be born to them, Courtney interrupted them and explained what really happens. As soon as you arrive in heaven you are allowed to rest for a while. After this holiday you have to work. You have to think about what you want to learn in your next life on earth. Then you choose a family that will help you to learn the things you have decided to learn. Her mother was most surprised and asked her daughter whether she had seen God in that place. To this the little girl replied that she had only seen God with her soul.

At the age of six Courtney saw a mother on television who was weeping for her son who had been sentenced to death for a crime he had committed. Courtney's mother listened with utter disbelief while her six-year-old told her the following: 'The mother on television doesn't understand that the death of her son is no punishment. He has messed up his life and has been given another chance to begin a new life as a baby with a new family in order to learn the things he needs to learn. So the woman doesn't need to be sad.'

How would you feel if your six-year-old child had revealed such other-worldly things to you? Courtney could not have picked up any of this from other adults since her parents strictly followed a Presbyterian belief. A wise initiate could well have said everything this child has revealed. In this book we will frequently hear about children speaking of higher knowledge, which they brought with them into their present incarnation from the 'afterlife'.

THE THREE-YEAR-OLD WHO
CONVICTED HIS MURDERER

I have been a friend of the well-known Israeli doctor and professor of medicine, Eli Lasch, for ten years now. He served for a long time as senior consultant responsible for the health services in the Gaza Strip and temporarily for the whole of the Israeli-occupied Sinai. Yet his own experiences gradually helped him to find his way back over the Kabbala to the inside, where he rediscovered amazing abilities that he had possessed in a past life.

After he had completed his career as a highly decorated medical doctor, he opened a practice in Israel where he worked as a regression therapist and spiritual healer. In 1989 he came to Berlin where I took part in his seminars and where we ended up leading each other back into past lives. A few years later he appeared on television several times where he successfully conducted healings from a distance. All of a sudden he had become a well-known personality throughout the country. In 1998 his highly interesting book appeared with the title, *From Doctor to Spiritual Healer*.[8] Eli told me several amazing stories about reincarnation, which had helped him to revolutionise his entire conventional doctor's way of thinking. In December 1998 I visited him in his flat in Berlin, where among other things he recounted the following event, which I will now tell you in my own words.

The Druse is a nation of approximately 200,000 people who settled in Lebanon, Syria, Jordan and the region that is now Israel a long time ago. They are neither Muslim nor Christian, for they have their own religion. In Israel they are mostly found on the Golan Heights. They are the only non-Jewish Israelis to serve in the Israeli army. Reincarnation forms the basis of their beliefs.

As soon as a child is born its body is searched for birthmarks, since they are convinced that these stem from death wounds, which were received in a past life. If such marks are found on a child they try to discover something from his or her past life as soon as the child is able to speak in order to get the first clues to the circumstances of his or her former death. They are aware that small children often confuse past and present events and so experience everything, as if it were the same life. Therefore as soon as the child is three years old and is able to distinguish between events from the past and its present life, the child is taken to the place it has talked about and where it claims to have lived in a past life (provided that the child in question did mention such a place). Since this is usually a special occasion, a kind of native board of inquiry is formed, led by several respected village elders.

When a certain boy became three years old, on whose upper forehead a long red birthmark stretching to the centre of his head was found, a group of 15 men was formed. This group consisted of the father and other relatives of the boy, several elders of the village and representatives from the three neighbouring villages. From what the boy had said they were quite sure that he had lived in their immediate neighbourhood in his past life. Professor Eli Lasch was the only non-Druse who was invited to join this group because they knew that he was interested in reincarnation.

When they arrived at the first neighbouring village with the boy, he was asked whether it seemed familiar to him. He told them that he had lived in a different village, so they walked on to the next one. When they arrived there and questioned him again he gave them the same answer. Finally they reached the third village. Now the boy told them that this was where he had lived. All of a sudden he was able to recall some names from the past.

He had told them months ago that a man had killed him with an axe, but he had not been able to remember his own name and that of his murderer. He now remembered both his first and second name as well as those of his murderer. One of the oldest people of this village who had joined this group had known the man whom the boy named. He said that he had disappeared without a trace four years ago and had been declared missing. They thought he must have come to some harm in this war-torn area, for it often happened that people who strayed between the lines of the Israelis and the Syrians were taken prisoner or shot if suspected of being spies.

They went through the village and the boy showed them his house. Many inquisitive people had gathered around. Suddenly the boy walked up to a man and said, 'Aren't you . . . (Eli forgot the name)?' The man answered, 'Yes.' Then the boy said, 'I used to be your neighbour. We had a fight and you killed me with an axe.' Eli told me how the man had suddenly gone white as a sheet. The three-year-old boy then said, 'I even know where he buried my body.'

How could he have known where his former neighbour had buried his body after his death? Almost daily, my clients describe to me the following post-mortem scenario during regression therapy: after death the soul leaves the earthly body and in most cases is able to see the body from above. Often it hovers there for a while and can see exactly what happens to the body. We will hear more about this from other children later on in this book.

Some time later the whole group followed by many inquisitive people were seen wandering off into the nearby fields. The man whom the little boy had recognised as his murderer was asked to come along. The boy then led them to a particular field and stopped in front of a pile of stones and said, 'He buried my body under these stones and the axe over there.' They now removed the stones and underneath discovered the skeleton of a grown man wearing the clothes of a farmer. A split in the front of the skull was clearly visible. Now everyone stared at the murderer who finally admitted to this crime in front of everyone. Then they went over to the place where the boy said the axe was buried. They did not have to dig for long before they held it in their hands.

Reincarnation is a fact of life for the Druse; they need no proof to secure this belief; and yet it always amazes them every time reincarnation reasserts itself in cases like this one. The Druse also believe that they are always reborn as Druse. Perhaps group regression among their people would prove whether this statement is true. Eli then asked the people what would become of the murderer. They said they would not hand him over to the police, but they themselves would decide on an appropriate punishment for him.

MY WIFE WAS MORE BEAUTIFUL THAN YOU, MUMMY

In this story we shall once more focus on the Druse, a minority in all three countries mentioned above. Where numbers are concerned they are most strongly represented in Lebanon, which is one of Israel's neighbours. This time I present you with a case researched by the famous Professor Stevenson,[9] about whom you will get to hear a great deal more in this book.

In 1962 he spent some time in Brazil looking for children that are able to remember their past lives. His privately hired interpreter was Lebanese and was very interested in the professor's work. He told him that in Lebanon in the village where he came from there had been, and possibly still were, a number of children who were able to remember their past lives, and whose statements had been proven to be correct. He also gave him the address of his brother who lived there. Following these suggestions Stevenson travelled to Lebanon two years later. To his disappointment, the brother of his Brazilian interpreter, Mr Mohamed Elawar, was not in the village of Kornayel at the time. Stevenson, who had brought with him a French interpreter, had him ask the villagers whether there were children in this place or surrounding area who had memories of past lives. It was discovered that Imad, the five-year-old son of the absent Mr Elawar, was able to remember a past life. With the aid of his interpreter he then asked Mrs Elawar many questions concerning the things her son had told them about his past.

Imad started talking about his past life at the age of one-and-a-half to two years. He mentioned many people from the family and friends of the man he used to be. He was able to remember his surname, which was Bouhamzy, but his his Christian name. He was also able to tell them about his village, which was called Khirby. He described his house, which was built on a hillside and had a garden in which apple and cherry trees grew. He also talked about having had a yellow car as well as a bus and a lorry of his own. He had used the lorry to transport rocks.

Imad's father forbade him to speak about his past life, even though he was a Druse; in fact he called his son a liar. This is why Imad never mentioned his past life in the presence of his father after that, but kept on revealing details about it to his mother and his grandparents. He told his mother about Jamileh, a woman whom he had loved very much. She had been very beautiful and loved wearing red clothes and red stilettos. He often compared Jamileh with his mother, always talking more highly of the former. He also spoke of owning a double-barrelled gun as well as a shotgun, with which he often went hunting, accompanied by his dog. One day his dog fought with another dog and he remembered having beaten the other dog. Imad begged his parents again and again to take him to Khirby, so that he could show them everything. One day at the age of two Imad was in the street with his grandmother. Suddenly he saw a man and ran over to him and hugged him. The man asked the little boy, 'Do you know me?' 'Yes, you were my neighbour.' (Only later did they discover that this was really so.)

Imad's father was notified that some of his brother's friends from Brazil had come to visit him. On hearing this he immediately returned to his village. He told them that three months ago he had been to Khirby for a Druse burial and had made enquiries about the Bouhamzy family. But his son's statement had been self-contradictory. He had told them about a car accident and about having lost the ability to walk. It turned out that there really had been a man in the Bouhamzy family who had died from the consequences of a car accident, but his father had mistakenly thought that this accident related to his son and had mistaken him for the other man. Mr Elawar agreed with Mr Stevenson's suggestion to drive to Khirby with Imad the following day. Stevenson noticed the joy on the face of the five-year-old boy when he was told about these plans.

Even though Khirby is only about 20 kilometres from Kornayel as the crow flies, we are talking about two mountain villages linked by winding roads across the mountains. On the strength of the boy's and his father's statements, Stevenson assumed that Imad could be the reincarnation of Said Bouhamzy, who had died in a car accident. Several people were interviewed once they arrived in Khirby. Stevenson now received even more contradictory evidence about what the boy had said about himself and his past life, so that by the end of this visit they returned more or less empty-handed. Imad had been asked to show them his house, but he was unable to recognise it – the reason turned out to be the fact that much had changed in the village since his death.

Even so Stevenson did not give up. He returned to Khirby the following day with his interpreter. He had made notes of Imad's many statements about places and events, and wanted to further investigate where these had apparently taken place. Stevenson questioned several members of the Bouhamzy family and soon noticed that their descriptions about Imad's past life did not fit those of the deceased Said. This man had not had a wife by the name of Jamileh. Apparently another boy had already been identified as the reincarnation of Said, after the case had been thoroughly investigated by the relatives of the deceased. However, Imad's statements seemed to fit Said's cousin, whose name was Ibrahim Bouhamzy. This man was said to have had a beloved named Jamileh, whom he had never married. This man had owned a yellow car, a lorry for transporting rocks and even a bus at some time. Ibrahim had died at the age of 25 on the 18th September 1949. He had been suffering from a sickness of the lungs for a long time, which had made him completely bedridden. He'd had tuberculosis of the spine that can be highly contagious and had been unable to walk for the last three months of his life.

Convinced of who Imad could have been in his past life, Stevenson now returned to Kornayel and persuaded Mr Elawar to accompany him to Khirby with his son once more. Imad was really happy to be taken to Khirby again for he was convinced that he had lived there in the past. Once there they first visited the house of the deceased Said Bouhamzy. Imad was led through the house but he was unable to recognise anything. When he was finally shown a photo album depicting the Said family, again he was unable to recognise anyone. He did show great interest in two partridges in an enclosure and asked to be allowed to take them home, but his father managed to talk him out of it.

After this they went to the house in which Ibrahim had lived, where he met his mother, his sister and a neighbour from the past. These people had already been informed of the reason for the five-year-old's visit to their house. Strangely enough he did not recognise his mother, for she had changed so much in the last 20 years that she hardly resembled her previous self. When his past sister asked him whether he knew who she was, he immediately said, 'You are Huda', which was correct. Then he was shown an oil painting on the wall depicting the youngest son of his mother from his past life. When questioned about this Imad correctly named the person as Fuad. He also recognised his favourite brother Fuad on a photograph, which he hugged tenderly. Stevenson remembered that Imad had supposedly mentioned early on that his past mother had once trapped her finger in a door. He now noticed that one of the woman's fingers appeared a little flattened. When questioned about this she confirmed Imad's story. He was then led through the house and into his old bedroom in which were two beds. When asked which bed used to be his, he pointed to the right one and said that it used to be positioned diagonally across the room. He also told them that he used to sleep in it with Jamileh who had visited him frequently. His mother and sister clearly remembered this since it had been a public scandal at the time. When he was asked where Jamileh lived, he pointed in the right direction of her village.

Due to his sickness Ibrahim had spent his last year in a hospital for lung patients, but had been brought back to the house a few days before his death. No visitors apart from the doctors had been allowed to enter his room. The visitors had had to talk to him through the window, which was why the bed was in that particular position where he could see them. Knowing this Imad was asked how he had been able to speak with his friends. He pointed to the window.

He had often spoken about having owned two guns and was now asked where he used to hide them, since it was forbidden by law to own firearms without special permission. He went to a cupboard and opened it. In the back of the cupboard was a partition behind which he had hidden his guns. His previous mother who was standing by him said that she had been the only person to know of this hiding place apart from her son. When he was asked what his last words had been before he died he answered, 'Huda, call Fuad!' This was also confirmed. He was repeatedly shown photographs and sometimes they deliberately tried to mislead him. For example they showed him a photograph saying, 'This is your cousin.' But Imad replied, 'No, that's me!' Out in the yard he pointed to the place where he used to tie up his dog. There were so many other clues relating to his past existence as Ibrahim Bouhamzy that his relatives from his past life no longer doubted that Imad really was the reincarnation of Ibrahim, a member of their family who had died at such a young age.

STABBED BY HIS BEST FRIEND

The Islamic faith is the main religion in Turkey. Officially no one believes in reincarnation, even though some Islamic sects either partially or completely acknowledge that reincarnation exists. The Sufis and the Allevites are two of these sects. Many children who remember their past lives have been found among the latter. The incidence of children remembering their past lives may well be the same among all nations of the world, yet among those who believe in reincarnation, the people take more notice of their children's early comments regarding past lives and do not ignore what they say. Professor Hemendra Banerjee reports about a case of reincarnation relating to the boy, Necati Unlutaskiran, from Adana in Turkey.[10] His actual name given at birth was Malik. His mother had a powerful dream a few days after the birth of her son, in which he appeared to her and insisted on being called Necip. She was happy to comply with her son's wishes, but was reminded that there was already a Necip in the family. To please everyone they chose the name Necati for the boy.

As soon as Necati was able to speak he talked about his past life. He described certain people and talked about those ones he particularly loved or liked. Finally he told them that his name was Necip Budak and that he lived in Mersin (Turkey), and was married to his wife Zehra with whom he had many children. He also spoke of his friend Ahmed Renkli whom he had often visited with his favourite son Najat. One day he had fallen out with Ahmed. Their argument had ended with Ahmed grabbing a knife and stabbing at Necip like a maniac. This is how Necati, who was then called Necip, had died.

Necati's parents had never heard of a family in Mersin by the name of Budak, so Necati was taken to the town, which was more than 100 kilometres away. He found the house he had once lived in. He recognised his wife, who was still living there, and was able to name all his children, except for the youngest whose name he could not have known since she was only born after his death. He was questioned about many things all of which he was able to answer easily. Sadly the report on these events was extremely short and therefore we do not have many details.

There was one other noteworthy detail however, which was put down in writing. Necati confessed to having had a dispute with Zehra, during which he had grabbed a knife and injured her knee. He pointed to the relevant place and Zehra lifted her skirt to reveal a large scar exactly where the young boy had pointed. Zehra and her children were soon convinced that Necati was the reincarnation of her husband and the father of her children. It was also confirmed that Ahmed had stabbed Necip Budak during an argument at that time. Necati had many birthmarks on his body, which could easily originate from the stab wounds he had received in his past life.

I would now like to focus on some more thoroughly researched and well-documented cases.

WEEPING IN HIS FORMER MOTHER'S ARMS

India with its population of many millions is regarded as the central homeland of reincarnation and the Law of Karma. All three of the original main religions, namely Hinduism, Buddhism and Jainism, to which Sikhism was later added, were founded on the belief in reincarnation. It was only Islam and later Christianity, which managed to successfully woo many millions of believers in reincarnation away from their faith, which was not too difficult since those joining belonged to the lower castes. Since they were seen as degraded people by higher castes, they were only too willing to join a new religion, which would free them from this stigma. It seems there have always been many children in India who are able to remember their past lives. Dr Pasricha conducted a field study with students whose job it was to enquire in a great number of villages whether there had been, or still were, children who were able to remember their past lives. From this survey they discovered that approximately one in every 420 children had this ability.

Professor Banerjee was head of the parapsychology department at the University of Rajasthan in Jaipur before being offered a chair at an American university. During his long term in office he was able to investigate many hundreds of cases involving children who remembered their past lives. For him as a scientist, as is the case with Professor Stevenson, the important issue is not that of converting people into believers in reincarnation. It is rather a question of intellectual curiosity which inspires them to carry out exact investigations (which will always include setting aside any cases that cannot be conclusively and scientifically proven). They frequently showed those addicted to finding proof of reincarnation that for some reason or other a case in question cannot be considered conclusive. Those concerned may frequently be disillusioned by this scientific approach, but science is science. All emotional responses must be avoided in order to maintain the greatest possible objectivity during the investigations and when compiling a summary of each case. Scientists are not permitted to openly declare their belief in reincarnation, for otherwise they would be classified as being biased and their research would be discredited.

I now present you with two cases from India, which were researched by the two above-mentioned scientists.

Professor Banerjee and his co-workers from the University of Jaipur investigated the first case and subsequently published it in scientific journals.[11]

At the northern end of the Ganges is the small village of Chandgari, consisting of barely a 1,000 inhabitants. In 1951 a woman gave birth to a son who was given the name Munesh. At the age of three, while playing with children of his own age, he told them about a place that he called Athanni. His friends laughed at him for they had never heard of a place with that name. One day when his mother was bathing him and he was being unbearably difficult, she smacked him. Munesh shouted at her saying 'Mother don't hit me or I will go away from here.' 'But where will you go?' 'I will go back to Athanni. That is my village. I live there. I don't belong here.' His mother had never heard of such a place. She questioned him further about this village and it became clear to her that he meant Itarni, but was unable to pronounce the word correctly. His mother told him, 'You must stop talking such nonsense.' 'But it is not nonsense. My name is Bhajan Singh. I live in Itarni. I belong there not here.' His mother replied, 'Belong there and not here with your family?' 'No, I don't belong here,' said Munesh, 'I have a house, a well, a garden and a farm there. I also have a wife, a brother, a mother and a daughter.' His mother then forbade him to continue going on about such childish things. Munesh stubbornly replied that he was speaking the truth. When he broke this rule of silence yet another time, she gave him a smack around the ears. Following this incident, he never again spoke about his past life at home.

When Munesh started school he told his classmates about his past life in a village called Itarni. He talked to them about many events in his life as Bhajan Singh. His classmates found this very amusing and teased him about his stories. Nobody wanted to believe him. His grandfather was the only person who would listen to him. He told himself that the easiest thing would be to investigate what Munesh was saying which would surely establish that there was nothing in it. This would dispel his grandchild's crazy ideas about a past life once and for all. He happened to know of a man who used to live near Itarni. He now went to ask this man whether he could remember a man by the name of Bhajan Singh who used to live in Itarni. According to his grandchild's statements Bhajan had died from a fever in 1951, leaving behind his wife and daughter. After thinking about this for a while, the man told him that he did know someone by that name who had died leaving his wife and daughter. He also believed that both of them still lived in Itarni. Without knowing the correct address, his grandfather wrote a letter to Bhajan Singh's widow, hoping that the postman would know whom he meant. In this letter he described who his grandchild claimed to have been in a past life and some of the things he had heard Munesh talk about.

A few days later Bhajan Singh's brother and brother-in-law arrived in Chandgari to find out whether there was any truth in this matter. When they entered the family's house Munesh was still at school. He was immediately collected, brought home and told that two men had come to see him. As soon as the boy saw the two men he ran up to the younger one, stood in front of him and folding his hands so they pointed upwards said, 'You are my brother, Bhure Singh.' He did not recognise the other man.

Mr Singh was doubtful about the whole thing. Maybe someone had enquired about him in Itarni and had described him to Munesh, who could now claim to know him. Mr Singh then asked the boy several questions about the past life he claimed to have lived. To his and his brother-in-law's amazement he was able to answer all the questions correctly. He was also asked who his best friend had been. To this Munesh answered that his friend's name had been Bhagwati. Now the two men were more than surprised. When the two visitors wanted to say goodbye, Munesh clung to his brother from the past begging him to stay. In order to pacify the boy he said, 'All right then, I will return in less than a week and will take you to Itarni myself.'

A few days later two women arrived to pay Munesh's family a visit. They were Ayodhya Devi – Bhajan Singh's widow – and her sister in law. They had both become curious after hearing reports from the two men. Could this boy really be Bhajan Singh reborn? They both kept their names a secret and remained veiled so that no one would tell Munesh what they looked like, or what their names were beforehand. Everyone was certain that these two women had come from Itarni. Rumours had already spread throughout the village that the two men who were seen a few days ago must have been relatives from Munesh's past life. It was obvious that these two women had come to put Munesh to the test. In no time at all numerous onlookers had gathered in front of their house.

When Munesh was taken to see these two women, whose faces he could hardly see behind their veils, his grandfather asked him, 'Do you recognise either of these two women as your mother?' Taking the hand of one of the women the young schoolboy answered, 'This is my wife.' But Mrs Ayodhya Devi immediately withdrew her hand, suspecting that this was some kind of rigged game, for it had been too easy for Munesh to recognise her as the wife of the deceased Bhajan Singh. Then the boy turned to the other woman saying, 'And you are Bhabhi.' The boy was so touched he began to cry. Mrs Ayodhya Devi then took him aside telling him the following, which she later confirmed in writing, 'If you are really my deceased husband, then surely you will be able to tell me something about our marriage that no one apart from us could know about.' The boy then reminded her that one day he had returned from Agra after sitting an exam to find out from his mother that she and his wife had fallen out with each other. He had been so angry about this that he had beaten his wife with a large butter spoon. The woman could well remember this unpleasant incident. She asked him about other experiences that they had shared and Munesh was able to tell her many things about their marriage. Mrs Ayodhya Devi was now completely convinced that this boy really was her previous husband. She then invited the boy to Itarni. His grandfather was willing to take him there.

When the boy arrived in Itarni with his grandfather, word had already spread about this incident of a past-life reunion, which meant that a large crowd soon surrounded them. Munesh suddenly recognised a man among the crowd and ran up to him saying, 'You are my friend Bhagwati Prasad.' This man replied that this was his name and also confirmed his close friendship with Bhajan Singh in the past. This man now had many questions to ask his previous friend and admitted with amazement that all his answers were correct. Bhagwati was now completely convinced that this boy had once been his friend, Bhajan Singh.

After this the boy led all his followers to the house he had once lived in. When he saw his mother sitting in a chair waiting for him he ran up to her and sat on her lap and began to sob uncontrollably. When he was later led through the house, he was able to point out all the changes that had meanwhile taken place. He recognised his coat from the past, his special chair and his books. Turning to his past wife he asked her, 'Where is your Dhoti [Sari], which I brought back from Agra for you?' By now everyone was completely convinced that Munesh really was the deceased Bhajan Singh.

How many other children may well remember their past lives, not only in India but all over the world? They may beg to be taken back to their past homes, yet no one believes them and they are left with this knowledge all by themselves. Luckily the grandfather in this case had at least partly given his grandchild the benefit of the doubt, which finally led to a complete confirmation of the boy's claims. Even in India, where the belief in reincarnation is an intrinsic part of life, it is difficult for those children who remember their past lives to appear believable and be taken seriously. I believe that we adults should listen much more carefully when children talk about unusual things. In fact we should encourage them to tell us everything that is important to them and allow them to speak without dismissing what they say, or even worse, shutting them up.

Stevenson has collected over two thousand reports about cases of reincarnation to date and has published detailed accounts of several dozens of them in various magazines and books. The following story is a case that this great scientist and his colleagues researched in 1961. Once again, the boy's relatives did not want to believe the statements of a mere child.

THE BOY WHO WALKED
'HOME' DURING THE NIGHT

In April 1950, a ten-year-old boy named Nirmal, who was the son of Sri Bholanath Jain, died of the pox in the town of Kosi Kalan in the State of Uttar Pradesh. Shortly

before he died he said to his mother, 'You are not my
mother. You are a Jatni. I am going to my real mother
now.' He pointed in the direction of the neighbouring
town, Chhatta.

*I was told about a kindergarten teacher who had a five-year-old
boy in her nursery who fell ill with a brain tumour. She often visited
him in the hospital. She was present at the bedside of the fatally ill
little Jakob, as were his parents, when he spoke his last words, 'I am
going to my real parents how.' His parents continued to be upset about
those last words for a long time, thinking that their son had not
accepted them as his parents. They also thought that they must
have treated him badly in some way. They did not understand what
their son was really trying to tell them. Either he meant that he was
returning to his parents from the past who were probably still dead, or
that he would soon be born again to different parents where he
would have another chance to grow up. We frequently make ourselves
very unhappy by being unaware of the way things truly work and
interrelate in the greater scheme of things, i.e. by our ignorance of the
true reasons why things happen. Once we have reached the higher
realms after death with the greater perspective and understanding that
this brings, we will say to ourselves, 'How I wish I had known the
true reasons behind the things that happened so I would not have
caused myself so much worry.'*

A couple by the name of Varshnay had a son who was
born in August 1951 and was named Prakash. They lived
in the small town called Chhatta mentioned above. When
the boy was about four-and-a-half years old he would
frequently get up in the middle of the night and walk off

in the direction of Kosi Kalan, which was approximately nine kilometres away. Each time he was captured he begged them not to stop him walking into the town. He repeatedly told them that he lived there and that his real name was Nirmal, the son of Bholanath Jain.

One day his uncle took him to Kosi Kalan as the boy had begged him to. Once there he was unable to recognise his father's shop since it had completely changed. Even so Prakash continued to ask to be taken back to this neighbouring town. He began to remember several names of his siblings, relatives and friends. Prakash's parents were becoming fed up with his constant begging to be taken to Kosi Kalan. They told him he was not to mention it again and beat him if he did so. When he continued to talk about his memories from the past, he was finally strapped to a potter's wheel, which was then turned anticlockwise in an attempt to drive out his past-life memories. This had apparently worked in many cases. But even this normally successful method had no effect on Prakash. He only stopped talking about his past life after his parents started beating him more severely.

Meanwhile Mr Jain from Kosi Kalan got to hear about this boy from the neighbouring town who claimed to be his deceased son Nirmal, who had died 11 years before at the age of ten. Early in the summer of 1961 he found himself on a business trip in Chhatta with his daughter. There he met Prakash who immediately called him 'father' and seemed very happy to see him. Prakash mistook Mr

Jain's daughter as another one of his sisters from the past. This mix-up was not surprising since the little girl had developed into a young woman in the past 11 years and looked quite different. The boy then accompanied them both to the bus station and constantly begged them to take him with them to Kosi Kalan.

Back home when Mr Jain talked about his meeting with the boy from the neighbouring town, his wife too wanted to get to know this boy called Prakash. She wanted to see whether he would also recognise her, and decided to visit him in Chhatta. Her oldest daughter and one of her sons accompanied her. When they arrived in Chhatta and approached Prakash he immediately recognised them. He called them by name and cried tears of joy. They went to see his parents and asked them to allow the boy another visit to their town. This request was granted.

Having arrived there, Prakash showed them the way to the house belonging to the Jain family. When looking at it from the outside, he was most surprised at how much it had changed. Inside the house he met other brothers and friends of the family from the past and called them by their names. He showed them where he used to sleep and where he had died. The Jain family was now utterly convinced that standing in front of them was the reincarnation of Nirmal. From then on they treated him as one of the family.

After Prakash had got to know his past family, he continued to express his wish to return to them. Despite his parents' strict rules he could not stop himself getting up at night and walking in the direction of the town. His father put an end to the boy's disobedience by beating him even more severely, for he must have been afraid of losing him and could see no other appropriate means of deterring his rebellious son from further plans of this kind.

The famous reincarnation research scientist Ian Stevenson, about whom we will hear a lot more later on in this book, happened to be staying in India when he heard about this fascinating case. In the summer of 1961 he visited the Varshnay family with Nirmal's oldest brother. Mr Varshnay was very reserved towards him and only reluctantly answered his questions. He suspected that Mr Jain had sent his oldest son and this foreigner to take Prakash away. Even when Stevenson finally got to see Prakash, the latter refused to answer his questions, even though Stevenson could see in his eyes that he was happy to see his older brother from his past life. His father had probably drummed it into the boy not to talk to these two visitors nor answer any questions under any circumstances. Stevenson, who follows up on every interesting case with utmost exactness, went to visit the Varshnay family again three years later. He was pleasantly surprised to find that Prakash's father had lost his fear of losing his son to his previous family. Meanwhile both families regularly exchanged gifts, and Prakash was even permitted to visit his other family in Kosi Kalan from time to time.[12]

Accounts of children who remember their past lives similar to the one above are comparatively frequent, especially in countries where the possibility of having lived past lives is accepted. As you can see, these memories from children often cause unease in 'Western' adults, who then dismiss their children's statements about people, places and situations from past lives as fantasy, without giving them much thought. This is why these cases appear to be relatively rare in Europe and in the United States. This rather biased behaviour by parents towards their children when telling them about past lives will gradually change. Our knowledge is constantly increasing and life is full of surprises. It seems to me that we still only know very little about what really holds our inner and outer world together.

THE BOY WHO CONFESSED TO A
MURDER HE COMMITTED IN A PAST LIFE

Wijeratne was born in 1947, the son of Tileratne Hami in the village of Uggalkaltota, Sri Lanka. Even at birth, it was obvious that the right side of his ribcage was deformed, due to one of his vertebrae being too short. His right arm was also shorter than his left and on his right hand the fingers were partly grown together. Apart from this his skin was particularly dark, which was not usual in his mother's family nor that of his father. However there was one exception: Mr Hami's brother who had been executed

19 years before had also had the same skin colour. Shortly before his death he had told Mr Hami that he would be reborn as his son. When Mr Hami became aware of other marks on the body of his baby son, some of which were similar, others exactly the same as those on his late

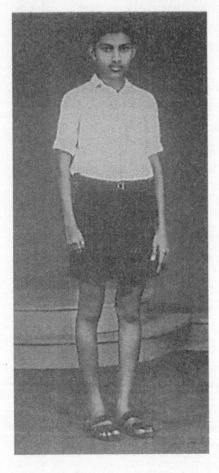

Wijeratne, when he was 18 years old. His right arm is markedly shorter and underdeveloped compared with his left arm.

brother's body, he declared, 'My brother Ratran has returned!'

When this boy was about two-and-a-half years old, his mother overheard him talking to himself saying that he had murdered his fiancée, which is why he was born with a crippled arm as a punishment. She then asked her son to explain what exactly he was talking about. He repeated again and again that he had killed his wife with a knife and that his father was actually his older brother. (He had not been officially married, but in Sri Lanka it was the custom to regard your fiancée as your wife.) His mother was shocked and went to talk with her husband to find out whether there could be any truth in what her son was saying. Her husband then confided in her a family secret that had been kept from her all this time. His deceased brother Ratran had not died a natural death; on the contrary it had been extremely gruesome. This is why, her husband said, he had not told her about the true events surrounding his death.

Even though his father forbade him to talk about his past life, Wijeratne could not refrain from talking to himself and to others who felt sorry for him because of his crippled arm. He would explain to them that it was a punishment for having murdered his past wife Podi. During the following years he uncovered more and more details about his past deeds. His wife Podi had refused to leave with him when he had gone to her village to collect her. He had seen her with another man and knew she had fallen in love with him, and that the man wanted her for himself.

In his anger he had walked home, sharpened his knife, returned to find her, and then stabbed her in the back. The other man and others in the house had then knocked him to the ground and the police had taken him away. In court he was adjudged the sole responsibility and was hanged for his crime. He could even describe the details of his hanging. Before he was hung he had seen someone testing the ropes with a heavy sack by taking the ladder away from underneath it. After this test had been successful they had put a black hood over his face and the noose around his neck. He remembers a Buddhist monk being present.

A monk, who was a well-respected professor of Buddhist philosophy, heard about this case, because Wijeratne's mother had gone to see the monks to ask them for guidance relating to her son. The boy continued to talk about his past misdeeds even though his father had forbidden it. After the monk had had a long talk with Wijeratne, the boy stopped his incessant talking to himself and others about his past life. This monk had also shown Professor Stevenson the notes he had made about his conversation with the boy. Wijeratne had confessed to his crime in the presence of the monk and later to Professor Stevenson, but had shown no remorse. He said that he would have to respond the same way if a similar situation arose. In his opinion, preserving the deceased husband's self-respect called for his kind of action. The boy also told the monk that his brother from the past (who is his present-day father), had given alms to the poor before the hanging in order to redeem the terrible deeds that had been committed in his family.

What is interesting is that when Wijeratne was visited by one of his relatives, he recognised the belt this man was wearing as one he had left at his aunt's house when he had been Ratran. The truth of this was also confirmed. In 1969 Wijeratne became mentally ill. He was temporarily admitted to a psychiatric hospital. He was diagnosed as suffering from hebephrenic schizophrenia. Professor Stevenson visited Wijeratne on six of his visits to Sri Lanka in order to collect even more details about this case. The fact that his father had known about virtually everything the boy had talked about, made this case unacceptable as a 'solved case'. This was because it is possible that Wijeratne had tapped into his father's knowledge via some kind of telepathic communication. Contrary to this hypothesis is the fact that the boy was able to talk about things such as the details of his hanging, which his father could not have known about since he had not been present.[13]

In my opinion it is more likely that Ratran's dead, yet temporarily earthbound, being had possessed Wijeratne. Ratran had already spoken through Wijeratne when he was a young boy, causing him to talk to himself incessantly even though his father had forbidden it. Later the monk may have succeeded in banishing Ratran from his body since after their conversation, as if by magic, the continuous talking to himself had ceased. To my mind, the likeliness of Wijeratne having a propensity to being possessed is borne out by the fact that later he was apparently taken over once more, resulting in his admission to a sanatorium. This is why I do not consider this case cogent enough to serve as convincing evidence of reincarnation, no matter how interesting it may be. Even so, I wanted to present you with this case to point out the need to proceed with caution before jumping to conclusions when handling a seemingly conclusive case of a child claiming to have been somebody else.[14]

In the following case from Thailand, the evidential gap remaining is minimal, yet surely big enough for hardened critics to question the truth of it.

THE UNCLE WHO WAS MURDERED
RETURNS AS HIS OWN NEPHEW

When Thiang was born in July 1924 in the village of Ru Sai in Thailand, his parents discovered strange birthmarks on his body. A toe on his right foot was deformed and on his hands and feet they found markings that looked like tattoos. But who could have tattooed the boy whilst he was in his mother's womb? It was instantly clear to the father who it was his wife had given birth to. It could only be the reincarnation of his brother who had died three months ago when he was stabbed in the back of the head in the midst of a crowd of people who wanted to beat him up. At the time no one claimed responsibility for this crime. His brother Phoh had had exactly the same deformed toe on his right foot as this boy now had, as well as tattoos on his hands and feet. They were the same tattoos as before, just less pronounced. As expected they also found a clearly visible scar on the back of his head, relating to the deadly weapon that had killed him in his previous life.

When Thiang was four years old, he began to identify himself as his father's late brother. He told them the whole story about his death. He had been accused of stealing cattle when he had been at the market. Then an angry crowd had gathered around him. He had tried to protest his innocence. Suddenly a man whom he knew had pulled a knife on him. Thiang had tried to avoid being stabbed by turning his head away, but the weapon struck him in the back of the head. Next he saw himself outside of his body. He was floating above his earthly body, which was lying on the ground, and he could see the blood gushing out of the wound on the back of his head. He thought about returning to his body, but suspected that the crowd would kill him again as soon as he regained consciousness.

When he realised that in this strange form he was able to move around by just using his consciousness, he decided to leave the place where those gruesome events had taken place and go home. He was there in an instant. He tried to make himself noticed to his relatives, so that he could tell them what had happened and that he was still alive, but no one seemed to notice him. He then visited other relatives and friends, but once again no one seemed to be aware of his invisible presence. This filled him with grief. When he discovered that his sister-in-law was pregnant, he felt an irresistible urge to enter her womb. He was later born to her as her son.

Earthbound entities are ones that were unable to make the transition into the intermediate realm, the so-called 'hereafter' once they had died, as was the case with the man in this story. Sometimes these beings can live among us for decades or even for centuries since they are not ready to make the transition to the 'other side'. It is very rare for an earthbound soul to enter the womb of a pregnant woman in order to be reincarnated, before first having made the transition to the other world.

Meanwhile Phoh's widow found out that her husband had apparently been reborn to her brother-in-law's family. She gathered up several of Phoh's clothes and personal belongings, which he had left behind, and also borrowed some similar things from various neighbours. She wanted to make sure that it really was her husband who had returned. Such things will happen now and again and followers of Buddhism know how to carry out identifications such as these. For example, everyone knows that with this method it was possible to recognise the reborn Dalai Lama in Tibet, or any high-ranking reincarnation of a Buddhist dignitary. The child is shown several versions of the same thing and only one of them will have belonged to the child in his previous life. If the child reaches out for the object that it once owned, you can be sure that the child can clearly remember its own things from the past. This test is then repeated with a variety of objects.

Phoh's wife Pai then undertook to walk the 25 kilometres from her village Ar Vud to Ru Sai on foot. Sadly we have no in-depth report on the reunion of this 'couple', but it is safe to assume that Thiang immediately recognised his wife from the past when she was introduced to him. To test him, Pai then proceeded to show the four-year-old an assortment of objects that had once belonged to him, spread out on the floor among all kinds of other articles. Thiang found it easy to divide them all up into two separate piles – one of the piles being made up of all the things that had once belonged to him. He had not made a single mistake. Everyone was now utterly convinced that this boy was really the reincarnation of Phoh. Even so his widow wanted more evidence. She took the young boy aside and asked him about things that only she and the reincarnated Phoh could know about. After that Mrs Pai was more than convinced that Thiang was really her husband reborn.

The return of her husband now presented her with a problem. On the one hand she was a widow and was free to remarry. On the other hand her husband was still alive. How could she best cope with this situation? She subsequently decided that the best thing was for her to become a nun and join a nunnery. When Thiang was taken back to the place where he used to live, he was able to recognise which fields had once belonged to him. He was even able to describe the circumstances and people involved in acquiring them.

Mr Pramaun, the local police inspector, heard about Phoh having been reborn. He had been involved with his murder inquiry in the past, so he was keen to see for himself whether this was really so. He went to visit Thiang's family and was most amazed when the boy immediately recognised him and called him by his name. When the police inspector then asked him to describe the circumstances of the crime in sequence, the boy was able to describe what had happened in every detail from his perspective. He mentioned the names of those present and also the name of the man who had stabbed him in the head with the knife. The policeman inspected the scar on the back of the boy's head, for he had previously inspected this on Phoh's head at the scene of the crime. He now confirmed that this birthmark perfectly resembled Phoh's injury.

Even today he is convinced that Phoh had deserved to be killed by the angry mob, for he holds him responsible for the series of cattle thefts he had been attempting to solve for a long time. The people had taken the law into their own hands and had kept quiet about the name of the murderer. For him the case was closed. This is why the police inspector now encouraged Thiang to confess to the cattle thefts, for he was now safe to admit it. Thiang continued to plead innocence.[15]

In these first examples it will have become very clear to you that the phenomenon of remembering past lives is found among children all over the world. So far we have not been to all the countries in which this phenomenon is particularly pronounced, but I will go into examples from other parts of the world later in the book.

THE GIRL WHO IS ABLE TO
REMEMBER TEN OF HER PAST LIVES

In most cases children only remember the life they lived immediately before their present one. But there are exceptions. Joan Grant was famous for being able to remember ten of her past lives even as a child, and for keeping these memories alive into her ripe old age. She has written books about seven of them and all have been translated into many languages. She was able to remember three Egyptian lives so clearly that archaeologists and Egypt-ologists later came to her to have many long-standing puzzles explained or even solved. She was particularly good at remembering the different languages including the hieroglyphs and correct pronunciations and was able to correctly describe the religious and cultural environ-ment and conditions of the times. In her present life she had only been to Egypt for a few days and had read no history books about the country. All of her memories were stored in her subconscious to which she had constant access, which meant that the distant past constantly remained in her awareness.

The case of Joey Verwey was similar. Even before she started school the white South African girl talked about her past lives. The most interesting thing was that she was able to draw almost perfectly at a very young age. She loved to draw clothes and buildings from her past life. Her parents were so amazed at this phenomenal gift that they called in an expert on parapsychology to advise them. Professor Arthur Berksley described Joey Verwey's ability in the following words: 'Before she could write she was able to draw the fashions of ancient times with the most minute and accurate details. She later described objects, customs and dress of those times in a way that by rights only someone who had lived in those times could have known how to. Her accuracy is uncanny and other than the possibility that she had indeed been reincarnated several times I can find no other explanation of her amazing knowledge.'

In one of her past lives she was a black slave in North Africa. In another life she found herself in Roman times where she took part in stoning a man who prophesied the imminent arrival of God's son. In another life she experienced herself in the time of the Renaissance, and in yet another she was a primitive native in a country she was not sure of, where she dug up eggs that crocodiles or ostriches had apparently buried. When Joey became six years old her mother bought a diary in which she wrote down all her daughter's comments regarding her past lives. Mrs Helge Verwey was especially interested in her daughter's previous life in which she personally met the past president of the Boer republic, Paulus Krüger.

One of the entries in her diary in which her daughter describes her past life as a slave went as follows: 'Our cave had only one entrance because it was too dangerous to have more than one, since the wild animals would otherwise find their way inside at night. As slaves, we were never allowed to speak in public; if we did we ran the risk of having our tongues cut out.' She continued to tell her mother, who diligently made notes, that the king at that time was extremely cruel. For example when he became angry with his very beautiful wife, he ordered her to be executed. He then ordered one of his tall slaves to bring him her head on a large copper dish, with her hair draped over the sides of it.

Joey was questioned by many inquisitive people and also by experts about further details of her past lives. Everyone was amazed at the degree of accuracy and detail with which she was able to describe things from the past.[16]

I have led thousands of people back into their respective past lives, and many of them have seen and/or relived a whole string of past lives in great detail. Many were still able to remember the details of what they had seen and experienced years later. For others the memories they experienced in my seminars soon faded. This is why it is beneficial to make notes of what happens during regression, like Mrs Verwey did with the memories of her daughter, in order to be able to refer to these experiences at a later date.

2

Children who are reborn to the same family

I DREW THIS PICTURE A LONG TIME AGO

As we will hear confirmed by children later on in this book, our soul enters an intermediary life after death and the time spent there can vary a great deal. As a general rule one might say that the sooner a soul leaves its earthly body the shorter the time before it enters a new body; yet there are of course exceptions. Even among deceased adults, their stay in the intermediary life can vary greatly from a few weeks to many hundreds of years.

As mentioned earlier, in most cases the soul is able to choose its next parents, if this is part of the plan for its new life on earth. In cases where the soul is still lacking the maturity to make its own decisions that will benefit its spiritual growth and higher good, other wise souls will take responsibility for making this choice. They know best which circumstances the individual needs to be born into in order to evolve spiritually to an ever higher understanding of love.

Stevenson writes about a wife from Myanmar (Burma), whose parents had died.[17] When this woman was pregnant she had a dream in which she was told that she

64

would give birth to twins who would be her reincarnated parents. Sure enough she gave birth to non-identical twin girls who were named Gyi and Nge. When they both began to speak Gyi made many comments referring to her life as her grandfather and Nge talked about her deceased grandmother. Even though Gyi was a girl her build was rather masculine and she always wanted to dress like a boy. They were completely different in looks: Nge was, and still is, very delicate; whereas Gyi looked rather masculine, which was particularly noticeable in her legs which were rather stocky in contrast to those of her sister Nge.

In the intermediary life, or 'afterlife' as it is often called, the soul prepares itself for its next life on earth. When requested, 'advisers' make themselves available to the being to help plan its next life on earth. At this stage we frequently make mutual arrangements to again meet with acquaintances, former relatives or friends who are also planning on reincarnating. It is usual for us to feel most happy and at ease with those we already know. As beings on 'the other side', it is possible to visit those on earth – provided that the higher plan allows such an intervention – to help, encourage and support them. If we perceive a person who is mourning our death intensely, we are frequently drawn to being reborn to this person in order to comfort them. This could be one of the reasons why the deceased couple mentioned above chose to be reborn to their daughter as twins. There may of course be many other reasons why they chose this woman as their new mother.

Having witnessed many regressions, I can say that approximately 25 per cent of the white population will choose to be reborn to parents who used to be members of their family in their last life. Very often it is the case that grandparents or great-grandparents are reborn as grandchildren or great-grandchildren. Yet the percentage of people reincarnating into the same family can be a lot higher, as is the case for instance among many African tribes. We have very much to learn as yet before we understand the overall scheme and conditions that govern these matters. The children can help us understand these things if only we give them more attention and take their comments seriously. Elisabeth Kübler-Ross often talked about children having been her greatest teachers. I am sure we will understand more fully what she is likely to mean by that as we continue with our 'tale'.

The author Carol Bowman, who has been mentioned in this book before and who will be speaking to us in more depth later on, was told the following story by a grandmother.[18] This woman called Hilda Swiger had a father who was a minister in the Church of God in Indiana. Her upbringing expressly excluded any belief in reincarnation and yet this woman had always believed in the possibility of repeated lives on earth. In 1977 her son Richard died in a car accident. She prayed to God for his return. One day she met her son in a dream and begged him to return to her. He replied, 'No, I have been here for so long that I have no wish to return.'

Once we have received a glimpse of how beautiful the afterlife can be, we would surely understand Richard's reason for not wanting to return to her. For anyone wishing to get an impression of 'the world beyond', I suggest watching the film Beyond the Horizon *starring the actor Robin Williams.*

Mrs Swiger reassured her son, 'I would make sure that you have a good life with me.' Following this her daughter gave birth to a son whom they named Randy. Two weeks later Mrs Swiger visited her daughter to see the boy. When she approached him he stretched out his hands towards her. Mrs Swiger then said to her daughter, 'I know who this soul is. It is Richard.'

You could well say now that Mrs Swiger's wishful thinking gave her the idea that her grandchild was her reincarnated son. This argument will no longer hold true when you find out what happened next.

Mrs Swiger had recently moved and was sorting out her things in the presence of her grandchild. She found a picture of an angel, which her son Richard had once drawn. Randy saw the picture, took it from her and ran to his father saying, 'Look Daddy, look! I drew this a long time ago!' When he was three-and-a-half years old he said to his grandmother, 'I was in your tummy before I came to Mummy. But then I died and went to heaven and that's where I met Grandpa John.' (John had been Richard's grandfather.) 'But I knew that you needed me and so I decided to go into my mummy's tummy so that I could be with you.'

This example shows us how a loving relationship on earth will continue after the physical death of a beloved person. The beings after death can be motivated to return to their beloved or those who love them on earth in a different form. How often do people look into the eyes of a newborn child and say, for example, that the boy looks just like his deceased grandfather, father, uncle or someone else. Each soul has a particular individual vibration unique unto itself, which it continues to have in all its lives on earth. Others can pick up on this vibration and instinctively be reminded of a certain deceased person.

This story is not yet finished. When Randy was four years old, his parents visited a particular restaurant. The last time they had both been there was five years previously. Randy noticed that his father had chosen a different table than before. In the past they had sat at another table at which the little boy now pointed. It was obvious to his father that he was speaking the truth. But how could he know this when he hadn't even been born at that time? When Randy was asked how he knew where they had sat before he answered, 'Oh, before I was born I followed you and Mummy all day long on the day you came here.' Randy's numerous statements about Richard's life had long since convinced this family that their son was both the brother and brother-in-law. Mrs Hilda Swiger could say with certainty, 'I knew it from the beginning.'

It is interesting to hear from a child that this soul, before it was reborn as Randy, was already following its chosen parents. Before our conception or before we decide to fully enter the growing foetus, we often remain in the proximity of the parents in order to become used to them. With our spiritual eyes we can recognise our parents as well as all physical things. We are particularly attuned to the thoughts, feelings and conversations of the parents. If, for instance, we hear or feel some lingering disharmony between the parents, we may choose to wait a while before entering the mother's body. If we decide not to enter the foetus of this already pregnant mother, the physical body will remain without a soul and is sure to die and be miscarried shortly after.

THAT IS MY WATCH!

Professor H. N. Banerjee whom we have met before is, apart from Stevenson, the most remarkable research scientist on the subject of reincarnation. He describes the following case in his book, *Lives Unlimited*.[19]

William George was a fisherman from the Tlingit Indian tribe. He knew that he would be reincarnated after his death. (The belief in reincarnation is widely spread among the North American Indians.) He wanted to be reborn as his grandchild. This is why he approached his son Reginald and told him, 'Listen carefully. If there is any truth in this idea of rebirth, then I will return as your son.' His son then replied saying, 'How will I know that it is really you father?' 'You will recognise me by my birthmarks, which will be exactly the same as the ones I now have.' He then pointed to the birthmark on his left shoulder and to another on his left forearm. During the following weeks he reminded his son again and again about what he had told him. Reginald promised him each time that he would not forget, even though he himself did not believe in repeated lives on earth.

Among the Tlingit Indians it often happens that a soul is reborn to the same family. Sometimes they already know to whom they will (or want to) be reborn while they are still alive. There may be several reasons why they have this confidence and knowledge. One explanation might be that they were given these insights from a higher source during their dreams, or that this knowledge was intuitive, possibly transmitted to them by their spirit guide or a deceased member of their family.

Reginald's father gave him his watch saying, 'You look after it for me!' Several days later the fisherman, William George, took his boat out onto the lake seeing that it was reasonably calm. He never returned. No one could imagine what had happened to him, since he was considered a skilled fisherman who was unlikely to make any mistakes out on the water. All search parties returned without finding a trace of him. Nine months later to the day, on the 5th May 1950, Reginald's wife, Susan, gave birth to a little boy. Shortly before the baby emerged from his mother's womb, Susan fell into a kind of coma. She suddenly saw a vision of her father-in-law, William George. A moment later she was completely conscious again.

Even though the soul of the deceased William George was already reincarnated in the baby's body which was emerging from her womb, Susan saw a vision of her father-in-law in that unconscious state. Again there are several possibilities to explain this incident in relation to the higher laws of life. One possibility is that William George had asked his spirit friends to show Susan a vision of him shortly before his birth, so that she and her husband would be convinced that it really was him who had returned.

Reginald immediately searched the body for birth-marks, and found the two marks that his father had pointed out to him on his own body. They were in exactly the same places. He and his wife were now convinced that William George had returned to them, which is why they christened him William George, Junior.

How many parents give their children the name of one of their deceased parents or other deceased members of their family? By doing this they believe they are preserving the memory of the deceased loved one or person who was very important to them, not knowing that it is extremely likely that their child actually was the deceased member of their family from whom they took the name in the first place.

As William was growing up, he exhibited more and more character traits as well as outer characteristics of his grandfather. The latter had injured his right ankle so badly that it never really healed again and he therefore dragged his foot behind him slightly. The grandchild also dragged his right foot behind him in the same manner, even though he had never injured himself in this life. He even closely resembled his grandfather in looks, which means very little since it is common for grandchildren to resemble one of their grandparents. Even his gestures and facial expressions were identical to those of the deceased. On the one hand he showed fear when taking the boat out into the water. On the other hand, to the amazement of everyone else, he often knew just the right places for fishing even though these changed regularly. This last trait had been one of his grandfather's strong points, but he had never shown fear when taking the boat out in water.

His fear of going out into deep water may well stem from the fact that he had drowned when he had been the grandfather and his fear was programmed into his soul. If we have suffered a traumatic death, the memories of the circumstances that led to our death are stored in our subconscious, which the soul then carries over into the new incarnation. As soon as the soul, which is now in the new body, is confronted with the same or a similar situation, the fear rises 'automatically', which is a kind of warning signal as a protection against experiencing the same thing again. We will be hearing more about the above 'mechanism' in other cases, which will be discussed extensively later on.

William showed some odd behaviour towards other people. He treated his grandfather's sister as if she too was his sister in this life. When speaking to his uncles and aunts, who were his deceased grandfather's sons and daughters, he addressed them with 'my son' and 'my daughter'. One day he came into his mother's room just as she was sorting out a small jewellery box. Suddenly he saw the watch, which the grandfather had given his son Reginald to look after, and said while grabbing the watch and holding it up, 'That is my watch!' When his mother wanted to take the watch away from him he refused to give it back and repeated again and again that this watch belonged to him alone. Susan finally managed to talk him into putting the watch back into the jewellery box by explaining to him that he could have it, but that she would look after it for now.

DO YOU REMEMBER SITTING ON MY LAP?

Diane Williams mourned the death of her beloved grandmother, Nanny Wyatt, very much. She had died on 4th October 1974. They had both been very fond of each other and it was only when Diane's third child, Kelly, was born on 4th May 1975, that she was finally able to get over the death of her grandmother. It was after the child's second birthday that it began to become evident that her daughter used to be her own recently deceased great-grandmother. Pam, her mother's sister, who was visiting them at the time, took the little girl on her lap who turned to her and said, 'Do you remember when you used to sit on my lap like this?' Diane and Pam laughed, since they thought it was just her childish fantasies running wild. But their laughter soon ceased when Kelly continued, 'And I used to comb your hair for you.' She now described in detail the hairstyle that Pam had worn at the time. The two-year-old said that the hairstyle had been like Cleopatra's. From where did she know this word? This particular hairstyle was out of fashion today and no one talked about it any more.

Both sisters now remembered that in those days, about 20 years ago, when they had been young girls, they had worn exactly that hairstyle and had sat on their grandmother's lap to have their hair combed. The little girl had not finished yet. She reminded Pam about the white dress with red dots that she had given her, which was also true.

Kelly's mannerisms and peculiarities were in many ways similar to those of her great-grandmother. She had never asked anyone to tell her about her great-grandmother and yet she was able to imitate her spontaneously. When the little girl sat down in the armchair she put her child's handbag on the floor between her leg and that of the chair, exactly as Nanny Wyatt had always done with her handbag. Just like her great-grandmother, Kelly continually tidied her handbag so that everything was in its right place, which seemed almost obsessive. As Kelly grew older she often enjoyed talking about her Victorian clothes, which she had worn in the past. She was able to describe them in detail even though she had never been shown any pictures. When asked how she knew about all this she said, 'I secretly used to watch the dancers in the ballroom.' She always talked in the first person when mentioning anything about her great-grandmother and she never changed her statements, even if they had first been made weeks or even months ago. She used numerous words like 'ballroom' or 'Cleopatra hairstyle', which no one uses today because they are just no longer fashionable or out of practical use. She told them that she used to live in a bungalow and was able to describe the furnishings in detail. At first Diane was unable to remember how it used to be, but gradually her memories returned and they were exactly the same as Kelly's.

When Kelly was seven years old her grandmother died, which caused great sadness in the family. Kelly comforted the mourners by saying, 'Nanny's at rest now with all the people she loved as much as us. She is with Grandad Wyatt.' They were all amazed to hear a seven-year-old express such knowledge. From where did she know all this? No one had ever talked to her about life after death.

Children often remember more than just their previous life on earth. For instance they may remember what happened after their death, including details of who came to meet them and what happened to them in the 'afterlife'. If children speak about these things, it is worth encouraging them to tell you more. Those among the Africans whose knowledge has not yet been destroyed by Christianity, listen carefully, particularly to their youngest children's statements, for they know that having just returned from 'the other side', they might have brought important things with them which are as yet unshared. After all, those on the other side have greater knowledge than we mortals.

One day an old friend of Diane's visited her and they talked about experiences that they had shared. Diane mentioned a holiday trip, but could not remember whether it had been the year 1958 or 1959. Suddenly the seven-year-old girl, whose presence the two friends had all but forgotten, said, 'I can remember it. It was the year in which we had the plague of ladybirds.' Kelly's mother was used to the fact that her daughter unexpectedly piped up with something relevant from the past. On hearing this, her friend pricked up her ears. 'Did you hear what she just said?' Diane answered her with a laugh, 'Well, she comes out with things like that from time to time.' But her friend did not want to let it rest at that and continued asking,

'How does she know about the plague of ladybirds?' Then the daughter took over the conversation and explained, 'I know it was the year of the ladybirds, because when you went on that holiday to the seaside, you wore that big funny hoop thing under your dress to make it stand out more. Your mother and I kept teasing you about it and called you a walking bell tent.' Now even Diane was nonplussed. She clearly remembered wearing a kind of hoola hoop under her dress, which had been fashionable among teenagers at that time. It was also true that her grandmother and her mother had made fun of them.

During a discussion with visitors in the sitting room about the war in the Falklands and the bombings that took place there, Kelly suddenly said, 'It was the same during the last war when they dropped the bombs. It was awful. Everyone knows that Birmingham was badly damaged.'

Later on Diane admitted, 'I never used to believe in reincarnation, but since I have had Kelly I have changed my mind. My husband Clive and I have become convinced that somehow Nanny Wyatt lives on in our daughter. I know it sounds completely ridiculous, but Kelly actually speaks as if she really is Nanny Wyatt. It is as if she is one and the same person with the same store of memories.' According to her mother, Kelly was very grown-up for a seven-year-old to the point of being able to converse with adults on their level.[20]

3

Children who are reborn as the opposite sex

THE GIRL WHO REFUSED
TO WEAR GIRLS' CLOTHES

In the autumn of 1972 Mr U. Tha Hla took his four-year-old nephew, Maung Pho Zaw, by the hand and walked across several fields in the highlands of Myanmar (Burma). They were both barefoot as was the custom among country folk. Suddenly the boy screamed. At first his uncle thought the boy had hurt himself on a thorn, but then he saw a snake quickly disappearing in the undergrowth. Farmers are familiar with this kind of snake. It was an extremely poisonous field viper, whose bite is usually fatal. Several women who were in the fields heard the scream and rushed over to see what was happening. One of the women was holding a hand-rolled cigar in her hand, which they had been smoking. When she saw what had happened, she quickly pressed the still glowing end of the cigar into the wound on the underside of the boy's left foot. This method of cauterising the snakebite is an old folk custom, which in the rarest of cases achieves the desired effect. The uncle then took the boy still shaking with agony to the nearest hospital. Once there the boy was given an antidote. The doctors were indignant about the unnecessarily large wound, which had been inflicted on the boy on top of the original bite by trying to burn it out. All attempts at saving his life were useless and the boy died that same evening. His parents were deeply upset to have lost their only child.

Their grief may have been somewhat lessened by the visit of a neighbour, who told the parents that their son, Pho Zaw, had appeared to him in a dream, telling him that he would be trying to return home to his parents.

During sleep our astral body often leaves the physical body and is able to travel through walls and through the roof of the house. We may travel vast distances in an instant and even visit the spirit world. While we are out of our physical bodies we will frequently encounter others who have also gone on an astral journey. Yet should the occasion arise, we can also meet those from the spirit world in the earthly realm, i.e. without having to make an astral journey. These beings sometimes leave their plane of existence and – invisibly to most mortals – will for instance look after someone in their charge and give that person guidance and comfort in their dreams. When a soul has decided to be reborn on earth, it usually visits its prospective parents and the surroundings where it intends to reincarnate. In the above story the neighbour had seen the deceased son in a dream and was then able to tell his parents of his wishes to be reborn to them. This was joyful news to them, since they then knew that the deceased was among them, even if invisible, and was hinting at the possibility of his return to the fold.

The deceased also met his father in a dream and reassured him that he would be reborn to them. Not long after, his wife became pregnant. When their daughter was born they noticed a round birthmark on the instep of her left foot in exactly the same place where their son had been bitten by the snake. This birthmark was also the same size as it had been on their son's foot, due to the glowing cigar having enlarged the original wound. The parents both knew that their son had returned to them in the form of a girl whom they called Myint, yet they had been looking forward to having another son and were therefore a little disappointed.

Sometimes we decide to be reborn as the opposite sex, as some things, such as motherhood or fatherhood for example, are only possible or easier to learn about in the body of a particular sex. As spirit beings we are strictly speaking sexless. In the course of our many incarnations we want to try out, if possible, all aspects of human existence on earth. We usually think about what we want to be reborn as while we are in that place we call the 'afterlife'. If for example we decide to explore and experience all the aspects of motherhood, we may choose to incarnate as a woman for the next ten lives. When this 'programme' is completed we can decide to experiment with another aspect of life on earth. If for example we choose to experience power, we would in most cases opt for a series of male incarnations. Apart from those who are on earth for the first time, there are presumably very few souls who have never experienced being the opposite sex in a previous life.

When Myint was two years old and beginning to speak coherently, she said that a snake had bitten her, and pointed to the sole of her left foot. Another time she mentioned the name of the boy she had once been in the past. She also displayed a great fear of snakes.

As we have already touched upon earlier, events related to wounds that we died from remain with us and frequently trigger phobias or allergies in later lives. If for instance you fell off a cliff in a past life you are likely to have a fear of steep cliffs or of heights in your present life. If you were attacked by a large wild cat and had died that way in the past, you are very likely to develop an allergy to cats and cat hairs in this life. In such cases regression therapy is highly recommended, since this can often clear the problem in a single therapy session.[21]

The rather masculine behaviour of this girl had been noticeable from the beginning. When someone tried to put earrings on her at the age of two she refused to wear them and her parents had to relinquish their wishes. From an even younger age, she stubbornly insisted on wearing her deceased brother's clothes. Her parents had to give into this for they knew that their daughter was their son from the past, reborn in a girl's body.

Thank goodness that these parents showed understanding for the behavioural differences of their daughter. She was fortunate to have been born to a family like that. Perhaps this was one of the reasons why the boy had wished to be reborn to his past parents, knowing or having been informed that they would be tolerant if he was born to them as a girl with male tendencies. You can imagine that most children, especially in the Western world and if they were growing up among people with strict orthodox religious beliefs, could have great difficulties with this kind of behaviour, which could lead to the child suffering from psychological disturbances in later life.

Even when they had become used to the fact that she only wanted to wear boys' clothes, the next thing they had to put up with was the fact that she only felt at ease with boys of her own age whom she played with. Her gait was noticeably boyish. At school she sat at the desks meant for the boys. Her teacher, who must have talked to her parent about these things, allowed her to sit there among the boys. When Myint was nine years old a school inspector visited her class. He was shocked to see the girl among the boys and immediately ordered her to change places and to wear girls' clothing from then on. Myint cried terribly because she absolutely refused to be seen as one of the girls. Her inner world and much of her outer appearance were boyish. Her parents, who were deeply affected by their daughter's pain, went to see the headmaster of the school and explained the circumstances to him. It was finally decided that their daughter should at least wear girls' clothes on two school days each week. Myint did not keep to these rules. She just refused to wear girls' clothes. The director and the teacher finally gave in and decided to overlook the fact that this girl ignored their wishes. She only began to menstruate at the age of 17, and was married at 18. Apparently her female hormones increased a great deal during motherhood and she then became more feminine and eventually her male tendencies steadily became less and less. Professor Stevenson once asked her father how he coped with the fact that his daughter wanted to be everything other than a girl. He intimated that he had actually wished for a boy and that his daughter gave him the illusion of having a son. He mainly tolerated her unusual behaviour so as not to cause her unnecessary pain.[22]

It would be wonderful if more parents adopted the attitude of this father. In Western countries left-handed children are still forced to write with their right hand. How do we then deal with children with homosexual tendencies? Society has doubtless become much more tolerant in regard to these issues. If we think back to what children who were drawn to the same sex (for reasons which have only now become clear to us through research into reincarnation) have had to suffer in past times, it is obvious how much harm has been done to these children and youngsters. Had reincarnation been generally accepted in those days these children and adults would have been treated with more care. It is high time that we not only accept reincarnation as a fact, but also consciously integrate it into our daily lives.

Professor Stevenson and his colleague Dr Jürgen Keil often visited Myint and her parents, not only to research this case from scratch, but also to follow up on the development of this girl. We must repeatedly thank Professor Stevenson and his many colleagues for their outstanding and often laborious research work, which not only serves to prove reincarnation but also helps to solve many riddles, both in a medical and interpersonal field.

The following examples about changing sex from one incarnation to another are further extracts from Stevenson's monumental work entitled *Reincarnation and Biology*. One of the many questions for which Stevenson's research has provided a preliminary answer is: At what stage of soul development does a sex change occur? At least for Myanmar he is able to answer this question based on the evidence collected there. In 26 per cent of all the cases investigated there, he found that the soul had undergone a sex change from one life to the next.[23] When we extrapolate from these results a prediction for the whole of mankind, it would mean that we change sex every fourth incarnation.

These results coincide approximately with what I know from my own experiences as a regression therapist. But it can of course vary a great deal. It is possible for someone to live for 20 or 30 lifetimes without changing sex. If someone has lived 800 lives so far, it is possible that 600, 400, or in exceptional cases just a hundred of these were male or female respectively.

THE BROTHER WHO RETURNED AS HIS OWN SISTER

In the autumn of 1967 the 13-year-old Apirak drove to Pakchong with his parents and other members of his family. The town was situated about 180 kilometres north east of Bangkok. On the way there their car collided with a lorry and the 13-year-old boy died immediately. His grandfather was badly injured whereas the rest of the passengers got away lightly only suffering from shock. There was blood on the face and head of the dead boy, which contrary to the local customs was not wiped off. It took a week before the dead boy's body was returned to Bangkok and finally cremated. Apirak had been a strange boy; even as a child he had only played with girls. He had wanted to be a 'girls' girl' and had only seldom worn boys' clothes, preferring to wear those of the opposite sex. He loved to paint his lips and blacken his eyebrows and colour his cheeks with rouge. He walked like a girl and later on like a young woman and often expressed the wish to be reborn as a girl. The problems he encountered by being so different often caused him to feel depressed. He mentioned in passing that he would love to know what happens after death. Perhaps he was even toying with the idea of suicide? He had developed a passion for drumming, which seemed to help him forget his troubles. Now he had died.

About three months later Nitaya, the mother of the deceased, had a dream in which her son appeared to her, asking her whether he could be reborn to her and her family. Her sister also had a dream at the same time in which Apirak told her that he wished to return to his family. On the 7th November 1968 Nitaya gave birth to a girl whom she gave the name Ariya. They were all shocked to find a large port-coloured birthmark on her left cheek. A similar birthmark of the same colour was also found on the top of her head. On her back they discovered an indentation, which was in precisely the same place where Apirak had had a birthmark of the same size and depth. The family was of course aware of the fact that the deceased had announced his intention of returning to the same mother, and that she had agreed to this at the time. So now they knew that Apirak had been granted his wish to return in a girl's body.

Sometimes we are born into the 'wrong' body in order to balance out a karmic debt. Maybe Apirak had made fun of another boy in a previous life, who had felt uncomfortable in his body and therefore wore girls' clothes. The distributive justice of the Law of Karma will always ensure that where we behaved unlovingly towards another person in the past, we will find ourselves – usually in a future life – on the receiving end of similar circumstances. It is possible that Apirak was meant to die at the young age of 13, since he had suffered enough due to his painful experiences in a body that had been 'wrong' for him. Now he was allowed to return in the body he had often wished for. This time his face was disfigured. Even in this girl's body he had decided to pay his karmic debts. It is likely that in a past life he had made fun of someone or had harmed someone who had unfortunate looks. Now she was bound to experience being made fun of by other children, by having a similarly unattractive and conspicuous mark on her face.

Everyone wondered what might have caused these two large repulsive birthmarks on the face and head of the child. At last they had an explanation that seemed to fit. A superstitious belief in this country is as follows: If blood is left on the body of the dead and is not washed away, they are likely to be born with a birthmark in their following life. They remembered that blood had been left on Apirak's dead body before his cremation, which had been in exactly the same places as the birthmarks that now appeared on the body of their daughter Ariya.

When their daughter was only a few weeks old, the papers published a report about her case saying that it was, 'an interesting case suggesting that reincarnation exists'. Stevenson heard about this girl through these news reports and went to visit the family in order to find out the details. After that he frequently visited the family on his visits to Thailand in order to follow up on Ariya's development. They were curious about whether the girl would say things that would reveal her knowledge of being her own deceased brother. In order to research this as a true case of reincarnation, Stevenson must have urged the members of her family beforehand not to tell the girl anything about her deceased brother, so as not to influence her.

At the age of two-and-a-half, Ariya began to talk about herself as the deceased Apirak. When asked where she got the birthmark on her cheek from she answered, 'injury from car'. When she was shown some photographs she pointed to one on which her deceased brother was and said, 'Ut'. This had been the boy's nickname. Her aunt wanted to make sure her niece really was her nephew reborn, so she used an accepted, tried and tested method of detection. She took Apirak's toys and clothes, mixed them up with many other things belonging to other children and teenagers and stood the little girl in front of this pile of things asking her to pick out everything that used to belong to her. As the witnesses had assured Professor Stevenson, she did indeed pick out exactly those things that used to belong to her brother. As time went by they noticed her fear of lorries. The following is even stranger: If you thought that Ariya would finally be able to live out her life as a girl now, you are mistaken, for this girl moved like a boy and preferred to wear boys' clothes.

We can see from this that there is still much that is unexplained and many things left to discover and research relating to the laws under which we set out on our earthly and spiritual journeys. As soon as public money becomes available for research into reincarnation, many riddles will be solved. Everything takes its time. Meanwhile we must be thankful for the new questions that have arisen for us to solve out of Stevenson's research. By the way, at the age of two-and-a-half Ariya already showed the same passion for drumming as her deceased brother.[24]

THE GIRL TWINS WHO
USED TO BE BEST FRIENDS

The following is one of the most interesting cases ever to have emerged from all the research into reincarnation.

Whom do you think we must thank for this story? Once again it is Professor Stevenson. The story begins in a past life lived in southern Sri Lanka.

Johnny and Robert had been inseparable friends since childhood and had been to school together. As they grew up they showed no interest whatsoever in the female sex. People began to say that they must be homosexual, and this talk was not kept secret from their families and others in their village. The boys showed no signs of being effeminate; on the contrary it was in fact the opposite. Even as boys they were active climbers who effortlessly climbed the coconut palms. They were also excellent swimmers who loved to dive for lobsters even in deep waters. Johnny worked in a factory making frames for spectacles, while his friend was a casual labourer carrying sacks of cement and stones on building sites.

At this point in the story it is worth mentioning an important event. One of Johnny's work mates in the factory was a man called Amarapala Hettiaratchi who had become good friends with him. He had invited Johnny and his friend Robert to his wedding, where he was to marry Yasawathie on the 20th October 1966.

At the end of the sixties when they were in their twenties (Johnny was 26, Robert 25 years old), a growing disaffection with the government was spreading especially among the young people. There were direct clashes between the rebels and the police. In the region of Galle, Johnny was their leader and Robert his representative.

Groups led by Robert and Johnny secretly crept into police stations at night and attacked the unsuspecting policemen who were asleep at the time. The aim of these actions was to acquire weapons in order to carry out their rebellion more effectively. They also produced bombs from the simplest ingredients. The government took severe action against these surprise attacks, and in 1971 the biggest confrontation with government troops took place. Within three weeks the rebellion was over. Altogether about 1,200 people were officially accounted for as having died in this rebellion and were being mourned for on both sides.

A search was launched for Johnny and Robert. They had both been staying in Johnny's house up in the hills, the place where the uprising had been prepared and rebels had been trained for the last year or so. Just before the soldiers stormed this building, the two friends managed to find a cave to hide in, which was out in the stony countryside surrounding the house. Some days later someone gave the police a tip-off as to where they were hiding. The desperately wanted men were finally arrested at the bus station of Galle and were then interrogated at the police station. Robert had thought of a plan for his escape. He claimed he could show the police a stash of weapons, which had apparently been hidden near the sea. On the 19th April five policemen led him with his hands handcuffed behind his back to the place he had described. It was situated on a cliff, which dropped several metres straight down to the sea. Being a strong swimmer Robert had planned to break free from the police and to leap into the sea to escape by swimming, even if he couldn't use his arms. He pushed one of the policemen aside, head-butted another and was about to leap into the sea, when he was hit by a bullet in the stomach on the right-hand side in the area of his liver. His lifeless body fell head first into the sea. Angered by Robert's deceit, the police then carried out an even harsher interrogation with Johnny, which ended in his death. His body was hung upside down, and was later cremated.

On 3rd November 1978, seven years after the death of the two friends, non-identical twin girls were born in the hospital of Galle. The twins' parents were Amarapala and Yasawathie Hettiaratchi. (You may remember that Johnny and Robert had been invited to their wedding.) The twin girl who was born five minutes before her sister was given the name Sivanthie, and the other the name Sheromie. Sivanthie had a noticeable birthmark just below her last rib on the right-hand side of her body, but they found no birthmarks on her sister. The family lived in a small village called Pitadenyia, which was 14 kilometres north of Galle. When they were both about two-and-a-half years old, the older one of the two began to talk about her other home where she apparently had a father, a mother and a sister. She talked about how she had to hide in a cave with 'Johnia'. She described how they had been arrested and how they had had their hands handcuffed behind their backs, and how she had been shot when she'd been trying to escape by leaping into the sea. When describing this she pointed to the birthmark on the right side of her stomach.

Sivanthie also begged to be allowed to go home. She said that her mother was called Mary Akka and her father Kalu Mahattaya. She mentioned a temple by the name of Yatigala, which she used to visit in the past. When the twins were three-and-a-half years old they were taken to visit this temple that was 15 kilometres away. Sivanthie noticed that the temple had been rebuilt. While visiting the temple she suddenly remembered more details from her past life. It was here that for the first time she mentioned that her name used to be Robert. Her sister Sheromie had not mentioned anything about a past life yet.

At last they had a name. The parents remembered the man called Robert who had been involved in a rebellion against the government and had been shot whilst trying to escape in April 1971. The rumour about one of the Hettiaratchi twins being the reincarnation of Robert, spread like wildfire throughout the region. Robert and Johnny had become national heroes of sorts whose story must have been well-known to everyone. During May and June 1982 several members of Robert's family and friends visited the Hettiaratchi family to ask Sivanthie some questions. One of the first to visit her was Grananadasa, one of Robert's old friends, who was Johnny's brother. When the four-year-old twin saw this man she said, 'My younger brother has come to visit.' She had until now not mentioned anything about her previous identity.

Visiting certain places or meeting certain people we once knew in the past often triggers past-life memories. This is how we can explain the déjà vu phenomenon. When we arrive in a new town and suddenly notice that everything seems familiar to us, this is because in many cases we have already been there in a past life. If we meet a person with whom we had either a positive or negative connection in a past life, our reaction to that person may be determined by that past. This also explains love at first sight, or the initial feeling towards another person whom we have only just met. Every place and every person radiates a certain vibration. If these emissions are strong enough they resonate with our own vibration, which has been stored in us. In the case of Sheromie, Grananadasa's specific vibrations were strong enough to make an instant recognition possible.

Suddenly even Sheromie's blocks to her knowledge of past lives seemed to have been removed. She remembered that she had been Johnny in her past life and recognised her friend Robert in her twin sister. They both now recognised several members of their past family and acquaintances and called them by their names. On the 18th July Johnny's mother and his younger sister visited Sheromie to see whether she would recognise them. When the visitors entered the house, the four-year-old said to the others, 'This is my mother and this is my Nangi' (a name used for a younger sister). Two newspapers published reports about these sensational twins. A research scientist by the name of Godwin Samararatne took this case on board and questioned eleven relatives and acquaintances of the twins and took them to various scenes and venues of their past lives.

Sheromie was asked to show him and the people accompanying him the way to Johnny's house. The little girl confidently led them uphill into the rocky countryside, until they stood in front of the ruins of a mud house. This was the place where Johnny's hidden house had been, which was later demolished. Sivanthie was able to show the police the exact path she had taken, when she'd been Robert, to show the police the place where weapons were supposedly hidden. In this place she was able to describe the exact events leading to Robert's death. Three months later Stevenson walked this way during a five-day investigation of this case and found the track to be overgrown and difficult to navigate. This is why he was amazed at how the little girl Sivanthie had been able to show people the way with such ease. Naturally the twins' family, the family of the two deceased and their close friends, no longer were in any doubt about the fact that these twins really were the reincarnation of Johnny and Robert.

When I enquired about these events in the area in December 1998, every adult I questioned knew about the past incidents concerning Johnny and Robert and their rebirth as the twin sisters. They had become local celebrities.

Both the girls had phobias. They were afraid of people wearing khaki-coloured shirts like the ones the police wear in Sri Lanka, and they cowered from fright whenever they saw a Jeep in which there were policemen or soldiers.

Whatever resulted in a highly painful experience or even in traumatic death in a previous lifetime, remains stored in the subconscious, or the emotional body, which we take with us from one life to the next. This part of the subconscious is like a storage chamber for our emotions. Receiving the same or similar input again in the present can reactivate these stored emotions. In the above-mentioned case we are dealing with the police, their uniforms and shirts (they rarely wear jackets due to the hot weather) as well as military Jeeps serving as triggers for the fear stored in the subconscious of the girls. This fear can suddenly reappear during a renewed confrontation, resulting in fearful reactions. Such fears stem from past experience and serve as protection against subjecting ourselves to the same situations again. These fears are often completely inappropriate in the present (for instance the fear of being hanged), so it is a good idea to free ourselves of this baggage from the past as quickly as possible by making use of regression therapy for instance. During regression the energy that has once been attached to the hidden fears is released, enabling us to put it to better use, thereby benefiting our lives and rekindling the joy in living.

To a certain extent, Robert and Johnny's peculiarities and even their outer appearance had been imprinted on Sivanthie and Sheromie. The older of the twins, who was able to remember having been Robert, was more robust in stature than her sister, as had been the case with Robert. Sheromie had darker skin than Sivanthie, just as Johnny's had been darker than Robert's. Both girls enjoyed making bombs out of clay or sand just as they had done in their previous lives.

They even explained in childish terms exactly what was needed to make them. Both girls also had the habit of putting sticks in their mouths and pretending to light and smoke them. The two deceased friends had been heavy smokers. We now come to an important detail, which is why this chapter was included under the heading of 'sex changes' in this section of the book.

Both sisters displayed very clear manly behaviour. Much to their parents' displeasure, they both urinated standing up even when they were very little. The girls only gradually gave up this habit. They both liked wearing T-shirts, an attire usually reserved for boys in those days, and rolled them up from the belly upwards, to expose their stomachs and part of their chests. Johnny and Robert also used to do this. Both girls developed a passion for climbing trees and riding bikes, which was just not done by other girls in those days. Even at a young age they stroked their chins saying that they had beards, just like the two young men they had been in the past.[25]

Having reached this particular part of the story while writing my book, I took a break and made my way to the restaurant. I had heard from a Ceylonese man, who was fluent in several languages, that Johnny's brother was running a diving school here on the beach of Unawatuna, only a few hundred metres from my hut where I was spending my time writing. This Ceylonese man had been the captain of a luxury yacht belonging to the weapons dealer and millionaire Adnan Kashoggi for a long time and was now living nearby. I mentioned that I was interested in meeting this brother of Johnny's. In the restaurant he introduced me to Chandra Soma who had spent practically all his life here and was certain to be able to tell me something about Johnny and Robert. Chandra came over and sat down by me while I gave the waiter my order. Chandra was 53 years old with a white beard and only three fingers on his left hand. He had lost one when trying to intervene during a violent clash. He told me that he had been a close friend of both Johnny and Robert's.

At the end of the sixties, radical communist beliefs had crept into the minds of the people, especially the youngsters. They wanted wealth and work to be distributed more fairly and hoped to achieve this by bringing about the collapse of the privileged ruling classes. Johnny and others, teachers in particular, gave public lectures. Johnny was radically left wing and was involved in encouraging everyone to help in bringing about the downfall of the system. Chandra's father and mother were policemen who Johnny spoke out against in their discussions together. Chandra supported the rebels financially. He himself had spent several years in Colombo, the place of his childhood, working in a factory that produced batteries. Robert, who was Johnny's right-hand man, was responsible for acquiring weapons and the manufacturing of bombs. Chandra also helped Robert to get work in the battery factory in Colombo with the sole purpose of acquiring the necessary knowledge and materials to make bombs. Their first bombs were tested on the beach of Unawatuna. Even though they must have heard explosions from time to time, the local people kept quiet, for most of them belonging to the poorer part of the population supported the communist activities. It was during one of these operations that Robert burnt his hands and injured his face, resulting in long-term eye problems.

Chandra knew them both very well and said they were not homosexual, contrary to what others had said. He felt that the reason for their not being interested in girls was their total immersion in the *idea of communism to the point of not wanting to waste any time on private affairs. Their main aim, namely the collapse of the class system, was a far more important goal, for which it was worth putting their lives at stake and sacrificing any personal and private interests.*

Until the outbreak of the great rebellion in the spring of 1971, the majority of the population living on the south coast of Ceylon supported the rebels. Johnny had been one of the leaders. By Chandra's estimation at least 3,000 people in southern Ceylon lost their lives during this rebellion. A great number of children who were later born in this area can remember having been among those that died, and now know that they have been reborn. Chandra had heard of at least ten cases in which children were able to give exact evidence of their past identities as one of those killed during the riots.

Any researcher wishing to work in the field of the demonstration and documentation of reincarnation would find much scope for this type of endeavour in the region of Galle; there are many cases just waiting to be thoroughly investigated and evaluated. Chandra promised that during the next few days he would show me the places nearby where Robert and Johnny had carried out their rebellious activities.

He turned up that same afternoon on 22nd December asking me whether I was ready to take a walk. We left the beach and headed west up a narrow path. We finally arrived at his parents' house, which he had since sold. He led me around to the back of the house and told me the following.

In the summer of 1970 he was sitting in one of the rooms with Robert and Johnny, who were both being searched for by the police, when they heard noises outside. As they were used to constantly being on the lookout for unexpected visits from the police, they jumped out of the back window and rushed across streams and bogs on wooden walkways and hid themselves in the undergrowth. The policemen must have caught sight of them, for they sent many volleys of gunfire in the direction where they suspected them to be heading, but none of the policemen dared to follow the two armed men into the bog.

Later on Chandra led me to the demolished house, which had once belonged to Johnny's parents. Johnny himself had lived there until shortly before he was arrested. It was this ruin that Sheromie had led the group of people to, who had been keen to check out her story. Sivanthie had also been among this group. From here they walked about a kilometre to the house Robert had grown up in and had spent most of his life in until shortly before his death. This house now stood empty, but was still habitable. Apparently this was where Sivanthie had revealed further details about her past life. When I asked Chandra whether it would be possible for me to visit the twins, he told me that they no longer wished to see anyone interested in their past or their past lives. They had had to experience enough disturbance and excitement in recent years and now wanted to live in peace. He did give me to understand though that he would see what he could do to help. He pointed to the rugged countryside leading down to the sea and told me that there were caves up ahead, where the weapons and bombs had been concealed. Even though Johnny and Robert were close friends of his they had never shown him those hiding places.

Chandra had only been involved with their affairs half-heartedly, since he was a landowner and his father had been a police inspector in Colombo up until his death in 1965. Chandra's brother was also in the police force. Even among his friends they had to be very discreet among those who knew what was going on. Even so Chandra was arrested after Johnny and Robert's death and was sentenced to one-and-a-half years in prison.

On the 3rd January I finally met Johnny's younger brother Grananadasa, who runs an international diving school in Unawatuna. We had arranged to meet at eight o'clock and now sat opposite each other in the diving school restaurant. His story, which I managed to get out of him by asking him endless questions, went as follows.

He had known about his older brother's plans because Johnny was involved in the rebellion both verbally and actively, which his brother Grananadasa who was only three years his junior could hardly fail to notice. He too had been enthusiastic about the idea of communism; that is why he moved to the north of the island after the rebellion failed and the police stepped up their search for accomplices. He returned from there a year after Johnny's death and was immediately arrested and sentenced to two years in prison.

Several years later a woman who was originally from Unawatuna and was visiting her family there told him the following. She said that in her village, which is about 14 kilometres from Unawatuna, were some twins who claimed to be the reincarnation of Johnny and Robert. This sparked off Grananadasa's curiosity, so he jumped on his bike and rode straight to Pitadenyia to the house where the twins lived. When the three-and-a-half-year-old Sheromie saw him she happily ran up to him and hugged him. The visitor claimed to be able to see a slight likeness to Johnny in her face. Even though they did not talk to each other, he was convinced that this really was his reincarnated brother standing there and he began weeping uncontrollably. The parents had recorded the twins' statements on tape. They talked about having been Robert and Johnny, about their involvement in the rebellion and about having made bombs and also about their own deaths. After Grananadasa had listened to everything he left promising to return soon.

One day later he returned with his mother to see the twins. When Sheromie saw her she ran up to her and hugged her saying, 'Sisel Hamy!' (this was the woman's name) and, 'Ama', which means mother. Then everyone cried. As soon as everyone had recovered, Johnny's mother began asking Sheromie many questions, for instance: 'Where were you on the morning before your death?' All this time Sheromie was sitting on her previous mother's lap. Three hours later when Grananadasa motioned to Johnny's mother that it was time to leave, the latter got ready to take the girl off her lap. But Sheromie did not want to be parted from her 'mother' and kept repeating: 'Take me with you!' Finally her real mother lifted her down. The two girls cried inconsolably when the visitors left the house. All they could do was promise to return soon, which was little consolation to Sheromie.

Meanwhile word of this reunion had spread throughout the village and many inquisitive visitors had gathered outside the house. It was only three days later that Grananadasa returned to Pitadenyia. He once again listened to the cassette, which apparently still exists today. When answering his questions Sheromie told him among other things that shortly before 'his' death when he was being tortured in the interrogation chamber and was hanging upside down, he remembered seeing a picture of Buddha hanging on the wall upside down.

Some days later, when the papers were already publishing reports about the twins, the three-and-a-half-year-old twins were taken to Unawatuna accompanied by about 20 people. Apart from the press there were several neutral observers present, whose job it was to take exact notes of everything. I'm sure Stevenson would have loved to witness this. He was to be granted many such firsthand experiences in his life with other children who remembered their past lives.

Grananadasa joined the team of investigators, while the two girls strode ahead. Their first stop was Johnny's house where they were asked many questions. Then Sivanthie led the way to the place where Robert had died on the cliffs. After that they went to see Robert's house. Wherever they were the two girls answered the numerous questions asked of them. Sheromie only gave brief answers whereas Sivanthie gave them detailed descriptions.

The two girls are now 20 years old. They visit Grananadasa in Unawatuna between two and four times a year, whereas he drives over to visit the twins four to six times a year. They always exchange gifts. Their mother was naturally concerned that they may wish to return to their previous family for good, however, these fears have long since disappeared. Sivanthie (the one who used to be Robert) attends a college and is interested in gaining a higher education just like Robert had been keen to. Sheromie on the other hand enjoys helping her mother around the house. Grananadasa assured me that if the twins get married, he and his mother would definitely be there, since they were one big family. Every time the twins come to Unawatuna to visit Sheromie's mother from the past, they all end up crying. The man telling me this story observed that the twins are both still rather masculine. He promised me that if I return in a few weeks he would *take me with him to visit them. He also agreed to introduce me to his mother.*

On my return to Unawatuna on 26th January I once more visited Grananadasa accompanied by my partner. There were still some questions I wanted answers to. On each of his first three visits Grananadasa had listened to the cassette and had frequently visited the twins in the following weeks. During this time many friends and relatives of Johnny and Robert had turned up asking him to take them to the twins' family. On the cassette Sivanthie's and Sheromie's voices were clearly audible. When I asked Grananadasa where exactly the shot wound was on Sheromie's body, he said that he had seen it long ago, but could not remember whether it was on the right or the left. When I asked him whether he could have another look next time he visited the twins, he said that it would not be proper for a man to ask a young woman to bare her abdomen so that he could look for a scar.

At their first meeting when Sheromie had slung her arms around him, Sivanthie had also recognised him. She had smiled at him and had said something to him that he could not remember now. When on his second visit he had turned up to see the twins with his mother, Sheromie had called him 'my brother' and his mother 'Mother'. The twins as well as Grananadasa and his mother all cried. Grananadasa thought the tears were mostly due to the sadness they felt about no longer belonging to the same family.

He was particularly angry when I told him that after questioning many people, Stevenson had concluded that Robert and Johnny had been homosexual. Grananadasa had revered his brother, who appears to have been an example to him.

Up until three years before he died, Johnny had always dressed smartly as far as his finances would allow. He and Robert had both been smokers. They had looked and acted like two gentlemen. In 1968 they had become completely obsessed by the idea of communism. They joined this forbidden party and read their underground papers. The workers committee of the communist party organised a special group of 'jungle fighters', who had to keep to the following rules: no girlfriends, for they could betray the secrecy of their actions. No alcohol or drugs, and no sex, either heterosexual or homosexual, were permitted. Not even cigarettes or visits to the cinema were allowed, since these were seen as capitalist influences. They were also expected to dress very simply. The money saved in this way was supposed to benefit the communist organisation. Had Johnny and Robert really been homosexual, they would surely not have volunteered for this specialist training. Johnny had even become a leader in the region of Galle due to being a gifted speaker.

Finally Grananadasa gave us his mother's address, for I still hoped to visit her. He also promised us that we would get to meet the twins, but that he first wanted to visit them himself to get their permission and to arrange a date.

I visited Johnny's mother on the 10th February 1999, who had been living in her daughter's house in Unawatuna for years. This 88-year-old, white-haired lady is partially blind and is suffering from Parkinson's disease in her hands. At first she thought that we (my interpreter Aki, my partner and I) had come to find out about Johnny's communist past. This is why when mentioning his death she began to cry and said that Johnny had once explained to her with great passion

103

that his only reason for fighting for social justice was so that one day his children and grandchildren would have a better life.

Above all else I was interested to know how her first meeting with her reincarnated son had gone. When her son told her about the twins, Johnny's mother, her daughter and Grananadasa travelled by bus to the village where they lived. When they entered the house, Sheromie came running up to them happily and called Johnny's mother 'Ama' (Mother). The little girl also recognised her sister from her past life and called her 'Nangi' (younger sister). After this Johnny's mother picked up the girl who was Johnny's reincarnation, followed by her daughter who sat the girl on her knee. The twins' parents as well as their grandmother were also present at the time. They were all extremely touched and were all crying tears of joy mingled with sadness. In no time this news had spread far and wide, so it was not long before dozens of inquisitive people filled the house.

It was not long after this event that the twins visited Unawatuna in order to lead the group accompanying them, including the twins' parents and Grananadasa, and a number of inquisitive people to Rumasala, a village in the bush outside Unawatuna. Johnny's mother saw the two girls leading the group to Johnny's house, which by now was a mere ruin. After that they led everyone to Robert's house. An interesting detail is the fact that when the twins walked through the village they recognised several local people and are reported to have made comments about who had once been their enemies.

Sivanthie had recognised Johnny's mother on her first visit and had called her 'Ama', just as Robert had done in the past. Aki explained that it was the custom in Sri Lanka for close friends to call each other's relatives by the same names (i.e. acting as if the respective person were their own mother, father, uncle, etc.).

Both Sheromie and Sivanthie had often asked their mothers from the past whether they would be allowed to return to them for good, but their present parents forbade this of course.

Sheromie calls her mother from the past 'Ama' to this day. She visits her frequently and was with her only three days ago to ask her to help her find a job, since her former mother has several relatives by the sea that may have heard of work in the area. Apparently the 21-year-old is about to start work in a factory on the south coast. On meeting Sheromie for the first time Johnny's mother noticed the determined expression on Sheromie's face, which was much like her own. Sivanthie's former mother later expressed herself in similar terms about Sivanthie knowing that she was her reincarnated son.

Due to my wish to leave Unawatuna shortly thereafter, I was not sure whether we would get the chance to see either of the twins face to face, and as it happens we never did get to meet them.

The day before I was due to leave, Chandra Soma led me through the woods to the place by the sea where Robert had intended to leap into the water in the hope of escaping his captors. This path was difficult to find and I was not sure whether I would be able to find it again on my own. Is it not then astounding that the three-and-a-half-year-old Sivanthie had had no problem in leading the group unerringly and without so much as a moment's hesitation to that rocky place?

You may have noticed that some of the statements seem to contradict each other. This is understandable when you consider the long time lapses during which facts may have become somewhat *blurred in people's memories. Even so I think that this does not detract from the significance of those past events.*

THE BEARDED WOMAN

José Martins Ribeiro was born in 1872 and was called Zeca by his friends and relatives. As a young adult he was interested in politics and revolutionary activities, but then became a businessman, got married and settled down in Dom Feliciano in southern Brazil. His wife became pregnant, and during this time he fell ill and died before he was able to see his child. His cousin Georgeta, who was married to Patricio de Albuquerque, gave birth to a daughter in 1919 who was given the name Dulcina. In the beginning, this girl tended to be often ill even though her body seemed to be strong. She first started talking about her past life at great length at the age of five. She said that she was a man called Zeca who was married and insisted on being called by this name. One day she asked her mother, 'Why have I changed sex? I used to be a man and now I am a girl.'

Children often have great problems dealing with a sex change. Sometimes their past life is still so strongly in them that they want to, or seemingly have to, continue living in it. Once reborn they are forced to be the new person. Sometimes they just don't know which person or sex they are, for at times they will feel more certain of one identity while at other times the opposite will be true. It all seems to make no sense to them, especially when adults choose not to tell them the reasons or are unable to do so. Many parents think that their children are inventing stories when talking about their past lives as the opposite gender, even though it may set them thinking when their children eventually start to exhibit unmistakable characteristics in their looks or behaviour. Most doctors when asked about this matter will try to explain away these crazy ideas coming from children who are confused about their sex by blaming the condition on an over-production of the opposite sex hormone. They always know best. Nonetheless the question still remains unanswered: Why do some children have more of these opposite sex hormones than others? Is it not because they belonged to the opposite sex in their previous life? There is one mystery that remains to be solved. How is it that both the physical and character traits relating to the sex of the person in a previous life can assert themselves in the new body that is now the opposite sex?

Dulcina, who was now five years old, looked into the mirror and sadly asked her mother, 'Why are my eyes a different colour now?' She sat on her horse like a boy and looked masculine. She even grew muscles like a man. After puberty she grew hair on her arms, her legs and above her top lip, which soon looked like a moustache. Her breasts remained underdeveloped. Even so there was a man who wished to marry her. She and her newborn child died during childbirth, even though she had a caesarean birth.[26]

Now that we know the reasons for such specific sexual deviances, what will we think when we next see a woman with a moustache? How will we respond to transvestites from now on? Will we still be able to make negative comments about such people as we did in ignorance? There is something we must remember: everything we do to another person in thought, word or deed that puts them at a disadvantage or even hurts them, we will one day have to experience ourselves. This is how God's Law of Karma works. People who are born into the 'wrong' bodies and have visible physical characteristics of the opposite sex, may need this experience to balance a karmic debt. (They may well have chosen this fate for themselves in the afterlife, where they were able to see things from a higher perspective.) Apart from this these people serve as a test for us to determine how loving we have become.

At this point I wish to present you with an interesting case about a girl who was not only born as the opposite sex, but was also born into a completely different culture. This case is taken from Stevenson's incomparably rich collection of cases dealing with children who remember their past lives.

THE GIRL WHO WAS A
JAPANESE SOLDIER IN HER PREVIOUS LIFE

In the Burmese town of Pyawbwe in northern Myanmar, lived a man called U. Aye Kyaw and his wife Daw Hkin Win. On the 17th February 1962 Mrs Win gave birth to a daughter who was given the name Ma Win Tar. (I shall call her Ma Win for short.)

Imagine how shocked her parents must have been when they saw that some fingers were missing on their daughter's hands and that others were crippled. The middle and ring finger were hanging loosely from her hand. They also discovered strange indentations on her wrists, which looked as if she had been tied up tightly with a rope. The doctor decided that the least they could do was to amputate the two loose fingers.

When Ma Win was three years old she began to tell her parents about having been a Japanese soldier in Burma in the past, where she had been captured, tortured and finally burnt alive. To explain this I have added the following comments. In 1945 the British troops reclaimed Burma. The japanese army had occupied Burma in the years before that and had often mistreated the local

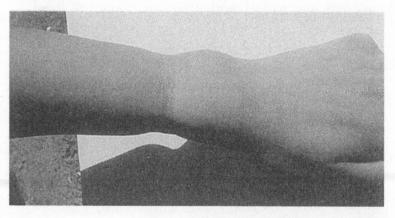

View of Ma Win Tar's left forearm as it appeared in 1978. One can see a pattern of three separate depressions extending around the arm and corresponding to the grooves that a rope might make if wrapped tightly around the arm three times.

population, thereby instilling a great hatred for the Japanese in them. With the invasion of British troops many of the Japanese units were separated from each other, which meant that many of them did not find their way back to their own country. They retreated into the forests hoping to survive there as long as possible. Many Japanese soldiers lost contact with their widely dispersed companies and so tried to survive on their own. They had to protect themselves against the indigenous people particularly in those places where the Japanese had caused gruesome suffering among the locals. These local people now took ruthless revenge on anyone they captured that once belonged to those occupying troops. Hundreds if not thousands of those falling into the hands of the Burmese must have died a cruel death at that time. Many of those Japanese soldiers who died in Burma have been reborn in that country and have remembered their previous lives. Several of them were reborn with white skin and were therefore considered to be Albinos. (Stevenson writes about this in his reports.)[27]

It is also possible for dark-skinned children to be born in countries populated by white people. The genetic parents of these coloured children were both white-skinned, including all their ancestors. Why children are sometimes born with a different skin colour to their parents in spite of their spotless genetic heritage is likely to remain a scientific mystery for a long time. I could well imagine that there are karmic reasons for this, for anyone who made fun of people with a different skin colour, put them down or intentionally harmed them in a past life, will in some way or other have to experience a similar fate. Regression therapy could go a long way towards determining the truth of this matter.

It had not been forgotten that in the region of Pyawbwe Japanese soldiers had been tortured to death towards the end of the war and even after it had ended. Sometimes they had been burnt to death, which was what had happened to the Japanese soldier whom the three-year-old Ma Win claimed to have been and had started talking about.

The soldier must have accumulated some terrible karma for himself in his past lives to have come to such a gruesome end. All those who were involved with his torture and murder will also carry a tremendous karmic burden, which will have to be balanced out in a future life in a similar way. It seems to me that during a person's early incarnations on earth, the cruel behaviour patterns still present in him or her can only be gradually made to fade by experiencing the same cruel and unloving behaviour as that which he once inflicted on others in one of his past lives. We gradually seem to be conditioned into loving earth beings over many lifetimes. I feel almost inclined to put it the following way: the age of a soul can be determined by how loving a person is.[28]

It is true that Ma Win had apparently never mentioned a Japanese name in her youth, unless of course they had not understood her due to the unusual sounds she used. Her behaviour was very Japanese. She did not like the Burmese food because it was too spicy for her. She preferred sweet food and pork, which is absolutely forbidden for Buddhists. She was very brave when hurt, never feeling sorry for herself. Unlike her peers she loved to work conscientiously and hard just like the Japanese. Stevenson discovered that she had a tendency to be cruel and wasn't afraid of hitting other children in the face. This was highly frowned upon in Myanmar, for this kind of punishment is seen as a terrible insult. As the Burmese remembered with horror, it was apparently this type of chastisement that had been routinely administered by Japanese occupation forces on the locals. Ma Win also found it impossible to get used to Buddhism and lacked respect when meeting monks, even though her parents repeatedly reminded her to fold her hands and bow down in front of monks when she met them. She also preferred to crouch down and sit on her heels like the Japanese, whereas in Buddhist countries they crouched or sat very differently.

Should you have a child that exhibits unusual behaviour, that child is not necessarily rebelling against the adults or trying to see how far it can push its boundaries; so do not punish the child for this. It could well be that the child brought this behaviour as well as other peculiarities with it from a past life, and is therefore only able to gradually adjust to the changes required to fit in with its present culture or social setting. This is why I suggest to all parents to exercise circumspection, understanding and tolerance when dealing with children that portray unusual behaviour.

Ma Win insisted on being seen as Japanese among her playmates and if anyone tried to say otherwise she answered proudly, 'I am Japanese. What do you take me for?' Several years later when a Japanese Graves Commission came to Pyawbwe, Ma Win said to her friends, 'They are part of our nation.'

As you can imagine from having read these reports so far, Ma Win's behaviour was completely boyish. She dressed like a boy, wearing trousers and shirts and had her hair cut the way boys like it, until her parents finally forced her to stop looking like a boy. She gradually got used to the fact that she was becoming a woman and when Stevenson visited her when she was twenty-two years old she told him that she no longer wished to return to Japan.[29]

4

Children's sudden panic attacks

A PHOBIA OF THE SOUND OF CANNON
FIRE, RELATING TO A BATTLE IN THE
CIVIL WAR, IS CARRIED OVER INTO
THE PRESENT-DAY LIFE OF A CHILD

In her book *Children's Past Lives*, which I recommend to all
parents, Carol Bowman explains how she came to accept
reincarnation by witnessing the panic attacks of her own
children. She had a nine-year-old daughter, Sarah, and a
son called Chase. 4th July, Independence Day in America,
is celebrated every year with huge parades, various forms
of popular entertainment, dancing and firework displays,
and plenty of entertainment for the children. This national
holiday was also celebrated with pomp and ceremony in
Ashville, North Carolina, where Carol and her husband
Steve lived with their children. For the children the day
usually ends with youngsters setting off bangers and flares
at dusk, before all eyes are drawn to a gigantic firework
display that lights up the night sky. While the rockets were
being fired into the sky sounding like cannons, and the

crowd was cheering with amazement, the little boy, Chase, suddenly began to cry inconsolably. When his mother asked him what had happened he did not answer. She then hugged and comforted him, but the crying did not stop, in fact it became worse.

Carol then felt that the best thing to do was to take Chase home immediately. She told her husband that she would go on ahead. The five-year-old sobbed so much that she had to pick him up and carry him home. Once they got there she sat down in a rocking chair with the boy on her lap. When his crying had subsided a little, she asked him what the problem was and whether he was in pain. He just shook his head. When she asked him whether the rocket noises had frightened him, his tears started flowing profusely again. It took a long time before he finally went to sleep. His mother came to the conclusion that the crying was due to him having had a long, strenuous day, since he had never behaved like that during the same festivities in the previous years.

Several weeks later the same thing happened again. The weather was hot, and Carol had taken her two children to a swimming pool, where hundreds of children were shouting loudly, screaming and playing happily. Chase once more began to cry terribly, sobbing and screaming almost hysterically, begging his mother to take him out of there. Once outside the swimming pool premises the five-year-old gradually calmed down, but was unable to tell his mother the cause of his upset. When she suggested going back to the swimming pool he refused to go. Carol now remembered the time he had cried like that at the Independence Day celebrations and asked him whether the noise of the divers jumping into the water and the general echoing noise in the pool had frightened him. Chase nodded. So that was it! Chase had developed a phobia of loud noises. How could this have suddenly developed in him? What would happen if she were not present to comfort him during such a crying fit? What should she do now to help him to overcome this noise phobia as quickly as possible?

As fate would have it, a hypnotherapist came to visit her a few weeks later. This man was holding seminars in the town and was also treating private patients in the Bowmans' home. He also conducted regressions into past lives, which Carol was now interested in finding out more about. When she was sitting at the kitchen table with Norman, the hypnotherapist, and her children, she told him about her son's strange behaviour when subjected to loud noises. She asked him whether he had any suggestions for helping her son. Norman asked her and Chase whether he could do an experiment right there and then. Since they trusted him they both agreed. Norman asked Chase to sit on his mother's lap and close his eyes. 'Tell me what you see when you hear the loud frightening noises.'

It is a real phenomenon that many children are able to go into themselves in an instant and access their subconscious, where they can retrieve the past-life information stored there. Adults often need a longer phase of inward contemplation to be able to reach the storeroom of their subconscious through the alpha mind state. Children are often able to tune into their inner images with surprising ease if they are not being highly energetic at the time. This may be because we as adults cannot imagine that it is possible to access the subconscious so easily, and so automatically create a block which children simply have not developed yet.

Chase immediately began to describe his life as a soldier. He held a gun in his hand which had a sword blade on the end of it. (He was describing a bayonet.) 'What are you wearing?' asked Norman. With his eyes closed Chase described that he was wearing torn clothes and brown boots. He described that he was in the midst of a battle and was hiding behind a rock. Now and then he would carefully peep out and shoot at the enemy with his gun. Carol and Sarah looked at each other in amazement when hearing these statements. Chase had never said anything about war or fighting before now and had shown no interest in playing with toy guns like other boys his age. He continued to describe what he was experiencing. There were loud bangs going off, and flashes like lightning were coming from guns and cannons all around him. Calls and screams were mixed in with the general noise of the battle. With the dust whirling about and the smoke from the gunpowder he could no longer distinguish friend from foe. He was very frightened and shot at everything that moved. He kept saying that he disliked being in this battle where he had to shoot at other people.

It was amazing what was suddenly coming out of the mouth of this five-year-old boy, for he described this battle as if he was really experiencing it right then. How could he know about all this when he had never watched any war films? In films the war is usually glorified, whereas the description Chase was giving them was far from that. Suddenly Chase shuddered on his mother's lap as he described how a bullet hit him in the hand. He was now holding his painful hand from which blood was flowing. Then he told them how another soldier took him to a kind of field hospital where the wounded had to lie on wooden stretchers. After receiving a makeshift bandage, he was sent straight back into battle with orders to assist in manning the cannon. He talked about his fears and admitted that he missed his family.

He suddenly became restless, opened his eyes, and looked around his familiar home with shining eyes as if he was glad to have escaped the battle unhurt. Then he leapt off his mother's lap and when asked how he felt he said, 'Great', grabbed a biscuit and ran into his room.

Everything described here took place during only 20 minutes. Norman was sure that Chase had really relived a past life and that his phobia of loud noises may well have its roots in the life he relived. Had he not gone into that life quite spontaneously when asked to find the cause of his fear? But Norman suggested that they wait to see whether there were any changes in the behaviour of the boy. He had never worked with such a young person before. He was surprised how easy it had been to transport the five-year-old into the past without the help of any hypnotic induction methods, which he would normally consider indispensable when dealing with other clients. Sarah remarked that Chase had a patch of eczema in precisely the place that the bullet had hit him in his past life. This reminded Carol that Chase had had this rash on his hand since birth. This rash itched so much that he frequently scratched it until it bled; Carol had often found it necessary to bandage his hand. She had visited several doctors with her son because of this scratch wound, but none of the medications were effective. Even allergy tests gave her no indication of the cause of this irritating, sore wound.

You will hear more about scars which children are born with relating to previous lifetimes. In short, birthmarks can be traced back to a past life in which we experienced a painful or even traumatic injury in the place where they later appear as birthmarks. This is usually the case in a so-called 'life spent as a victim'. You can read about this in detail in my book, Das Grosse Handbuch der Reinkarnation (The Great Handbook of Reincarnation). *These birthmarks may be dormant in the present lifetime or active such as the wound on Chase's hand.*

During regression therapy the subject is asked to go back to the time and place where the root cause can be found which made it necessary for him to experience a traumatic event such as being shot in the hand. This then takes us into a so-called 'life of the victimiser', in which the same soul in a different life and in a different body committed something unloving with that hand. Perhaps he had chopped off someone else's hand, or committed a murder or some other crime with this hand. Every regression therapist knows from the work he does that the Law of Karma always sees to it that a just balance is reached. If Chase had brought with him an active birthmark into his present life from which he still suffered, it shows that his karmic debt had not yet been fully paid for with the shot wound received in the war. This means that some sufferings still remained to be experienced in order to finally balance things out. If reliving the past injury should have dissolved the associated painful experience (in this case stored in the hand), then the corresponding karmic debt created in an even earlier life would usually also be dissolved.

Amazing as it may be, this is what happened. Within a few days the unsightly patch of eczema completely disappeared and never came back. At the same time an even greater miracle occurred: the fear of loud noises also vanished for good.

As a regression therapist I witness such miracles almost daily, so it came as no great surprise to me. Clients with all kinds of mental, psychosomatic or somatic disorders and malfunctions are able to experience the origins of their present-day problems, most of which can usually be found in their past lives. They can usually free themselves of these with the help of specific rituals of forgiveness and affirmations suggested to them by the therapist. Frequently a single session with a regression therapist will suffice to bring about the required healing.[30]

The story about Chase does not end here. Later in this chapter I will say more about the things that came to light when Sarah experienced a regression with Norman. Carol made it clear to her children that they were not to talk to anyone about what they had experienced during regression, because they would surely be teased and would probably feel hurt by this. She explained to them that most people in their country were not ready to accept the possibility of reincarnation or memories of past lives.

Much is soon to change in the world in this respect, for the truth is being revealed at an increasingly faster rate, just like germinating seeds that have worked their way through the top layers of earth and now wish to grow bigger as quickly as possible. These seedlings are even happier to grow when there are gardeners present who lovingly water them and talk to them encouragingly.

A year later the Bowman family moved to Philadelphia in Pennsylvania. One day, when they had settled into their new home and the two children had made some new friends among their peers, the six-year-old Chase asked his mother, 'Mum, do you remember that time with Norman when I saw myself as a soldier?' Carol suddenly felt shivers down her spine. Her son had never talked about his past life since that regression with Norman, so she had assumed that he had most likely forgotten everything by now. He told her that during regression he had experienced his past life in detail. He remembered having used a particular dialect, common among blacks. He told his mother, 'Yes, I was black.' Carol was startled and asked him whether he had fought together with blacks. To this Chase answered, 'Yes, black and white soldiers were fighting together.' When his mother encouraged him to tell her more, he said that he had told her everything he could remember.

Whatever is spoken about during regression is often only a small part of everything that was actually seen, heard, smelt, tasted or felt by the client. This is why I suggest that you make notes immediately after regression about what has been experienced, for otherwise most of it will soon be forgotten. Even so, snatches of half-forgotten memories may suddenly surface, like in Chase's case. Had they been able to question him more thoroughly, or had the chance to conduct another regression soon afterwards, he would probably have talked about these events in much greater detail.

After her son had come out with these statements, Carol tried to recall in which war blacks had fought together with whites. According to her son's descriptions the war he had experienced must have been the Civil War between 1861 and 1863. But were blacks really recruited in those days? As chance would have it, the papers published a detailed and richly illustrated article the following day, drawing attention to an exhibition, which portrayed the extent to which black soldiers had been involved in the Civil War. Carol showed her son these pictures and asked him whether they seemed familiar to him, to which he answered a laconic, 'Yes.'

A year later, just when the ground troops in the Gulf had taken up arms against Iraq, Chase returned from school telling his mother, 'I shall never let anyone force me to become a soldier again!' The boys in his class had been following the war with great enthusiasm on TV and were telling each other excitedly about the latest events. They identified with their compatriots fighting there, seeing them as heroes and role models. Her son then asked her to conduct another regression with him, so that he could find out more about his past life. Carol had since learnt how to use regression techniques with Norman and Roger Woolger. She had secretly wished to take her son back into his past life once more, but had wanted to wait until he suggested it himself. Now she knew the time had come to do this with him.

We are dealing with an ideal case here, in which a mother who has learnt the regression techniques is able to take her own son back into his past lives in order to find answers to many questions. Under normal circumstances in whom could a child confide more easily than in his own mother? Only later on when children reach their teenage years and begin to have their own secrets, they may feel more at ease with a stranger than with their own mother.

In her book, *Children's Past Lives*, which has been an important contribution to the research into reincarnation, Carol writes, 'I knew from having gone through regressions myself that there was no danger involved. The subconscious, where the memories of reincarnation are stored, chooses precisely what to present to the conscious mind of the person; it allows the person to go as far and as deeply as is necessary but no further.'[31]

She asked Chase to lie down and close his eyes. Then she began saying, 'Go back to those images that you once

saw with Norman, to the time when you were a soldier.'
This time Carol had a note pad on her lap ready to write
down everything he said. Almost immediately her son
found himself in the midst of a battle, once more
describing how he was hiding behind a rock only daring
to look out once in a while. From time to time, when he
thought he saw the enemy, he would point his gun at
them and start firing. He was very frightened. Finally a
bullet hit him in the wrist and everything went black
around him. Until now he had made short statements
about what he was experiencing, but now he became
silent.

*At the time of this event he had fallen unconscious from the injury
in his hand. As a regression therapist, if I were to leave him in that
state without giving him further suggestions, it could be a long time
before he experienced anything else. His unconsciousness may have
lasted half an hour or more. This is why in these situations I will
often say, 'I will count to three and then you will find yourself at the
point in time where your next experience occurred.'*

'What is happening now?' Carol asked. Her son
explained how he was being sent back into battle with a
bandage on his hand. He was ordered to join a unit that
was manning a cannon that was strapped to a cart. The
fighting had apparently ceased for the moment. He
watched chickens running around on the road, and once
again felt the fear of having to be involved in the war.
Everyone around him felt the same way. Mrs Bowman
then wrote that she felt inspired to ask her son, who was

the black soldier at that time, to go back to the place where he had lived before the war.

Our invisible companions transmit this kind of inspiration to us, these being our inner spirit guides in most cases, for they are extremely keen to help us broaden our consciousness. Each regression serves us in this way.

Then the black soldier told Carol about his life, which I briefly want to outline here. He sees himself in a town with the name 'Colossi' (or something similar) and the year is 1860. (He even got the year right.) He lives in a suburb of the town where other blacks have settled. He owns a wooden hut with a veranda on which stands a rocking chair. He is about 30 years old and is very happy. He has a wife and two children and is smoking a pipe. He had arrived here as a child in a covered wagon.

His work consists of painting, decorating and carpentry. In his spare time he makes clay pots. Next he sees people in great excitement gathered around a poster on which is written, 'War'. Even though he is unable to read he knows what the word means and what it is about. The poster is calling for men to join the army and fight in the war. He is very excited. After all, this war is about freeing the many hundreds of thousands of black slaves in the southern States. He signs up voluntarily and signs the papers even though he could not read the contents, which then committed him to serving in the army. The saddest moment of his life is saying goodbye to his family and seeing his children crying. Finally he returns to talking about the events of the war. While manning his post behind a cannon he is shot and dies instantly. Then he described what happened to him after his death. 'I am floating above the battlefield. It feels good to have left everything behind. I can see the battle and the smoke below me.'

Most of my clients, whom I guided through experiencing the state immediately after death, floated above their earthly body. All the pain ceases, even if they had been tortured just before death. It is a wonderful state, which is particularly enjoyable if one has had to suffer terrible pain before dying. One then observes everything as if from a higher perspective. The most amazing experience consists of being able to go anywhere one wants to instantly. Many soldiers who died in the war thought about going home shortly after their death and were instantly transported there. They could see their family and wanted to tell them that they were all right. There are thousands of cases in which the relatives at home could suddenly feel the presence of their husband, father, son, or brother who was apparently still at war. Some could even hear their telepathically transmitted thoughts to comfort them. A day later they would receive a telegram telling them about the death of the person in question.

Chase now continued to describe what he experienced immediately after death. 'I am floating above my house and can see my wife and children. I say goodbye to my family. They cannot see me because I am in a spiritual body, but they know that I am dead.'

Is it not strange to hear about real-life truths from a seven-year-old, truths about which most priests know nothing and yet try to appear as if they were the only ones to possess them? To whom should we listen more: to the children or the priests?

To his mother's amazement the young boy continued saying, 'Everyone has to experience war at some time, because it balances everything out. You don't necessarily have to die in the war, but it is necessary to experience it. You can learn a lot about feelings in that situation. War helps you to understand how others are feeling. War is a terrible thing.'

When the human mind is in the 'alpha state', even children will often be aware at a higher level of consciousness. In this state they may come out with things as wise as those spoken by the wisest people on earth. When someone reads channelled material supposedly from beings on the other side, then one could say that this wisdom comes from the subconscious of the medium. Therefore it is debatable whether the material thus transmitted is really based upon any higher truth at all. By contrast, a child in his everyday state may know very little about how things work on a higher plane and may have great difficulty expressing these truths. So when you are fortunate enough to witness a child talking about this kind of thing while in a trance state, you will begin to wonder whether there is after all some truth in that which is written in many books of wisdom (most of which are repudiated by dogmatic religions). A nine-year-old girl, who had already experienced a great deal during regression, was sitting with a group of adults one evening. They were arguing with each other about war. On her way to bed the girl said the following, 'Wars exist so that we can learn about love.'

Then Chase continued, 'I avoided the Second World War. I was up there and was waiting to be reborn at a more peaceful time. I had another short life in between that.'

So Chase remembered the life as a soldier that had been prior to another life. Most of the children, which Professor Stevenson examined on account of their past-life memories, described the life immediately before their present one. It would be interesting to see whether Chase's incarnated soul also carried the same 'active' birthmark on the hand in that other life in between. Based on my research up to now, I must assume that we carry birthmarks around with us on the relevant areas of our bodies until the messages relating to the birthmarks have been fully understood by the soul and are therefore dissolved.

Then Chase opened his eyes again. He felt really good, leapt to his feet and disappeared into his room where he was building something with his new Lego set. Carol was speechless and remained seated. What had he meant by 'up there' where he'd waited until his present incarnation?

Even among people who believe in reincarnation, there often seems to be a great deal of confusion and half-baked knowledge passed around which is marked by prejudice instead of true knowledge. By means of regression, even if only children are chosen for this, we come to a new understanding of how things really work in this arena. The Indians, for example, still believe that humans reincarnate as animals. I have never seen any evidence of that in the numerous regressions I have facilitated. Rabbi Luria, who lived and was teaching in the 16th century, claimed that as a Jew you would always be reincarnated as a Jewish person. I have regressed many of today's

Jews and have seen for myself that this is not true. Regression will put an end to such erroneous ideas. Many others assert that one is forever reborn to the same people, the same race, the same religion or the same family. The example of Chase having been black in his former life is proof enough that this is not so.

If Carol Bowman now took the chance that presented itself to her through the extremely good regression qualities of her son, she could lead him during regressions into the planes 'up there' where we dwell between lives and could find out more truths from him than all the books of academia and churches combined have ever given mankind. She did indeed conduct several other regressions with her children and gained a lot of insights into things that were new to her. After Chase had experienced death in another life Carol asked him about what happens when we die. The seven-year-old replied, 'When you die you can choose what you want to do. You can have another look at scenes from the life you have just lived, in order to gain answers to questions relating to that life. You can choose to see what happens to the people you have left behind, and you can return to them in spirit form and say goodbye and then observe what becomes of them in the future. If you see that everything is going all right for them you are then free to leave the earthly plane.' Carol emphasised that these were the exact words her seven-year-old had used. The only way to describe it is: unbelievable but true. Even so she continued to ask Chase what happens if one sees someone one loves having problems. The boy whose consciousness was broadened explained with his eyes closed that it was possible to return to loved ones in a different body – he meant the astral body – in order to be with them. It was possible to move very quickly in this new body. You could choose to float to any place you used to live, in order to watch what happens on earth. Yet you live in a different time than on earth. After that you go back to heaven before deciding to return to earth in a physical body.[32]

In this way our children can become like living books containing secret treasures and occult knowledge, if only we learn to open these books and read what is written there with an open heart. Carol Bowman, who grew up in an orthodox, Jewish family, admits that the regressions she experienced served as a turning point in her life.

BURNT TO DEATH IN A HOUSE FIRE

On the day that Norman led the five-year-old Chase into regression, his mother and his nine-year-old sister Sarah had been present and had been amazed at what the young boy had said. When Chase had gone to his room, they talked about what had just happened. Sarah asked the hypnotherapist whether he would do a regression with her, because for as long as she could remember she had always had a huge fear of fire. Carol had only become fully aware of Sarah's fear of fire about a year before. Sarah had stayed the night with her friend Amy, which she often did.

The two girls had stayed up late watching a film in which a house caught fire and a person was burnt to death. Suddenly Sarah began to sob inconsolably, so much so that they were unable to comfort her. Amy's mother had to ring the Bowmans in the middle of the night to tell them that she would have to take Sarah home immediately.

When the still crying girl was back in her mother's arms, she told her parents about what had happened in the film. She had always had a fear of fire breaking out and therefore always kept her favourite doll and a bag containing her most important things under her bed, so that she would be prepared and able to escape should there be a fire. It was only now that her mother realised why she kept these things at hand under her bed every night. Sarah was otherwise very sure of herself and had no tendency towards snivelling and being fearful. Her mother promised her that there would never be a fire in their house and that as parents they would always be there to support her. She also showed her all possible escape routes out of the house. Even so her fears about fire became more acute in the days that followed, so much so that she even rebelled when her parents wanted to light a candle. Sarah's parents hoped that in time these fears would disappear on their own. And now Norman was there, who had just managed to take Chase to the origin of his irrational fear of loud cannon fire.

Norman then encouraged Sarah to close her eyes and to allow herself to feel the fear that she had experienced the last time her fire phobia had surfaced. 'What do you see?' he asked. The nine-year-old described a life in which she was twelve years old and was growing up with her parents in a two-storey wooden house. She also had a younger brother who appeared to have been handicapped. She helped her mother with the housework and made herself useful in the shed where the animals were kept. She was not allowed to go to school since it was thought that girls did not need any further education. Then Norman asked her to move forward to the time when her fear of fire had started. Until now she had spoken from the perspective of an observer, but now she was suddenly immersed in an event, which she described in a highly excited state.

She is waking up in the middle of the night and can smell smoke. She immediately knows that something is burning in the house. She jumps out of bed and hurries out onto the landing. Despite the thick smoke she sees the flames leaping up all around. She runs through the flames to the other rooms but her nightdress catches fire from flames coming through the gaps in the floorboards. Even so she manages to reach her parents' bedroom, but they are not there. Their beds have not been slept in. Where are they? A sense of fear and utter helplessness sweeps over her. Wherever she tries to go to escape the flames, she is faced with more. Finally a beam from above crashes onto the floor ripping a hole in it. At this point she knows that she will not be able to get out of this inferno alive.

Breathing has become very difficult. Finally Sarah stopped talking. She had apparently died at this point.

I always allow my clients to experience their death, if their symptoms were created at the time of or because of their death. For a complete recovery to occur it is necessary that the information related to the death experience, which is stored in the emotional body, is brought into motion in order to live it out and clear it out for good. This results in an incredible emotional liberation, which can be felt as an immediate, most welcome effect as soon as the therapy session has ended. Some therapists are afraid to subject themselves to these death experiences. They miss them out by telling their clients, 'I will now count to three and then you will find yourself in the time after the previous event where you are happy again.' By avoiding the death experience and therefore not stirring up the emotions related to that experience, they will to a large extent remain locked in, and in most cases the therapeutic benefits will be halved or very poor.

Norman then continued by asking, 'What are you experiencing now?' The girl answered saying that she is floating over the treetops and feels light as a feather. She feels no pain whatsoever and is relieved to know that she had died and that it is all over.

This feeling of lightness, relief and painlessness after a gruesome death that has just been experienced, is normally identical for all clients who have gone through an agonising death. The floating sensation is experienced as unexpected and pleasant, which is reflected in what I would feel tempted to describe as near ecstasy upon the face of the person recounting their story. Many clients also express surprise at what is happening to them. They have no way of explaining it.

I then allow them to look down at their dead body so that they realise that they have died.

When Norman continued questioning Sarah about what was happening to her, she said that she was now floating above the blazing house. She sees her family standing in the yard: her brother sitting on the ground and her father holding his wife in his arms who is stretching her arms out towards the house in despair. Suddenly Sarah began to cry uncontrollably. From the perspective of her higher consciousness she could now see the deeper reasons why she had taken this phobia, as well as her unspoken resentment towards her present-day parents, into her present lifetime.

As in Sarah's case, it can happen spontaneously that after re-experiencing a previous death we suddenly see the connection between the past life and our present one. After having viewed some past lives I always take my clients up the 'mountain of knowledge' from where they can get an overview of the lives they have just uncovered, in which various causes of their present-day symptoms were revealed. They can then clearly see the true connections between their problem and everything that led to its manifestation. At this stage they are then able to let it go.

Sarah is now able to see how her parents had done everything they could to save her, and how the heat and the flames had driven them back. Sarah was really touched by her parents' despair and helplessness. Until now she had programmed into her subconscious her final impressions from before her death during the fire, that her parents had only cared about their own safety and had left her behind, completely helpless. She now discovered that they had in fact done everything they could to save her. A deep sense of relief then spread across her face.

Then she opened her eyes, sniffed a couple of times and looked at the faces looking back at her full of anticipation. Her face was now beaming with joy. They then discussed what had just happened in more detail and, since Sarah had only expressed a part of her experience during regression, she now filled them in on some of the events she was still able to remember. She confessed that during her search for her parents she had been overcome by intense anger, thinking that they had forsaken her. She had later brought this anger with her into her present life.

The last emotional impressions are imprinted on our emotional body and continue to make themselves felt in our next life. People with choleric tendencies are usually among those who died feeling anger and rage at the time of their previous death.

Then Sarah made a wise observation, saying that her fear of fire was there to remind her that there had been something as yet unresolved that she was carrying around with her.

A few days later something amazing happened: Sarah fetched her doll and the bag containing her most important things from under her bed, for she knew that her fear of fire had vanished, and indeed it never returned after that.

It seems too easy to help children to let go of their phobias, fearful dreams, wounds that won't heal, allergies, breathing problems, bed-wetting and many other problems, by using regression therapy to identify the cause of their symptoms. Many children may respond to regression as easily as Chase and Sarah, whereas others would require more patience and would require the therapist to wait for an appropriate moment. I can picture a future not too far from now where it will be common for parents to take their children to regression therapists in order to free them of unpleasant symptoms. It will be a joy for children to live in such a future. Can you imagine a world where fear no longer exists? Are not all wars born out of fear, which in turn create more fear? This chain of 'fear creation' followed by fearful reactions has been perpetuated from one century to the next. It is now possible for this chain to be broken, which will be a blessing for all mankind.[33]

5

Children who speak in foreign tongues

THE AMERICAN BOY WHO
SPOKE A TIBETAN DIALECT

There are many cases of children as well as adults speaking or writing in languages that they are not familiar with. The scientists talk about Xenoglossy (speaking in foreign languages) and Xenography (writing in foreign languages). Critics have tried to discredit such evidence by saying that the child must have heard someone talk in that language at some time and that the child's subconscious had registered it. At certain times or during sleep the child would then repeat the previously stored information. According to this, Xenoglossy has nothing to do with past lives. Other critics, who may have a deeper insight into things that most people are as yet unable to understand, try to dismiss Xenoglossy as possession. In such cases (and it goes without saying that they do occur) a deceased person whose soul has not managed to reach the 'beyond' moves invisibly among the living, or actually enters into them, and at times speaks through an individual.

There is also a phenomenon in which the dead or higher beings that dwell on higher vibrational planes speak through someone. This is done in a completely different language, or with a strong accent, a very different pitch and articulation or even using a completely different vocabulary than the person normally possesses. From time to time it also happens that during regression the person speaks the language that he or she spoke in the life they are remembering. I will write more about this in another book. In this book I want to tell you about children who spoke in a foreign language, which was later determined to be in all probability the language they had spoken in a past life.

Professor Adrian Finkelstein, a very famous author and psychiatrist in Los Angeles, tells the true story in his book *Your Past Lives and the Healing Process*[34] about a boy who remembers his past life as a Tibetan monk. This boy was called Robin Hull and was five years old at the time. The boy often spoke a completely different language, which his mother could not understand. When Mrs Hull's friend came to visit, she witnessed Robin speaking in that strange language. This friend believed in reincarnation and thought that the boy was speaking a real language that he may well have learnt in a past life. She said that she knew a professor of Asian languages whom she would love to invite to listen to the language the boy spoke.

Some days later she came to visit the Hull family accompanied by the professor. He asked Robin to speak in his foreign language and Robin complied happily. After having listened to the boy for some time the professor told them that it was a dialect spoken in the northern regions of Tibet. He then asked the boy where he had learnt this language. Robin answered saying that he had learnt it at school. His mother then interrupted their conversation by saying, 'But you don't go to school yet.' 'But I did go to school a long time ago.' Then, to the amazement of his mother, the boy said that he had not told her about his past life in Tibet because, one day when he had tried to tell her something, she had ignored him and so he had kept it to himself. He then described his school to the professor. He called it a school, yet it was likely that he meant a monastery, but did not know the correct name for it. Robin then described what the teachers were wearing and the size of the 'school'. This five-year-old boy talked for over an hour to the professor, who was so impressed with this information and exact descriptions that he decided to go in search of the place. After a long journey through northern Tibet he found the monastery in the Kuen Lun Mountains.

It is a great shame that I do not have a more detailed account of this case to offer my readers, since I imagine that a lot more evidence could otherwise have been shared. The following account is equally amazing.

THE GIRL WHO SPOKE FRENCH IN HER SLEEP

Roger was an employee at a bank in Evanston in the State of Illinois. One evening when he was sitting in the lounge with his wife, they heard their six-year-old daughter's voice coming from her bedroom. They were amazed to find her fast asleep in bed, talking in her sleep. The language she spoke was not English but French. Her parents only knew very basic French, which they had been taught at school. This was enough for them to understand a few words of what she was saying, even though she spoke very fast. How could their daughter suddenly speak fluent French? She had never been abroad, and as far as they knew she could not have heard this language anywhere. They were puzzled. When their daughter began to speak in French again during the nights that followed, her parents desperately wanted to know what their six-year-old daughter was saying, as neither of them understood enough to know what she was talking about. They decided to borrow a tape recorder with which they recorded their daughter's voice speaking in French while asleep. They then took the tape to a French teacher and asked her to translate it for them.

While listening to the recording, it soon became evident to the teacher that it was about a little French girl searching for her mother. When Germans had raided their village her mother had escaped and could not take her daughter with her for some reason. The little girl was most alarmed. From having heard these statements her present-day parents are convinced that the events described by their sleeping daughter relate to a past life in which she lost her mother and most likely also her own life.[35]

People, especially children, often talk in their sleep and sometimes in other languages. While dreaming, the soul often taps into memories from the past, possibly from hundreds of years ago, which have been stored in the subconscious. How loud or how moving the words or fearful cries uttered during sleep are may depend on how upsetting or traumatic the experiences had been in the past. Regression therapy has proven that nightmares are usually related to traumatic experiences in past lives. If these events are relived during regression therapy by leading the client back to the event where the problem originated, then the traumatic experience stored as a negative memory can be dissolved. The nightmares never return after that.

THE BOY WHO SPEAKS A FOREIGN LANGUAGE AND REMEMBERS THE NAMES OF HIS MURDERERS FROM A PAST LIFE

In the village of Don Kha in northern Thailand, a boy named Bongkuch Promsin was born in 1962. When he was about two years old he started to talk about having been murdered by two men at a fair, and that he was called Chamrat, not Bongkuch. He mentioned the name of his former parents and also the name of the place he had once lived, Huan Tanon, a neighbouring village only nine kilometres away. He had been a young man at the time, and the murderers, whose names he later remembered, had stabbed him in several areas of his body. After that they had taken off his watch and his necklace and had finally dragged him into a field. The little boy continued to use Laotian words instead of his Thai mother-tongue. As they later discovered Chamrat had belonged to a Laotian refugee family, which had settled in the neighbouring village of Huan Tanon. Yet there was no one who spoke this language in the village where he was now living.

One day the relatives of the deceased Chamrat were informed that living not far from them the murdered Chamrat had been reborn. They went to visit him and were able to translate the boy's Laotian words. This is a very impressive case of Xenoglossy. What the boy had said about who his murderers had been also seemed to be correct, since both had been suspects at the time. One of them had avoided being arrested by disappearing, while the other was later released due to a lack of evidence. When this boy had grown up a little he swore that he would revenge himself on his murderers and was sometimes seen beating a post with a stick whilst shouting out the names of his murderers.

When a person is murdered very suddenly and unexpectedly, the reincarnated soul in its new body may think itself to be at the age at which it had died. Stevenson referred to this kind of behaviour in children as, 'bouts of adultness'. In many ways Bonkuch behaved like a Laotian. He also preferred to eat rice the way the Laotians prepared it. He brushed his teeth just like an adult, even though it was unusual for any other children to do this. He also went to the village barber and asked him to shave him. The young boy even showed an interest in girls who were in their puberty, making advances and stroking their legs, while ignoring the younger ones.[36]

IS DAVID MORRIS THE MESSIAH REBORN?

David Morris was the son of Samuel Morris, an oral surgeon from Jerusalem. At the age of three David began to go into a trance-like state in which he spoke a language that was unfamiliar to his parents, from which they were only occasionally able to decipher a few words. Since they were unable to understand this 'double Dutch', they dismissed it as gibberish. They seemed to have become so used to the strange language he spoke from time to time that they paid little attention to it. One day when David was 12 years old, his mother telephoned her husband at his practice sounding rather upset and asking him to come home immediately. David was sitting on the floor in front of a castle he had constructed out of all his building blocks and other things, and the whole thing looked like a fortress. Somehow this building seemed familiar to Mr Morris. He knelt down on the floor next to David and asked him what he was building. His son replied in the foreign language. His father was only able to make out the word 'temple'. He then noticed that this temple looked similar to a reconstruction of the temple of King Solomon, which he had once seen himself. After having put the tape recorder on, he asked his son to tell him more about this temple in order to record his words. He then took this cassette of his son's spoken words to Dr Zevi Hermann, a scholar and authority on the subject of ancient Semitic languages. This linguist was amazed to discover that what Mr Morris had called gibberish was actually ancient Hebrew, a language which differs in many ways from today's Hebrew in inflection, accent and grammar. Mr Morris' son spoke this old language perfectly. One of the sentences went as follows, 'The king speaks to his people: follow me and I will lead you to greatness.'

It took Dr Hermann and his colleague Dr David Auerbach a long time to translate the whole cassette. They started to work intensely with David, often successfully assisting the five-year-old to go into his familiar trance-like state in which he was able to answer many of their questions using the ancient Hebrew dialect. He always spoke in the first person, as if he was King David himself. Before the two language experts decided to publicise this exciting news, they decided to first go and see the rabbi Yedida Cohen, a member of the supreme council on religious questions. He told them the following, 'We cannot talk about this in public, since our beliefs are based on the revelation that King David is the Messiah who will return to earth in order to create God's kingdom on earth.'

Based on the advice given to them by this man well versed in the scriptures, they decided to keep quiet about this boy and the possibility that King David may have been reborn. The consequences of a public announcement would most likely bring thousands of believers flocking around David, treating him as their long-awaited Messiah. As Sybil Leek writes, the religious authorities do not want to tolerate anyone 'before' them who bases their credibility on memories of their past lives. Should it really be so that this boy is King David reborn, the long awaited and prophesied Messiah, then he will surely come forward to tell the world about himself and his mission on earth when the time is right.[37]

Should all these examples of children remembering their past lives have left the reader in any doubt about the truth of reincarnation, then the following accounts of children's memories presented to us by Stevenson will surely convince every reader that past lives really do exist.

6

Children that are born with birthmarks

SHOT BY A STRANGER WHILE RIDING A BIKE

Bua Kai Lawnak was the headmaster of a small village primary school in the Thai province of Phichit, situated between Bangkok and Chiangmai. He was 36 years old and was married to Susan. They had two sons as well as twin daughters, Tim and Toi, and Susan was expecting another child. The father was especially fond of his nine-year-old twins, and on his return from school by bike in the evening he usually bought some pieces of sugar cane for them.

Yet Bua Kai was not an ideal husband, since he had relationships with other girls on the side. He was also involved with other jobs, which must have put him in some danger for he usually carried a pistol and kept a gun at home. So it happened one day that someone shot at him when he was at a temple where he planned to participate in a Buddhist festival. The bullet must have only grazed his stomach for he soon recovered. Since he no longer felt safe in that village he asked to be transferred to another town.

He was offered a post at the school in Ta Paw, which was about 25 kilometres from where he had previously lived. On 23rd January 1962 Bua Kai was hit in the head by a bullet shot from behind and died instantly. The bullet had entered the back of his head and had emerged where his parting was on the left side, so that blood flowed from two wounds. The police never caught the murderer.

About 50 kilometres from the village where Bua Kai had lived, a couple by the names of Kamron and Somkid Choomalaiwong gave birth to a son on 10th October 1967 and named him Chanai. His mother discovered two hairless birthmarks on his head. The one at the back was approximately half a centimetre wide, whereas the one on the left side at the front of his head was about two centimetres long and half a centimetre wide. Mr and Mrs Choomalaiwong had separated before the birth of their son. When Chanai was two years old his mother moved to Bangkok leaving him behind with her mother, Prom. The boy's father and mother only visited him and Prom for a few days on the odd occasion. When Chanai was three years old his grandmother overheard him playing at teachers and pupils with the other children, asking them to bring him their notebooks. He had told them that he used to be a teacher and the children had presumably accepted this fact and went along with his games.

Could it be that most children love playing exactly those things that they enjoyed most in their previous lives? If it is true that we only change sex on average every fourth life, then 75 per cent of children are living as the same sex they belonged to before. Is it then not to be expected that little girls play at being mothers with babies since that may well have been their main occupation in the past? Many boys play with toy guns. Is it not likely that they remember the glory of being a soldier and wish to relive that in their present childhood and youth? Large areas of research remain open to future reincarnation psychologists.

Chanai then began to tell his grandmother that he used to be a teacher called Bua Kai. He also told her that he had a wife named Susan, two sons and twin daughters whose names he also remembered. He mentioned the village where he had been a headmaster of a school, and also explained to her that he had been shot while riding his bike. Apart from this he mentioned the names of his previous parents. He asked his grandmother to take him to his family or the people who used to be his parents. He told her that he knew the exact location of the village where his parents, Kiang and Yong, used to live. When his grandmother tried to talk him out of this he began to cry. He begged her again and again to either take him to his family in Ban Khao Sai or to his parents in Khao Phra. His grandmother threatened to hit him if he did not stop making this strange request. The three-year-old said he did not care about that and was not intimidated by her threats. Finally she gave in.

Why is it that children who remember their past lives (I will give you further examples of this) have this desperate urge to visit members of their families from a past life? Is it nostalgia? Or a kind of magnetism that draws them back there? Or are they after proving to themselves and their doubting parents that their knowing is correct and that their memories are no figments of their childish imagination. What is more likely is that the loving connection is still active in the emotional body that is now in a new body. All feelings are stored in the emotional body, and, since it is transferred to the same soul from one life to the next, feelings of love or dislike remain intact.

Grandma Prom and Chanai caught the bus to the town near the village where Chanai said his parents used to live. The grandmother later confessed to having felt awkward about driving there with her grandson, since she still believed that all Chanai's claims could have been made up. She was afraid to make an utter fool of herself, and yet she had given in to his demands to prove to him that all his claims were just borne out of his childish imagination. The three-and-a-half-year-old seemed to know his way around the small town. He knew how to get to the neighbouring village where his previous parents were supposed to have lived.

Finally they found themselves standing in front of the house, which the boy had previously described, and were knocking at the door. When someone answered the door the grandmother asked whether a couple with the names Kian and Yong used to live here. When the answer was yes, the grandmother must have breathed a sigh of relief. Chanai's stories really seemed to be true after all. When the two old people stood in front of the two visitors the little boy called them mother and father. Grandma explained that her grandson claimed to have been Bua Kai their son who was shot dead several years ago when working as a teacher. She asked them whether they had a son fitting that name who had died in those circumstances. They said it was all true. Chanai was overjoyed to see everyone so amazed. The grandmother then showed the couple the birthmarks on his head. Bua Kai's parents were now fully convinced that they were looking at their deceased son reborn. On saying goodbye they agreed to see each other again soon, since they wanted to inform other members of their family.

When they returned a few days later, numerous members of his family were there to see him. Among them was also Bua Kai's wife, Susan. When asked whether he knew this woman he said, 'Of course I do, that's Susan.' He also recognised other members of his family and called them by their names. Once again they looked at the birthmarks on the boy's head and Susan confirmed that these marks coincided with the wounds that had been on her deceased husband's head. At the time of his death she had seen the wounds caused by the bullets. When Chanai was asked about what he had been doing on the day of his murder before having been shot he answered, 'In the morning I washed my clothes. After that I took my Buddha necklace off and put it on the table. Then I had a shower and after breakfast I cycled to school. I forgot to put my necklace back on and forgot my pistol. Had I not forgotten them they would both have been stolen together with the other things.' Susan could only confirm all these statements.

Then he was asked what weapons he owned. He correctly answered that he owned one pistol and one gun. As you can see, they had prepared their questions well in advance in order to test him. The next question was whether he could remember anything that Bua Kai had owned. To this the three-and-a-half-year-old said that he had owned a Buddha necklace. When asked how many Buddhas hung on this necklace he raised three fingers. Then the little boy asked his previous parents whether they still had the small first-aid box that he had once given them. They said yes. Chanai then went upstairs and brought it down for them to see. He could still remember where he had put it at the time. When going through the house he commented on everything that had changed. He mentioned things he could no longer find like his books or pieces of furniture, or things that were new. Old Mrs Yong then fetched six ammunition belts and asked Chanai which one used to belong to him. He pointed to the right one. Now Bua Kai's mother was utterly convinced. She began to cry and many of those present joined in. After the old lady had calmed down she asked him why he had not been reborn in her family and instead such a long way away to another family. The little boy explained that it is impossible to choose where one wishes to be reborn.

The three-and-a-half-year-old was then invited to the home of Susan, who was Bua Kai's wife. When he stood face to face with one of his former twin daughters Tim, who was now seventeen, Chanai broke down in tears and asked her whether she recognised him, but she said, 'No'. Then he told her that he was her father, but Tim was not at all taken with what this boy was saying. Only after he had answered a whole string of questions correctly was she able to accept him as her father reborn. He asked after Toi, his other daughter from the past. Tim led him to her sister. After they had exchanged a few words the little boy asked her whether she still reacted in an oversensitive manner to everything like she used to.

Following this encounter Chanai frequently visited his former family and his parents. He often travelled there by bus on his own and sometimes he stayed there for several days or even weeks. He had now been fully accepted as the deceased Bua Kai reborn, and they respected his wish to be called 'Father' by his grown-up children. His former daughters had a problem with calling him Father at first, so they had agreed to call him 'little nephew'. Chanai was not happy with this and refused to talk to them until they called him 'Father' again. Bua Kai's younger brother could not accept the little boy as one of his family, which was why Chanai avoided him. Susan reminded him of his past life as a playboy and suggested that maybe he would again be like that when he grew up. The little boy answered, 'I've had enough of that, that'll do.' He behaved like an adult. When his former daughters were out for a walk with him one day, they met a man and one of his sisters asked him whether he recognised him. He said, 'Yes' and called the man Sam Am Sisawan, which was correct. After a while this man accepted Chanai as the rebirth of his friend. On another occasion he asked him what he would do if Susan decided to remarry. The indignant and angry boy replied that this idea was completely beside the point since he was her husband.

In all aspects of life Chanai behaved as if he was still the grown man Bua Kai. He took it for granted that he could wander around his former parents' house making comments about the things that he used to own, when he rediscovered them or found they were missing. He behaved the same in Susan's house. When he was unable to find something that he used to own he would ask Susan about it and she would tell him that she had given it away to a needy family. He usually praised her for that, but could also be annoyed if something he had been very fond of was missing. He once found a necklace on which he remembered having three amulets and now there was only one hanging on it. His former wife told him that his 'son' had removed two of them, which annoyed him very much.

Another time Sam Am asked him whether he knew who the murderer had been who had shot him from behind. The boy said that he knew. His grandmother had been told that a stranger had enquired from her friend whether

Chanai was able to remember who his murderer had been, and whether he wanted to report him. Her friend only gave him vague answers. The man was very nervous and hurried away. When the grandmother heard this, she thought it most likely that this stranger was the murderer who wanted to know whether her grandson remembered him. Should this be the case there was still time for him to murder this boy again in order not to be found out. This was why the grandmother probably warned her grandson never again to claim that he knew who his former murderer was. For the time being, she sent him to his mother in Bangkok to protect him.

Meanwhile this case had come to the notice of a reporter of a large newspaper, which led to a detailed report about this case of reincarnation being published. It was most likely that Bua Kai's murderer had read this article, which was why he now wanted to make sure that he was in no danger, since it was common knowledge that sometimes children who have been reborn have led their murderers to conviction.

His former parents had asked the three-and-a-half-year-old whether he knew what had happened to him after his death. He answered that he did not see who had shot him. (He must have known who intended to kill him, however, which is why this statement and the previous one need not necessarily contradict one another.) He said that he had been able to observe himself leaving his body. In his own words, 'I could see myself lying on the road. My feet were still twitching and my blood ran onto the road.' When questioned further about what happened to him after that the little boy said, 'I visited many places, but I can't quite remember where I went.'

Stevenson adds here that the Thai children who can remember their previous death and what happened afterwards, have often described being led away by a man dressed all in white.

This man is not necessarily European in looks. Relatives who have died, or spirit guides, often appear to people at the moment of death in a radiant white light or wearing a white gown.

Chanai took his former parents to the temple where he had been shot. Once there he explained everything that had happened to him at that time. Sometimes Chanai went to visit members of his former family without his grandmother's consent. So now and then, she would follow him and bring him back. Bua Kai's family asked Chanai's grandmother whether she would be willing to have her grandchild adopted, for they wished to have the boy living with them full time as had been his wish. She was strongly against this idea. During one of Chanai's father's visits she must have told him about his son wanting to be adopted by his former family, and so he strictly forbade him to visit any of his former family again.

Professor Stevenson had interviewed most of the family members and important people and visited the growing boy in Thailand on numerous occasions. As the years passed Chanai gradually forgot more and more of the things he had been able to remember in the past, yet some things still stuck in his mind. An interesting detail is the fact that Chanai always got headaches when talking about his past life.[38]

This may happen particularly when remembering the circumstances of his death. I have sometimes experienced this during regression therapy with my clients. As soon as they start talking about the events of their past lives they begin to experience pain in those areas of their bodies that were affected at that time. If the 'pain vibrations' recorded within the emotional body during a painful death experience are still lodged there (i.e. are still unreleased or unredeemed), the vibrations set up by remembering these events can set this past-life pain vibrating again. This may then be felt in the physical body and usually disappears during the therapy session, or vanishes within a short time after it has ended.

The following example was taken from Stevenson's mammoth work *Reincarnation and Biology*, in which he shows that more than 200 cases of birthmarks and birth defects derive from injuries demonstrably sustained in a past life. This example illustrates how important it appears to be for children who remember their past lives to return to their former families and surroundings.

A FALL FROM THE
RAILINGS AT THE AGE OF EIGHT

A girl by the name of Sakuntala was born in 1960 in a town named Kota in the state of Rajastan. She was the child of the Indian silversmith Prabhu Dayal Maheshwari. On 28th April 1968 when she was eight years old she was playing with her cousin on a balcony that had a low railing. She lost her balance, toppled over the railings and hit the concrete with her head. Her mother immediately took the unconscious girl to hospital. She had blood flowing out of her ear. It was only a few hours before she died. The cause of death was thought to be a fractured skull, which had caused internal bleeding and swelling.

On 19th September 1969 a girl named Sunita was born 360 kilometres away in Laxmangarh in the same state of Rajastan. Her father's name was Radhey Shyam Khandelwar, who dealt in grain, seed and fertiliser. He belonged to the middle class and was rather wealthy. As soon as Sunita was born they could see a large, bleeding birthmark on the right side of her head. They put powder on the wound for a few days, which eventually stopped the bleeding. This bleeding patch could not have been caused during birth, nor had the mother had any falls before the birth that could have caused this bleeding wound. It remained clearly visible since no hair grew on it and it was a darker colour than the surrounding skin and was slightly raised.

When Sunita was two years old she said that she lived in Kota where her parents and two brothers lived. Her father was a silversmith and owned a safe. She also claimed her family owned a car and a motorbike. She explained that she had had a slight fall and pointed to the marks on her head saying, 'Look at this. I had a fall.' During the following three years she begged her parents repeatedly to take her to Kota, because she wanted to see her previous family again. Sadly she was unable to remember the names of any of her family, but was able to describe to them that she had been pushed over the railings by her cousin when they had been playing together at the age of eight.

Even during regression many find it difficult to remember factual things clearly, such as names, places and dates, yet everything related to feelings and events is experienced in full detail.

When her parents refused to give in to her wish to travel to Kota, she refused to eat and lost so much weight that she had to be taken to hospital temporarily. In order to put an end to her stubborn refusal to eat and to satisfy her wish to go to Kota, her parents travelled with her to the nearest town of Jaipur for convenience. They told her that this town was Kota. The little girl was not misled for she knew immediately that this was not the town she was looking for, and was indignant at the fact that her parents had lied to her.

A friend of the family, who was moved by the little girl's incessant begging, pleaded with her parents to take her to Kota, for maybe she would be able to find her former family there. The little girl had even mentioned in which part of town her parents had had a shop, and also knew to which caste they belonged. This friend of the family was a solicitor. He contacted the reincarnation investigator Professor Banerjee in Jaipur, who later came to question Sunita. He was so persuasive with her parents that they finally agreed to comply with their five-year-old daughter's wishes to travel to Kota. He himself accompanied them in order to investigate the case in situ.

When they arrived there they were amazed to discover that the part of the town she had mentioned really existed. Even so their daughter was unable to take them to her previous father's shop, nor did she know his name. Only one solution remained; to go to all the silversmiths' shops and ask whether the family in question had a daughter who had had a fatal fall from a balcony at the age of eight. Finally they arrived at Prabhu Dayal Maheshwari's silver smithy. Sunita immediately recognised this shop as the one belonging to her former father. A man was sitting at the table working, and she recognised him as her father from her past. When they had explained to him why they had come he asked the five-year-old whose daughter she was. Sunita immediately explained that she was his daughter. Mr Prabhu Dayal had to admit that everything they told him was correct, for his daughter Sakuntala had fallen from the balcony at the age of eight and had died shortly after. He continued to listen with amazement as they told him more, and then he examined the birthmark on the girl's head. It was in exactly the same place as the wound had been on his daughter Sakuntala. He was convinced that this five-year-old was his fatally injured daughter reborn. Following this the girl led the group along many narrow streets and lanes to her former parents' house. Once there she made many statements relating to her past life, all of which were correct. One example was that she had also lived in another house before her family had moved into the house they were in now. Sunita's health rapidly improved after that, for now she had no reason to refuse her food because she had found her previous family again.

When Professor Stevenson heard about this case, he immediately sent his colleague Dr Satwand Pasricha to visit the family to investigate. before travelling to India himself to carry out more in-depth investigations. The two families visited each other from time to time during the following years, and when Sunita was a little older she travelled to Kota during special holidays so that she could spend the time with her former family. When Sunita married, at the age of 20, Sakuntala's father paid for the wedding, as if it was his own daughter's wedding. It is important to know that the father of a daughter is responsible for all the wedding costs, which often ends up being a small fortune, since hundreds of guests are invited to the wedding of a silversmith's daughter.[39]

One mystery remains to be solved. Why was Sunita's wound bleeding at birth? It is possible that when Sakuntala bled to death, a standstill in her physical programming occurred which was then reactivated as soon as she was born into her present body. It remains unsolved whether the foetus was perhaps already bleeding in this area, since the foetus itself is a highly developed physical body. In my opinion there must have already been a birthmark present on the foetus' temple, which was perhaps grazed during birth causing it to bleed. It is also possible that this bleeding was caused by a higher intelligence, in order to awaken the parents and later Sunita to the importance of this birthmark.

The following case is about another child that bleeds from a wound at birth.

SURROUNDED BANDIT SHOOTS HIMSELF

The story that I am about to relate may sound like a thriller and yet it has not been invented, but actually took place in the furthest southeastern province of Turkey called Hatay. Cemil Hayik was born to Mehmet Hayik in 1912 in a place called Kaharnub. He belonged to the Arabian-speaking minority of that region. After the French had taken control of the Turkish province, which caused much resentment among the people, many indignant people took to the mountains as bandits, where the French police, along with the local police force who co-operated with the French, had declared war on them. Cemil's father had been made one of the leaders of the bandits, so, at a very early age his son was introduced to the life of a band of robbers who were always on the run. Presumably, in order to survive, there was no other option for these outsiders than to rob people.

Cemil had two sisters, and one of her suitors was asked to back off by their father. In order to revenge himself and to humiliate the Hayik family, he and a friend attacked the two sisters and raped them. There was only one solution for dealing with such a deed: revenge. To carry out this revenge became the task of the then twenty-year-old Cemil, since he seemed to be well practised in these things. After all he had already killed two traitors who had told the police the whereabouts of his father. Therefore hunting down the two rapists in order to kill them did not take him long either. Now the police began their search for him in particular.

Cemil was sought by the police, and in the end must have been overcome by a feeling of hopelessness. His friends managed to persuade him to give himself up to the police – for, after all, he had only followed the vendetta laws, so he had reason to be hopeful (that local judges would grant him extenuating circumstances and thus give him only a short sentence or even let him off). Contrary to his expectations he was sentenced to death by the French court. Before his execution Cemil pretended to be in great pain. He was taken to hospital where his wife was allowed to visit him. He used this opportunity to exchange clothes with her and to leave the hospital undetected. Many of the inhabitants of the province of Hatay, who hated the

French government as a foreign body, celebrated this 'coup de maître' (masterstroke), which gained Cemil more and more respect in the eyes of the people.

After his death he was remembered as a kind of national hero. The French police managed to take Cemil's brother Ibrahim hostage, to encourage Cemil and his father to give up being bandits, unless something unpleasant should happen to their hostage. Ibrahim managed to escape and fight his way through to his brother in the mountains. The two brothers now became more and more well-known for frequently attacking travellers and robbing them without killing them. However, they badly treated the French and the local police who had been enlisted by them. Therefore these brothers soon became the most wanted bandits of the province in the mid-1930s.

One day at a house where they had found food and shelter, the man whose house it was secretly notified the police, telling them who was staying with him. The police surrounded the house. A huge shoot-out followed, in which three policemen were killed and seven were injured. The two brothers were shooting from the windows, which provided them with plenty of cover. They were skilled marksmen, whereas the police could only shoot at the two behind the windows from rather exposed positions. Finally they had the idea to set fire to the house by throwing petrol onto the roof and lighting it. When the brothers realised that they would not be able to escape the burning house alive, they decided to take their own lives rather than surrender. First Cemil shot his brother and dragged him through the pool of blood beneath him into a corner, so that his head was pointing in the direction of Mecca. Then he positioned the gun under the left side of his own jaw and pulled the trigger. He had positioned himself in such a way that his body too would fall with his head facing Mecca.

When the police heard the two shots from inside and no more shots were fired at them from the house, they carefully approached the building and found the two corpses. They were just in time to drag them out of the burning house. They then tied the bodies onto horses and took them into the capital Antakya like trophies. It was ordained that both corpses should be left in front of the courts for two days, as a deterrent to other bandits, before allowing relatives to collect the bodies for burial. Thousands came to look at these corpses.

All this occurred in 1935, four years before the French pulled out of the province. They had probably destroyed the legal documents and the autopsy reports, or had taken them with them, making it impossible for Stevenson to inspect the post-mortem reports.

Mikail Fahrici was a farmer in the province. His wife was expecting a child. One day, after the news of the Hayik brothers' death had spread across the region, Mikail, who was a distant relative of theirs, dreamt that the older of the two had entered his house. A day later his wife gave birth to a son whom they named Dahham. Under the left side of his jaw was a birthmark, and another one was clearly visible on his head. When Dahham was two years old he said that his name was not Dahham but Cemil. His father remembered having the dream about Cemil Hayik entering his house before the birth, and had believed from the start that his son was the reincarnation of the man who had shot himself.

News about his son being the national folk hero reborn spread like wildfire throughout the region. Many people came to see the boy to ask him questions about his past life. Mikail was not very happy about this, so he forbade his son to say that his name was Cemil. When this had no effect, they forced him to eat something very bitter or spat in his mouth every time he claimed to be called Cemil instead of Dahham. All these measures had no effect, and he continued to insist on being called Cemil. Finally they went to see a 'hoca', a religious leader, who strongly suggested to the parents to go along with their son's wishes.

His parents finally gave in and had him officially renamed as Cemil. The three-year-old continued to tell them more about his life as the bandit Cemil Hayik, who had recently shot himself. All the details he gave are said to have been correct. Members of Cemil Hayik's family heard about this boy and came to find out whether it really was the now famous bandit who had been reborn. They asked him who the three people standing in front of him were. The three-year-old called them all by name and told them that they were his sisters. When he was asked the name of Cemil's former wife, he answered correctly. When they showed him photographs he could tell them all the names of the people in them. The little boy's answers to their many questions, and trick questions, must have impressed those testing him so much that they were really convinced that he was the reincarnation of Cemil. He was also able to tell them the exact events surrounding his death.

When they finally took Cemil to see his mother she was very sceptical about seeing her son reborn in this boy. The correct answers to her numerous questions must have finally convinced her too that Cemil was indeed who he claimed to have been, so she and her husband asked the farmer Mikail whether they could adopt his son as their own, so that he could be with them again. The farmer would not hear of it. As Cemil grew up he often visited his former family and they exchanged gifts with each other. Each time he had to leave his former parents he cried. He did not seem to like his previous sisters overmuch. He once told his present-day sister that they had caused him too much trouble in his past life. Everyone where he lived just called him Cemil Hayik. This could either be because everyone believed that he was the reincarnation of their folk hero, or because they heard everyone calling him this, so they likewise used this name for him.

The reincarnated Cemil developed a fear of policemen and men in uniforms, and every time he saw one he became very angry. Even as a small boy he would pick up stones and throw them at the police. One day he took a stick and held it like a gun pretending to shoot at them. He was also born with a phobia of blood. When he was ten years old he saw a man who had been shot by the police lying in his own blood. The sight of blood always gave him headaches. He had nightmares about fighting the French police up until he was seven years old.

Nightmares often point to experiences from past lives. If these are confronted at their source and 'released and redeemed' during regression therapy, then they disappear for good.

Stevenson visited Cemil when he was 30 years old and working as a baker. He was still able to remember many details from his past life, but did not know at what age he had first remembered these things. Stevenson then examined Cemil's head and neck. Cemil told him that when the police had surrounded him and his brother and the roof above them had started to burn, they could see no way of saving themselves. That is why he had asked his brother to close his eyes and had then shot him. Finally he had put the muzzle of his gun under his chin and had operated the trigger with his toe. On the place under his chin where the bullet had entered there was a definite indentation, which was two centimetres long and one centimetre wide. According to his mother this wound had bled quite profusely at birth and needed stitching in hospital. Because of this operation the birthmark had become larger. The area around his teeth proved to be a weak point in his mouth, due to the bullet having gone through his jaw into the top of his head. He frequently experienced pain in this area. Even though the wound on his neck had been stitched immediately after birth, it still bled from time to time.

If a specific area of our body was injured in a traumatic situation in a past life, it tends to develop into a weak spot in our next life. Should someone have been killed by a lance in the area of the liver in a past life, it is possible for him to have a weak spot there in many of his lives that follow. Even if doctors come up with a feasible explanation for the pain, and are able to heal this weakness with medicines or an operation, it has actually not been cured. An accumulation of negative energy will still remain from a past-life

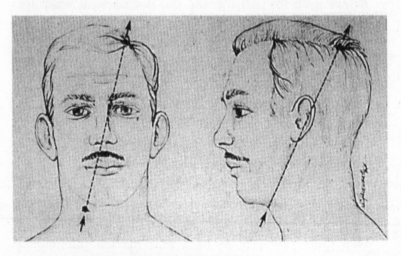

Artist's reconstruction of the trajectory of the bullet through the head of Cemil Hayik that would have caused wounds of entry and exit corresponding to the birthmarks on Cemil Fahrici.

experience, which can at any time make itself felt once again. However, should the origin of this weakness be uncovered and 'redeemed' during regression therapy, then this area will remain pain-free, and free of all irritation for ever. (This applies to this life and future lives after that.)

Stevenson could clearly see the other birthmark on his head when moving the hair aside. The scar, which was caused by the bullet leaving the skull, was two centimetres long and two millimetres wide. The scars of this kind of wound are usually larger than those caused by the bullet entering the body. The bullet leaving the body frequently tears or damages even more tissue or bits of bone, causing a larger wound on its way out than on the way in.[40]

An interesting question remains: how was it possible for Cemil Hayik's soul to enter the foetus just before birth, after having been 'dead' for only one or two days? And how is it possible for all the physical imprints on the new body to have been transferred in such a short time? Hundreds of my clients whose regressions I have facilitated remember having entered the foetus in the womb of their new mother. Some arrive in the mother's womb immediately after conception, which they often claim to have experienced; others waited at least a month if not several before entering the foetus and then identifying with it. Very occasionally it happens that the soul only enters the new body immediately after birth. One possible reason for this could be that the soul had experienced an extremely traumatic birth in a past life and therefore insisted on only being reincarnated if it did not involve passing through the birth canal again. As a general rule you can say that on average most souls enter the foetus during the second or third month of pregnancy. How it was possible for the death wounds of the deceased to have been transferred to the foetus of Cemil Fahrici, who was due the very next day, remains a mystery to me. In time we are gradually solving more and more of life's mysteries, which in turn reveal even more mysteries behind them. The whole of life seems to be a huge mystery. It is a joy to realise and marvel in love and humility at the wonders and secrets of creation and to be allowed to uncover a little more about them.

The following case is very interesting. Once again an imminent rebirth is first announced in a dream and a lot more is revealed about the intermediate state experienced as an earthbound entity.

MURDERED WITH AN AXE

Farmer Peng lived in the poorest conditions imaginable. His wife was called See, and she had borne a daughter in 1941 who was now two months old. They lived in a village called Nong Khun Puwa, which is situated in north-eastern Thailand in the province of Kalasin. Peng had a brother named Tao. On one occasion when Tao was visiting them, the brothers had an argument about an inheritance. Tao became so angry that Peng was in fear of his life. Thinking Tao wanted to kill him he left his own house in a hurry. Tao was so enraged and possibly drunk, and had worked himself up to such an extent, that he grabbed an axe and brought it down three times with all his might on the back of Peng's wife, See. She died immediately from these wounds. In no time at all, news of this extremely violent murder of Tao's sister-in-law had spread throughout the region.

Seven kilometres away in the village of Sao Lao lived the farmer Bai Poah Pah-Dee with his wife, Tam. They had two children. Approximately three months after the murder Tam's sister came to see her one morning to tell her about a dream she had had. In this dream she, Tam, and two other women were on their way home from the fields where they had been working when they saw a woman who was on her own. The woman came towards them and touched all four of them with her hand to determine which one of them had the coolest body. She had chosen Tam as the one with the coolest body, and had followed her home. Tam later told Professor Stevenson that it had been at that moment that she had realised that she was pregnant.

At this point I must add a remark so that you will fully understand what is meant here. In Thailand a woman who has a cool body during the hottest time of year is seen as particularly desirable. This is because she will not sweat so much and will therefore smell more pleasant. This superstition could well have other reasons why a 'cool' woman is more desirable, since even the king's bride is chosen for her 'cool' body.

Once again we have what Stevenson calls an 'annunciatory dream', which frequently occurs in many countries of the world in relation to imminent pregnancies or births. Either before or during her pregnancy the expectant mother usually dreams that a deceased person, who is maybe someone she knew or a stranger, introduces him or herself and either begs her to give birth to him or her or simply tells her that she or he will be her daughter (or son). It is also possible for relatives such as a husband, a brother or sister, parents or even friends or neighbours to have these 'annunciatory dreams'. These dreams are usually seen as very important, since in most cases they really do come true.

For me the most important question is: how do these dreams come about? I am convinced that coincidences do not exist and that everything is guided by a greater wisdom that makes perfect sense, for nothing sense-less exists in creation. Therefore even such dreams are arranged or allowed to happen – perhaps to show the dreamer or those concerned by the dream that a mysterious overall scheme exists, which as yet is not fully understood by we humans. We are given a taste of the numinous, mysterious connections that exist surrounding we humans and our presence on earth, which are not possible to unravel with our minds. Still the challenge is to continue facing these mysteries surrounding us with an ever widening understanding.

Nine months later in the early summer of 1942 Tong In was born. Her parents discovered three large scars on her back. From the top to the bottom they were as long as your finger. The top one was still partially open and bleeding, which only stopped after a week. Her parents Bai and Tam immediately saw the connection between these very obvious scars and the wounds that were inflicted on the fatally injured woman from the neighbouring village.

They believed that this deceased woman from the neighbouring village, whom they had never known personally, must have been reborn to them as their daughter.

When their daughter was three years old she began to talk more and more about her life as Mrs See, whose name she used. She also explained to her parents that Tao, who had been her brother-in-law, had killed her with an axe. Contrary to many other children who remember their past lives, she never expressed a wish to return to her village. It would seem that her memories of everything that had occurred there were too vivid for her to have any wish to return to the scene of the terrible crime. One day her mother asked Tong In whether she could remember what happened after her death. She told her that after Tao had hit her for the third time, he put his foot on her body now lying on the ground to pull the axe out of her back. She had been able to see all this and had remained in her house until they took her body away. She had followed it as far as the gates of the cemetery. Once there she had turned back. She also described how she had watched them all having a meal (which had probably been after her funeral) and had been very disappointed not to have been invited to join them.

As previously mentioned, we are usually met by a deceased person after death. If the death was unexpected, like for instance a sudden murder, then the soul is frequently so confused that it will often take some time before it realises what has actually happened. Even though the deceased See had been aware of her brother-in-law hitting her

*with the axe, she was unable to understand that she had actually died.
She must have been dead after the first blow and would therefore have
left her physical body immediately. Apparently everything after that
had been a mystery to her. Even at the funeral reception she did not
seem to understand that they were having this meal because she had
died. This was why she had been so surprised not to have been invited.
It often takes a long time before such earth-bound beings realise that
they are dead.*

The three-year-old then continued saying that finally
she left her village and had gone in the direction of Sao
Lao. On her way she had seen four women walking along
the road, and had touched them all in order to see which
one of them was the one that felt the coolest. She had
decided that it was Tam and had followed her home. She
was unable to tell them any more after that. It took until
she was 18 years old for her to visit the village from her
past where she had been murdered. She recognised a saw
that she had used with her husband in the past, and she
recognised a tree that she had once planted.

A monk who had heard of this American professor told
him about this case, and in 1984 when Tong In was
42 years old, Professor Stevenson, accompanied by an
interpreter, went to visit her. Tong In told him that when
she had been a child she had been able to remember many
details about her past life as See, but now very little of it
remained in her memory.

Stevenson then examined the clearly visible birthmarks,
which can be seen in two photographs in his monumental

book called *Reincarnation and Biology*.[41] All three birthmarks run parallel to the spine in a downward direction and are about seven centimetres long and about three millimetres wide. The upper one is the most obvious one and looks like a thick scar. It was this one that had bled during and after birth.

In the examples in this chapter, which were taken from Professor Stevenson's treasury of cases that he researched, the main theme has been birthmarks, which significantly differ from moles. Several birthmarks mentioned in these case histories were still active at birth, either bleeding or itching. Even those hidden in the hair are usually hairless and a slightly different colour to the rest of the skin. When the cause of death has been from being shot by bullets, then the place where the bullet entered is usually a little dented, whereas the area where it left the body is usually a little raised. Presumably, a well-practised expert on birthmarks could well determine, extremely accurately and just by looking at them, the past-life circumstances of a person, which later led to these birthmarks being formed.

From my experience as a regression therapist I can say that so-called moles, namely those brown and usually rounded marks that can appear anywhere on the body, were most likely caused by injuries in much earlier lives. In my opinion, they are the descendants of birthmarks. Apparently they gradually disappear after several incarnations. So it is safe to say that birthmarks and moles are a map of past violent or traumatic injuries. It is relatively easy to find the causes of these marks on the body by using regression therapy. In this way we are able to find out about all our past-life injuries to the skin.

We also carry in us an internal map of all still active injuries or death wounds received at some time in the past. These are not visible unless we undergo surgery, but we are frequently able to feel them. In my experience chronic pains are usually the after-effects of past-life injuries. In this category I also include migraines, asthma, as well as many other unpleasant symptoms of ill health. Medical research will make great discoveries by means of regression and regression therapy as soon as they get used to the idea that reincarnation is the truth.

I think that those readers, who did not believe in reincarnation when they started reading this book, will no doubt have changed their minds by now. Should any doubts remain then the following section will help to dispel any of those still deeply ingrained reservations you may have about accepting reincarnation as the truth. Stevenson was able to prove reincarnation scientifically for the first time, using cases where children are born with a birth defect. They are able to remember their past lives, and their statements have been double-checked and proven to be correct. Through this research reincarnation finally moves into the realm of science.

7

Children that are born with birth deformities

THE MURDER VICTIM WHO WAS
REBORN WITH CRIPPLED HANDS

U. Sein Maung owned a lorry with which he transported goods to and from Pyawbwe, the village where he lived, and the Burmese capital, Rangoon. He seemed to make a good living out of this. U. Sein was having an affair with a woman in Rangoon. When his wife found out about this she followed him there. There she discovered that it was true that her husband was staying with another woman. She was so distressed about this that she took her own life by swallowing battery acid. About five years later Mr U. Sein Maung went to visit his parents by bike. On his way back he stopped in the village of Okinnngone, which was near Pyawbwe, in order to speak with a couple he knew called U. Pe Tin and Daw Khin Hla. Following this, he got on his bike to go home.

Suddenly three men wielding narrow sabres barred his way and pulled him off his bike causing him to lose his glasses. They then began to attack him with their sabres. He held his hands in front of his face to defend himself against a blow and lost several fingers by doing so. He was stabbed by one of the sabres in the left side of his lower back, which proved to be fatal. At the same time another blow struck his neck almost decapitating him. When the police arrived at the scene of the crime they found the severed fingers lying next to the dead man. There was no sign of the murderers who were never caught. The strange thing was that the three men did not take the precious ring, the bike or any other jewellery belonging to the murder victim. Rumours were spreading about his mother-in-law wanting to revenge her daughter's death by hiring three murderers to kill her vow-breaking son-in-law.

That same night the farmer U. Pe Tin dreamt that U. Sein Maung came to him asking to be reborn in his family. Only the day before, U. Sein Maung had stopped at U. Pe Tin's place to say hello to him and his wife when he had passed their village on his bike. In the dream U. Pe Tin answered the man, knowing that he had died, 'You may come to us if that is your wish.' It was only the following morning that he found out about U. Sein Maung's murder.

Nine months later on 12th October 1956 a daughter named Ma Myint Thein (we will call her Thein hereafter) was born to U. Pe Tin's wife. The fingers on both hands were either missing or were short and crippled and only her left thumb was normal.[42] Since Mr U. Pe Tin was able to remember the dream in which the deceased announced his wish to be reborn, he knew that it really was his murdered friend who had been reborn as his daughter. It was some time before she began to remember her past life. When she was five years old and was playing with the other children, she must have once again noticed that she was unable to do things as well as the others because of her crippled hands. Her sadness about this must have triggered her memories of a past life. Her mother over-heard her little girl saying to her brother, 'I have got a wife who lives in the south. (She meant Rangoon.) I'll give you

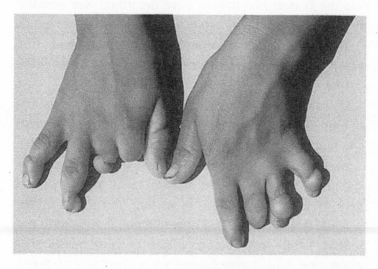

Ma Myint Thein's hands as they appeared in February 1977, when she was 20 years old. Most of the fingers and the right thumb show constriction rings. Only the left thumb is completely normal.

some sweets if you take me there.' After this she repeatedly spoke about her past life.

She said she was called Sein Maung and had a wife called Ma Thein and two children whose names she also knew. She said that she used to own cattle, a bike and a small lorry, which she had mainly used for transporting vegetables. It was not long before she also remembered being murdered in her past life. She said that three men had attacked her with big long knives (presumably, she was not familiar with the word sabre yet). She had fallen from her bike and in doing so had lost her glasses. She explained that the reason her fingers were deformed was because she defended herself by protecting her face with her hands so that the big knives would not hurt her head. She remembered having worn a ring, a watch and a gold chain on that day.

She was now able to remember all the circumstances surrounding the murder. She was sure that the woman who had been her mother-in-law had plotted this murder. Her uncle asked her whether she knew who her murderers were, to which she replied that she knew at least one of them. Her uncle pressed her to tell him who he was so that he could revenge himself. Thein told him that he must not do that. Later when she was asked the same question by others, she denied ever having recognised any of them. Thein showed signs of having a phobia about the place of her murder, for every time she passed by the place she began to shake. All the years that she went to school in

Pyawbwe she had to pass the place twice a day. Even as a child of school age she kept her hands hidden and sometimes got very depressed when remembering or being reminded of that past life.

Just like people, places have a particular vibration. If the vibration of a particular place is registered as negative in the soul's emotional body, such as the energy at the scene of a premeditated murder for instance, then the soul incarnated in a different body visiting that particular place may well experience an unpleasant connection with it. This can be so intense as to make the person faint. Agoraphobia is often confused with the condition previously mentioned because the symptoms are very similar. If for instance we were burnt to death in a certain place a few hundred years ago, and for some reason find ourselves drawn to visiting this place again in our present life, it could happen that a most unpleasant feeling wells up in us when we go there. When this happens we may not be able to set foot in that place, or we may panic and have to leave as quickly as possible. The emotional body wants to protect us so that we are not exposed to the same vibrations that caused us such terrible suffering in the past. The emotional body registers all vibrations, particularly those that were present at the time of a painful death. These vibrations could be those of the murderer, his weapon, or even the vibrations of his clothes and their colours, the energies of the place or even of the tree that stood nearby.

In a life that follows having been murdered, the mere sight of the colour of the former murderer's jacket (the vibration of which we have imprinted and stored as 'negative programming') perceived through our emotional body may be enough to make us feel uneasy. If you were very sensitive and you came across a tree that was the same type as the one that had stood near the place where you were murdered, the emotional body could react to the similar vibrations of the tree, and create an uneasy feeling in yourself. Regression therapy can follow up these vibrations, find their origin and then help the client to release them.

As you can probably imagine from having read about the sex changes from one incarnation to another, Thein had strongly developed masculine traits. She complained about being a girl, preferred to wear boys' clothes and behaved like a boy in many ways. She married when she was 20 years old and bore two children.

Many people feel as if they have been born as the wrong sex. Even when there are no homosexual tendencies many express the wish to be the opposite sex. It is likely that these people belonged to the opposite sex in their previous life and have a kind of nostalgic longing to continue being the sex they were then. Regression could surely shed light on this. Here you could ask your Higher Self, or your inner, all-knowing self, why it is necessary for you to live this life in the body of the opposite sex. Once you are shown an explanation from a higher viewpoint you will also understand why you chose your present sex, or agreed to it before birth. In this way you will then be able to accept your present sexual disposition without further conflict. Understanding the broader, higher reasons why things are the way they are makes it easier to accept an event or a situation as it is.

When Thein was eight years old she met her mother-in-law from her past life in the market place. She was friendly and asked her to come and visit her, but the girl said no.

Ten years later they met again. When Thein turned her back on her, the old woman began to cry saying, 'Now that my son has died I have no one left to look after me.' Thein turned around and said, 'Where is my lorry?' Three years later this woman came to visit Thein at her house. She was very friendly and wanted to ask her once more to come and visit her. Thein again refused her invitation. She simply wanted nothing to do with her, and did not want to be reminded of her past life. When Thein was nineteen she visited her former daughter in a neighbouring village. They both cried a lot when they met.

Professor Stevenson investigated this case in 1975, 1977, 1978 and 1984, and managed to gather much information from those he interviewed. It was only in 1984 that one of his colleagues found out from the murdered U. Sein Maung's mother-in-law's neighbours that after her daughter's suicide she was supposed to have said that her son-in-law must die like her daughter. Stevenson examined the birthmarks and the deformed fingers. Thein's mother told him that a long birthmark was visible on the right-hand side of her daughter's neck at birth, which curled around her neck like a ribbon. In 1984 when Stevenson examined her there was nothing left of this mark. Thein's mother also claimed to have noticed a birthmark at birth on her daughter's back in the area of her left kidney. Since Stevenson had no female translator with him at the time who could have had a look for him (it was unheard of for a woman to even partially undress in front of a stranger, not even a doctor), he could not continue this inspection.[43]

The following story is about another child that was born with several fingers missing. This child had died at the age of four in its previous life, three-quarters of a year after losing its fingers of the right hand during an accident.

LOST HIS FINGERS IN A FODDER MACHINE

Hukum Singh was the three-and-a-half-year-old son of a farmer Dwarka Prasad and his wife Raj Rani. This woman already had three boys and two girls, and was to bear four more children in time. The Prasad family lived in a small village called Nagla Tal. It is situated three kilometres east of the town Bewar in the Indian State of Uttar Pradesh. Behind a shed was a fodder-cutting machine, which was usually operated by two people. One person had the job of making bundles of corn, straw and various vegetable stumps, feeding them into the spinning cutting blades, while the other person turned the large wheel by hand on the opposite side. Hukum saw how his father turned the wheel while his uncle fed the vegetable stumps into the machine.

When the latter left his work place for a few minutes, the boy picked up a few stumps with his hands in order to feed them into the still rotating wheel, which his father was turning. The boy put his right hand too far into the machine, causing his fingers and the tip of his thumb to be severed from his hand by the sharp blades. Mr Prasad and his eldest son immediately took Hukum to the district hospital in Bewar. He only started screaming in agony once they had arrived there. They cleaned and bandaged the wounds, and gave him several injections. In the following month his oldest brother frequently took him for treatment at the casualty department of the hospital. Ten months later at the end of September 1971, Hukum developed a high fever. They called a doctor who gave him an injection. On the way home just minutes from their village, the four-year-old died. His mother suffered indescribable pain at the loss of her son. The deceased son appeared to her twice in dreams during the weeks that followed and comforted her and reassured her that he would return.

As I have mentioned before, the soul usually leaves the earthly plane after death to spend some time in an intermediate realm. This place generally appears much more beautiful and grander than the earth. Here we experience much joy, meet our deceased relatives and friends again, pursue our interests, which while on earth we may not have had the opportunity to do, and gradually prepare ourselves for a new incarnation. Children that die are usually taken to others of their age who are lovingly cared for by helpers on that plane of being. There they may enjoy an undisturbed, wonderful 'life', as they grow up surrounded by comforts that cannot be compared to those of the earth.[44] *As soon as someone mourns the death of the child, it can be ripped away from its carefree new state of being and be drawn back to the mourning person. It is then infected by this sadness and can fall prey to it. Children who have returned invisibly to a person who is mourning their death frequently try to comfort them. If this person is sensitive they can feel the presence of the child and can sometimes converse telepathically with it. Many people mourning the death of a child seek out a sensitive person through whom they can contact the deceased child. Sometimes they try to obtain comforting news about the whereabouts of the child by what has been dubbed electronic voice phenomena, i.e. the attempt to capture voices and receive messages of deceased loved ones on audiotape. The most common and simplest means of communication with those on the other side is through dreams. This is what the deceased Hukum used to comfort his mother. He seemed to know that he would soon be reincarnated and that it would then be possible to see his mother again.*

Thirteen months after Hukum's death a son was born to the farmers Sita Ram Jatav and Chiraunja Devi in the village of Nagla Devi, five kilometres south west of Bewar. His name was Lekh Pal Jatav (Lekh for convenience). To their horror they discovered that their child had several fingertips missing on his right hand. The fingers were over a third shorter than usual, whereas the fingers on the left hand were perfectly normal. The family was puzzling over why their son should have been born with a crippled right hand and for what karmic reasons this may have happened. A friend suggested that he must have been a tax collector in his past life who did many people wrong by writing and exacting payment with this hand. He claimed that as a punishment his hand was now crippled.

From the above statements we can see that karma is often erroneously seen as a punishment for previous misdeeds. This is not so since in its proper sense karma has nothing to do with punishment, for in God's creation there is no such thing. What karma actually means is that we reap what we sow. By observing which actions produce which fruits over many lifetimes, we will gradually learn to only do those deeds that produce sweeter fruits. The Law of Karma is a process that gradually helps us to sharpen our insights over many lives, the result being that through experience we eventually only live by God's laws, thinking, speaking and acting only from a place of love.

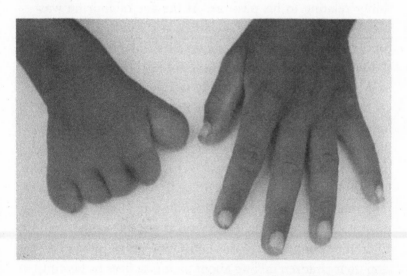

Lekh Pal's hands in February 1980, when he was just over 8 years old. The fingers of the right hand, including the thumb, are mere stubs, without any trace of bones. Rudimentary fingernails on three fingers of the right hand cannot be seen in this photograph.

In the first few years of his life Lekh was frail and sickly to the point that they often wondered whether he would survive. He was a late developer in all aspects and only learnt to speak fluently by the age of five. Since his parents often spent all day working in the fields, his older sister Rajan Siri usually looked after the boy. When her little brother was only a year old, she claimed to have overheard him using the word 'Tal' repeatedly, which as they later discovered was the name of the village where he had once lived. She soon seemed to have become used to his garbled speech, for already at a young age he told her things relating to his past life. At the age of four he was very clear about having a father, a mother as well as brothers and sisters in the village called Tal. He told them, 'I don't want to stay here. This is not my home.'

When her brother repeatedly talking about wanting to go home and occasionally also about his mother feeling lonely, the daughter must have told her parents that Lekh did not feel happy in this family and that he wished to go back to his family from a past life. In India you are shown in the Vedas already how to deal with children who remember their past lives. According to them, past-life memories must be expelled as soon as possible or the child could die young. Due to this belief, parents in India often stop their children talking about their past lives by beating them or punishing them in some way. The boy Lekh later spoke about having been beaten now and then for talking about past-life events in his childhood. When he was five years old and was able to speak fluently, he confided something in his sister (presumably swearing her to secrecy beforehand). He told her that he lost his fingers when he was a boy by getting his hand trapped in a fodder-cutting machine, which was being operated by his father and his uncle, whose turn he had taken. Two people had then taken him to hospital in Bewar.

The bonds of love between souls remain intact from one life to the next. The deceased Hukum had seen his mother crying a lot about his death, which is why he felt he must comfort her in her dreams. It is likely that the two of them had woven a special, loving bond between them long ago in other past lives. This could be why his mother mourned his death so much. In his incarnation as Lekh he still felt this love for his previous mother. Perhaps he could still vaguely remember having comforted his mother when she was mourning his death. This memory now prompts him to say that he wants to return to her because she is lonely. Everyone who has lost someone who they were particularly close to, usually feel very lonely at first and sometimes for a very long time.

Even when Lekh was very young, he not only threatened to go 'home', but was also caught attempting to walk to Nagla Tal. This must have been too much for his parents, which is why he probably received further beatings. When the boy was eight years old, Hukum's oldest brother Bharat Singh went to the village of Nagla Devi, which is about eight kilometres from Nagla Tal, to attend a wedding. Lekh recognised him and said to him, 'You are my brother.' He begged him to take him home with him, because everyone at home beat him. His brother realised that this boy must be his deceased brother reborn because of his crippled right hand, and upon returning to his village told his family about the member of their family who had been reborn.

A year later the Hukum family succeeded in persuading the Jatav family to trust their son to his former brother, and allow him to take him to visit Nagla Tal. When he arrived there he was subjected to a previously organised test. Hukum's mother, Mrs Raj Rani, had been asked to stand among a group of women and the boy was then asked to find his former mother among them. He pointed to the right person saying, 'This is my mother.' Then he pointed to several others who had gathered around him out of curiosity and picked out his brothers and sisters whom he had known from a previous life. He was then shown around the house and the yard and was able to show them the exact place where the fodder-cutting machine had been. In their eyes Lekh had successfully passed all the tests they had set up for him and was then accepted by everyone as a member of their family who had been reborn. Since Lekh's previous and present-day families were from the same caste and were equally poor there were no class differences between the two families. Class differences might have made a friendly relationship between them rather difficult.

The two families became good friends and exchanged gifts from time to time. Lekh was also allowed to spend two weeks at a time with his previous parents. Since they were very poor Lekh once brought his previous mother some rice, which she was very touched by. When Lekh was eight years old he moved in with his sister Rajan Siri who was married. The town was called Sirsa and was about 40 kilometres from his village, and this is where he went to school. His mother kept up the friendly contact with his former parents in his absence. It was in Sirsa that Stevenson met the boy in 1980 and was able to speak with him. As a medical practitioner he was able to ascertain that the third bone was missing from the tips of his fingers on his right hand. This birth defect is called brachydactyly. This defect occurs in one in 40,000 births and involves both hands. It is much rarer to find this defect on only one hand. In both these cases the fingers are usually normal but just smaller or crippled. In Lekh's case the tips of his fingers had no bones. Therefore we must be dealing with a one-off birth defect here. All genetic or endogenous reasons for this defect had to be ruled out.

It is possible that anybody who has gone through a similar experience in a past life would be reborn with a similarly stunted hand. Nonetheless it still remains a mystery why some reincarnated people are born with birthmarks or birth defects stemming from wounds from a past death and others not, or only with very slight defects. Why Lekh had no phobia about the fodder-cutting machine is also a mystery, since it was still there at his home and he could also see similar ones elsewhere. Other people may develop a fear or even a phobia about such tools that caused them great pain in a previous life.

Both children and adults sometimes show great fear of the dentist when he approaches their mouths with dental instruments. They are carrying conscious or unconscious memories of pains inflicted under similar circumstances in a past life. Maybe Lekh would have developed a phobia of fodder machines had the cause of his death been directly linked to his accident. Having understood the Law of Karma fully, it is easy to see that Hukum did not lose his fingers by accident. Most likely he had wilfully severed someone else's fingers in a more distant past life.

Stevenson and his assistant, Dr Pasricha, questioned everyone who had anything to do with this case during their several visits to Nagla Devi, Nagla Tal and Sirsa. When Lekh's former father died in Nagla Tal he attended his funeral and also his former sister's wedding. When Dr Pasricha asked him where he felt more at home, Lekh answered, 'When I am in Nagla Devi I miss Nagla Tal. And when I am in Nagla Tal I miss Nagla Devi.'

Children who are able to remember their past lives clearly, may have developed such a close connection and love for the present and former members of their families, that they no longer know where they belong. Apparently it is preferable to allow them to meet their families from a past life, in order to satisfy their longing for that past home and the people they once knew. Little children, usually those under two years old, often think that they are still living the same life. They think that somehow they jumped from one family to another, without knowing how it happened. They are often not aware of the fact that they died. This is why they use the present tense when talking about their past lives.

At the age of sixteen Lekh returned home to his parents to take care of the small farm. His parents tried to find him a wife, since at sixteen it was time for their son to have a partner. When Dr Pasricha went to see him he told her about his parents' futile efforts to find him a wife, for none of the local girls wanted to marry him because of his hand. When in 1990 Dr Pasricha visited him once more to clarify certain questions which were still open, he was still not married and complained bitterly about the fact that is crippled hand was a real handicap for a farmer.[45]

The two accounts above dealt with missing fingers on hands. In the first example it had been caused wilfully in a previous life, whereas the second one was caused by a former accident. I now want to give you an example of a case where the cause of a later defect stems from something completely different.

BORN WITH A HARELIP
AND A CLEFT PALATE

U. Paw Kywe, a farmer's son, was born in 1936 in Sipin Tabetkar. He was a part-time lorry driver and was married to a woman called Daw Aye Nyunt. She bore him three children. He especially loved his son and his youngest daughter, but not the older daughter, who was his second child Ma Ahamar Kyi. He often beat her and discriminated against her. U. Paw Kywe (Paw for convenience) seemed to have many talents as well as being socially involved in his community. He frequently applied his skills as an electrician and, since he seemed to have no fear of heights, he was entrusted with the task of climbing the village pagoda to install the electric lighting system, and then to be responsible for its maintenance.

One day when he was up there fixing something, he must have disturbed a swarm of bees. They attacked and stung him terribly. Not long after this incident he developed leprosy. The locals in this area, and no doubt others further afield, believe that leprosy is caused by bee stings or snake bites. Contrary to this, modern medicine believes it is spread by being contagious. Paw's leprosy spread more and more during the following weeks, until even his nose and mouth were affected and were gradually being eaten away by this horrific sickness. It also spread into the inside of his mouth right down his throat, so that his speech became more and more stunted. Within a few months his face looked terrible. Even his hands and fingers became infected by the disease, which soon made working impossible for him. Out of sympathy his boss gave him a small horse-drawn cart so that he could still go off on small errands. But even these quickly dwindled since everyone avoided him because of his sickening looks and his highly contagious illness. He was soon incredibly lonely and became very poor. His wife and children had already left him for the same reasons and had moved to Pyabwe.

Paw had a niece called Daw Win Kyi whose marriage to U. Kyaw Maung he had been violently opposed to. They had not spoken to each other for years. To his amazement they were now the only ones who would have anything to do with him. Win cooked for him and Kyaw brought him his food and water. Paw was extremely touched by this couple's compassion and charity, whose friendship he had once broken due to a disagreement. He apologised to them and asked them for forgiveness.

Having had much experience in the field of regression therapy, I could well imagine that these three people may have had issues to resolve between them, which may well span many lifetimes. For example it could well be that Paw was badly treated or even mistreated by Kyaw in a past life, which may even have led to his death. Our beings are always led back to each other over many lifetimes, until any remaining hatred towards each other has become love. This can take many lifetimes. This may well be the reason why Paw subconsciously rejected Kyaw as his niece's bridegroom. Kyaw unconsciously knew that he had something to make good in relation to Paw. It was probably these motives that got him to seize the opportunity that now presented itself to put things right. In this way the disharmony between them from a past life could be partially or completely resolved. Win was most likely also involved in those causative events of the past. It will be left to the psychologists and physicians of the future once they have grown accustomed to the idea of reincarnation, to follow up and constantly discover more about these physical and spiritual connections that reach far beyond our present lives.

In 1976 the now 40-year-old Paw kept completely to himself spending most of his time in his house, because he could not bear the looks from the people in his village and did not want to infect them with his sickness. Occasionally he ventured out to visit his best friend Ko Mya. Due to his infectious disease he never entered his friend's house, but sat outside on a large rock from where he was able to talk with his friend. Even though Win and Kyaw continued to care for the orphaned Paw, they sometimes spent time away from their village, so that Paw had to occasionally manage without their help for up to three days at a time. Returning after having been away for two days, Win and Kyaw found Paw dead in his house. No one in the village wanted to touch the body of a man who had died of leprosy. All they did was roll his dead body up in the plastic sheet he had been lying on, took it to the cemetery and buried it there.

In April 1978 the blacksmith U. Kyaw Maung and his wife Daw Win Kyi who had cared for the leper Paw until his death had a second child. They named him Maung Htoo (shortened to Maung in the following story). The boy's parents had a terrible shock when they saw what their child looked like. He had an ugly harelip that split his top lip, making an open channel that disappeared in his right nostril. Apart from this the child had a cleft palate which strongly affected his inner palatal organs. On top of all this the child screamed almost non-stop unless he was picked up and carried. As soon as they put him down anywhere he began to scream again. This tiresome condition only stopped when the parents had saved enough money for an operation on Maung's harelip when he was one-and-a-half years old.

At the age of two he began to give the first hints concerning his past life as his mother's uncle. He also exhibited some of Paw's typical mannerisms. For example, he liked to put one arm across his back when he wanted to say something. Since he found it difficult to talk due to his cleft palate, the two-year-old would frequently use gestures accompanying his speech, such as pointing in a certain direction to indicate where his mother lived. He also said that he lived near the pagoda and that his wife's name was Daw Aye Nyunt. After her husband's death, she had moved back into the empty house with her three children. When Maung was asked about his children he lifted three fingers and said, 'I have got three.' His parents had already suspected that they had given birth to their uncle, Paw, who had died such a gruesome death, and this was now confirmed beyond a shadow of a doubt. The two-year-old Maung now visited Paw's best friend with whom he used to talk from a distance while sitting on the stone outside his house. To test the boy, Paw's friend asked him to go and sit in his 'usual' place where he used to sit. Maung went outside, walked over to the stone and sat down.

As time went by, more and more details of his past life emerged from what he said. He told them about his death and about having been buried in a plastic sheet. (He could only have known these things through his own after-death experiences.) He also mentioned an accident that had been caused by his pony. The pony had bolted and the wagon wheel had rolled over his leg causing him great pain. His present-day grandmother was able to remember this incident, for she had been there watching it at the time. Even as a small boy he refused to enter the grounds of the pagoda. When asked about his he said that he had been badly stung by bees when he was on the roof in the past. (Localised phobia, agoraphobia, or both?)

When Maung was seven-years-old Paw's younger brother happened to be in Sipin Tabetkar for a funeral. He visited the house where the boy lived who claimed to be his reincarnated older brother. While he was talking with Maung's parents the young boy happened to walk into the room, and seeing Maung's parents the man immediately recognised him as his former brother saying, 'Hi Kaung! Since when have you been here?' The expression 'kaung' is reserved only for a man addressing his younger brother. If a young man addresses an older man in this way, it is seen as an insult. This is why his parents were shocked to hear their son call him by that name, and why Mr Kyaw was already on his way to discipline the boy. The visitor, who was not as yet convinced that this boy really was his older brother from the past, yet did not want to rule out this possibility, stopped the father from punishing the boy. He admitted that his brother always used to address him in exactly that manner in the past. This man stayed in the village for a whole week and talked a great deal with Maung in that time. By the time he left he was completely convinced that this six-year-old boy was his former brother who had died of leprosy, and had now been reborn.

At the same age, Maung also went to visit the house in which he had lived in his previous incarnation. His oldest son from the past welcomed him with open arms and allowed him to look around the house and to touch all the things that once belonged to him. His sister, Ma Ahmar Kyi, who used to have a hard time with her father, was not at all pleased to see him. She even threatened to beat him if he ever entered their house again. Maung dressed exactly like Paw used to, and even swore using the same words as Paw. (The outer and particularly the inner traits we are born with are to a much greater degree derived from past lives than they are inherited from our parents.)

Professor Stevenson visited and talked with Maung and members of both his present and former family at various times. It must have been quite something, even for him, to find that it is possible for a leper from a previous life to be reborn with a harelip and a cleft palate. He does mention, however, that defects such as these occur once in every 1,000 to 2,000 people. This condition is often inherited. Yet in the families in which Paw and Maung grew up, he could trace no relatives suffering from this hereditary disease. Maung's hands and fingers showed no remnants of his past life as Paw, even though the leprosy had also severely damaged these parts of his body.[46]

There are an incredible number of birth defects that the medical profession is unable to find the root cause for. Stevenson has clearly demonstrated through his investigations that one of the most influential determinants leading to birth defects is the transfer of physical conditions from a past life into a present incarnation. The following example is about a boy who was born with a flat area on the back of his head.

BORN WITH A FLAT AREA ON
THE BACK OF THE HEAD

Mehmet Bekler was born in 1938 in the Turkish village of Ekber. He was the son of Hamid and Katibeh Bekler. Apart from this child the couple also had another son and a daughter. At a young age Hamid Bekler took a second wife with whom he usually lived. Mehmet grew up with his mother. As soon as Mehmet had completed his national service in the army, he took over the running of a water mill that had been in the family for some time. This mill was right by the river that flowed past the village. Mehmet got married and had three children.

In November 1965 the following occurred. While several people were queuing up in front of Mehmet's mill to have their wheat milled, a man by the name of Bayrakdar arrived with a sack of wheat, pushed his way past everyone and insisted on Mehmet milling his wheat immediately since his family were crying with hunger. The miller told him that he would have to go to the back of the queue and, like everyone else, wait for his turn. Yet Mr Bayrakdar continued to insist on having his grain milled immediately due to the urgency he felt. An argument now developed between the two and, when the client's wheat, which was presently being milled, was done, Mr Bayrakdar took his sack and tipped it into the sloping compartment leading down to the millstones. Mehmet was so indignant about this man's audacity that he immediately stopped the millstones manually with a lever.

At this point the argument between the two men became violent. During this fight Mr Bayrakdar grabbed the flour shovel and brought it down heavily on the back of the miller's head. Then he threw himself onto him as he fell to the ground and madly beat and strangled the almost lifeless Mehmet. The others in the mill rushed over and pulled him off Mehmet, who was bleeding profusely from his head. He was immediately taken to the regional hospital in Iskenderun, but died from his injuries five days later on 28th November 1965. The post-mortem report, which Stevenson was later able to see, stated that an area of his skull as large as the palm of a hand had been broken and pushed in approximately one centimetre. Death was due to damage to the cerebral membrane and ruptured blood vessels. At both the first and the second instance, Mr Bayrakdar was sentenced to imprisonment since none of the judges would buy his claim that he had only acted in self-defence.

A few weeks after Mehmet Bekler's death Mrs Hekime Caspar had a dream. She lived in Madenli, which is a village 15 kilometres south of Iskenderun in the Gulf. In this dream a man on horseback appeared to her. She asked him why he had come to her. The rider answered, 'I was killed by a blow on the head with a shovel. I want to live with you and no one else.'

Such prophetic dreams are brought about by thought projections onto the inner 'screen' of the person who is dreaming. What is interesting in this case is that Mehmet, who planned to be reincarnated, apparently wanted to obtain the woman's prior permission to be born to her and to be accepted into her family. The woman who was to be his next mother was either recommended to him by other beings, or chosen by himself for whatever reasons. Since his new mother had possibly been selected for him by 'those above', he may simply have wished to introduce himself and to prepare her for his imminent arrival. He had his reasons for telling her that he had been killed with a shovel. He probably wanted to give her an explanation for the deformity on his head he was going to be born with. He was hoping that she would agree to his request.

It is also interesting that he appeared to her on horseback in the dream, which may have been intended to emphasise the importance of his visit. He may have wanted to make sure that she would remember this dream after waking, and would be able to tell her husband about it if she so chose. Ordinary dreams may be easily forgotten, but if the dream contains unusual imagery it makes it easier to remember it. I suppose this is the reason why we are often given symbolic dreams, which we feel compelled to contemplate after waking, in case they contain an important message. The true nature of many phenomena is as yet a mystery to us, and we would therefore do well to show a trifle more restraint in our scientific presumptions and arrogance.

In 1966, six months after the stranger on horseback had announced his imminent arrival, Mrs Hekime gave birth to a son named Süleyman. This was her fourth child, and she would have one more. When examining him the parents noticed that the back of his head was flat and slightly concave and felt soft. Before he was two years old he repeatedly talked about a river. At the age of two he began to speak more clearly about a past life, and always in the present tense. He would say things like, 'My name is Mehmet . . . I live in Ekber . . . I am married with three children . . . My father has got another woman . . . I am the owner of a mill.' It wasn't long before he started talking about the events that led to his death. 'Mr Bayrakdar killed me . . . He jumped the queue and wanted me to mill his wheat before anyone else's . . . I stopped the millstones and told him that I would no longer continue the milling. Then he hit me on the head . . . I died in the hospital.' His father, who had only known the deceased Mehmet Bekler by sight, had of course heard about what happened to the miller from Ekber, whereas his wife only heard about it now through her son.

The village of Ekber is only about two-and-a-half kilometres from Madenli as the crow flies, but by road it is at least seven kilometres. Since the boy told his mother so much about his life in Ekber, she took him by the hand one day asking him to take her to Ekber, and to her amazement he had no problem showing her the way to the village. Once there he showed her the mill and the house he had once lived in. Half a year later Süleyman's father took the boy to Ekber with him in order to double-check the statements he had been making about his past life.

While his father went to the mill to see whether the boy's descriptions were correct, the little boy had walked off on his own towards the house where his former parents lived. There in front of the house sat his former mother and the second wife of his father from the past. He ran towards the former calling her 'Mother'. Sadly this woman had little to say about this first meeting and reacted to Stevenson in a rather brusque manner. Even later on, she did not want to see her deceased son in Süleyman. The little boy, who frequently visited the village from then on, complained to her that she did not give him and his new family any olives even though she had plenty to spare.

Apparently Mrs Katibeh Bekler had the feeling that as soon as she accepted Süleyman as her son, he would want to take over her former son's rights, and would probably want to take control of everything he had once owned, which by the Caspar family's standards might have looked like a great deal. When the little boy was a couple of years older and people around him mentioned the name of his previous murderer, he always said that when he was grown up he was going to kill him. When the murderer happened to visit Madenli after his release from jail, Süleyman immediately recognised him. He pointed at him and told those present that this man was his murderer. He insisted that later on he would be borrowing his father's rifle so that he could shoot Mr Bayrakdar.

In his huge book on reincarnation Stevenson frequently writes about people who were murder victims in a past life. Apparently, even young children often display feelings of revenge towards their murderers from a past life. You would think that during their stay in the spirit world, they would have discovered more about the actual reasons why they had to be murdered, and would therefore have come to see their death as being just from a karmic perspective, and even possibly as having been their choice on some level. Most of my clients who have undergone regression therapy and are searching for the cause of their disturbing symptoms tend to discover a life in which they were the victims. When after that they continue to search for the reasons behind this life, they usually have no trouble finding a corresponding life in which they were the aggressors. If we then compare these two lives, we become aware of how perfectly logical and 'balancing' the life as the victim was, since the person had inflicted the same thing on someone in another life as the aggressor.

As soon as this cognitive leap has been made, it becomes easy to forgive one's malefactor either during regression into that past life or now in the present, should we meet the person again. This is one of the most important steps both to heal the symptom and to eventually achieve a holistic healing (a becoming whole) on all levels. Even if one had gained insight into the deeper connections at work after death, these insights are often forgotten as soon as one begins a new life, and so the old feelings that were experienced at the end of a previous life reassert themselves in the present. So, Mehmet's angry feelings towards Mr Bayrakdar were transmitted to Süleyman, and such feelings only begin to subside gradually as the person gets older and begins to forget the events of the past – as was the case for Süleyman as Stevenson was to find out later.

Stevenson thoroughly investigated Süleyman's head and found what he describes as a conspicuous birth defect. There must be many children that are born with flat areas on their heads. What was interesting and unusual was the indentation on the flat area on Süleyman's head. Stevenson could feel how the skull bones were dented underneath. On this area his hair only grew sparsely and irregularly. Even the skin felt uneven in this area. It is rare for this great research scientist from the University of Virginia to find an autopsy report belonging to a now reincarnated murder victim from the past. This time around he was lucky.[47] I will tell you more about Stevenson in a separate chapter.

One day when I visited a professor of medicine, who was also a regression therapist, to try to get to the bottom of my fear of the dark, I found myself in a life as a forester's assistant who was having a secret affair with the forester's wife. One night he followed me out of the house into the forest and hit me over the back of the head with the flat side of an axe. I died instantly. It was only after this regression that I became conscious of a flat patch on my head in exactly the place where I had been struck, and the indentation was the exact size of a lumberjack's axe head.

8

Reincarnation in the light of a new world view

IAN STEVENSON, THE FOUNDER OF A NEW AGE

By now you will have absorbed enough information about reincarnation in relation to children's discoveries and the stories they have shared with us, to reconsider your views on the subject. You have probably gained great respect for the achievements of Professor Stevenson, as have I. If Sigmund Freud is equated with psychology and Elisabeth Kübler-Ross with research into death experiences, then surely Ian Stevenson must be acknowledged in the same way for his research into reincarnation. In 1958 the American Association of Parapsychology organised a competition. The first prize was to be given to the person who could deliver the best scientific report about 'proof of survival of the personality after physical death'. The doctor and psychiatrist Ian Stevenson took part in this competition and won it with his report on: 'Proof of life after death through claims made by those who remember previous incarnations'.

207

Even though Stevenson had as yet no personal research to base this work upon, he commanded respect by the discriminating way of going about discovering the truth of the matter that he advocated. This work on reincarnation must have fascinated him so much that ever since that time he has dedicated himself mainly to finding and verifying cases to prove its existence. From 1961 onwards he began to examine the respective cases in situ by employing all scientific procedures available for this kind of research. Whenever he hears about a child somewhere in the world that is able to remember past lives, he travels there if he has the time. Once there he investigates the case, usually with the help of other scientists from the respective countries. With the help of these assistants they sometimes question 50 or more people as part of verifying the memories of an individual past life. He has collected more than 2,500 reports of cases of reincarnation. Seventy of these he described in great detail in various books and scientific journals before publishing his book *Reincarnation and Biology*. Anything suspect in the reasoning he would emphasise, and many reports that could be seen to contain ambiguity, which would discredit the authenticity of a case, he ignored. Stevenson was never satisfied with superficial information, so wherever possible he personally examined every case in situ, since none of his colleagues were more reliable and scientifically conscientious than he himself.

Before Stevenson appeared with his scientific investigation methods, there were many other reports of cases of reincarnation that had also been confirmed by witnesses. What was missing in these reports, however, was the scientific substantiation, the meticulous investigation and research down to the last detail that would separate, on the rock-solid basis of hard evidence and hard evidence alone, mere claims from real-life experiences. Stevenson's work as professor of psychiatry at the University of Virginia in Charlottesville, was the start of a modern approach to research into reincarnation.

We should all thank this great man for his relentless work with hundreds of children from all over the world, which served to lay the foundations for future research of this kind. In order to carry out a thorough investigation in situ, it was usually necessary to return to the same place several times. He would have to look up all the relevant people, who were not always all available at the time of his visits, and also follow up on the development of certain individuals. His research in these various regions was frequently an arduous task due to unexpected wars or rebellions arising in the area he needed to visit. Other times impracticable roads, storms, monsoon rains or other natural disasters would stop him from visiting his places of destination that were often out-of-the-way or difficult to get to. Sometimes even his return home would be delayed in this way.

Occasionally, inadequate translators made his laborious work extremely difficult, together with the refusal to testify of certain witnesses or the absence or unavailability of people who had gone on holiday or moved away. But Professor Stevenson did not give up. He travelled millions of miles by aeroplane and hundreds of thousands of miles by train and road all over the world to open and conquer a huge and as yet uncharted territory in the name of medical science. He can only be likened to great explorers such as Sven Hedin and Livingstone, with the previously undiscovered territory he explored bearing the name of 'Birthmarks and Birth Defects'. Professor Stevenson succeeded in putting forward conclusive answers to hitherto unanswered questions by presenting an impressive chain of evidence. His main work entitled *Reincarnation and Biology*, from which I chose several examples for this book, bears particular witness to this. Through his work as a pioneer Stevenson opened a new door for medical science, namely that of reincarnational medicine. (The combination of this and regression therapy could well be one of the blessings of the new millennium.)[48]

Elisabeth Kübler-Ross proved that there is life after death through her research at the bedside of the dying, especially dying children.[49] Stevenson brought about the next major step in the discovery of fundamental truths concerning our extended, larger existence, which we now know to consist of a chain of repeated lifetimes. He is the one that proved reincarnation conclusively once and for all, thanks to the children supplying the required body of evidence. He freed reincarnation from confinement to the sphere of believers and philosophers and to the 'dungeon of the numinous' and mere plausibility and brought it into the bright light of scientific research and scrutiny once and for all.

Since Elisabeth Kübler-Ross' pioneering work at the bedside of the dying, I know of no greater medical breakthrough than that of Stevenson's proof of the link between birthmarks and birth defects and reincarnation. He not only helped to reveal a great medical secret, but also has proven – as it were 'in passing' – the existence of reincarnation. I feel it would be appropriate to ask for this great research scientist to be awarded the Nobel Prize for Physiology or Medicine for greatly enriching the entire medical world as well as our outlook on life. (In my book *Rebirth – The Hard Evidence* I equate his achievements in broadening people's outlook on life with those of Copernicus.)

Stevenson's investigations heralded a new era as far as reincarnation is concerned. Before him reincarnation was the haunt of believers, followers of esoteric teachings and New Age adepts, or was mere speculation of philosophers and occultists. Now Stevenson has furnished the scientific proof of reincarnation. Inevitably, his work will bring in its wake major consequences for the world's entire way of thinking. Where previously people lived their lives from the short-sighted perspective of a single incarnation, they will now have to change their way of thinking to include having many lives on earth. In this way much will necessarily have to change in our consciousness on a personal as well as on a social level. In the rest of this chapter I will outline what the consequences of a general acceptance of reincarnation and the closely related Laws of Karma will entail regarding the way we think and behave.

THE INFLUENCE OF
REINCARNATION AT A PERSONAL LEVEL

1 I am no longer afraid of death, since I know that I have almost definitely lived before and am likely to reincarnate on earth again after an in-between life in a less dense reality.

2 When someone close to me dies it is natural to be sad. But my sadness is much reduced knowing that he (or she) has not died but continues to live on another plane of existence. I know that he is likely to be with me often, even if I cannot see him. I also know that it was right for him to die at that time according to his fate, which was decided by a higher consciousness. I also know that I will see this person again after my death and/or in a following life on earth. Goodbyes for ever do not exist.

3 I am tolerant towards all people as long as they do not restrict my freedom and that of others. I tolerate any form of religious practices and other people's opinions as long as they give others the same right to express themselves freely. By continually developing

from one life to the next, we humans broaden our awareness. I am never arrogant in my response towards other people's ways of thinking. I may have been that way in a previous life, and for that reason I never push my convictions onto others. Every human being reaches his time for broadening his consciousness when it is right for him. Besides, it is clear to me that it is most likely that I will often change, i.e. broaden my outlook in my future lives.

4 I will never discriminate against other people no matter who they may be. I know that it is futile for me to discriminate against someone of the opposite sex since I most likely belonged to that sex at some time myself. I will not condemn someone with a different skin colour or of a different nationality or race, since I could easily have been of this colour or race at some point in time, or possibly will be in the future. If I discriminate against someone on the grounds of his affiliation I will then have to experience being part of that nation, ethnic group or race in order to broaden my understanding and love for them. I will never look down on other people because they are poor, disabled, unattractive or in some way different, since every person has chosen precisely their circumstances, looks, and their particular disposition in order to learn from it.

5 I will never envy others, be they richer, more powerful or more respected, cleverer, healthier or physically

more beautiful, since they have created this learning situation for themselves in their life. They can use these means at their disposal to learn whatever they can in order to grow spiritually. I could possibly have had the same means at my disposal in a previous life or will have in a future incarnation. It seems necessary for us to experience all learning possibilities in order to evolve spiritually.

6 If I have a child I will give him the chance to develop his talents as long as they are not destructive. I will not force my will on him or attempt to break his, since I know that this child's past lives have played a major part in forming his present life. He will want to live out his learning programme in this life, which may be completely different to my own. This is why I will respect his individuality. Apart from all this I know that he has been an adult in a past life, possibly even one of my deceased relatives or friends. I would watch carefully whether he mentions anything about past lives. I will not forbid him these expressions or dismiss them as crazy talk. Perhaps this child has been my partner, mother, father or friend in a past life. I also know that it is possible that I could be reborn to my present child in a future life.

7 I know that I did not choose my partner by accident. I already knew her or him from an earlier life. We decided during our life after death to return to earth to continue learning from each other. Each

partnership is a learning situation in the school of life. I wish to make the most of all situations from which I can learn something.

8 I am able to accept my parents just as they are, since I freely chose them before my birth. They provided me with precisely those conditions that I need to accomplish my specific tasks in this life.

9 I see people, events and tragic blows which come my way as important pointers, which enable me to learn exactly that which is of importance to me. I allow no envy to develop in me towards others, since they most likely have very different issues to deal with and different means at their disposal for dealing with them. This is why I calmly face my specific life conditions seeing them more as learning opportunities than anything else. I do not complain about them but ask myself what it is I could learn from each situation.

10 The earth is a school of learning. With each incarnation we learn to be more understanding, more tolerant and above all more loving. If after many incarnations we have become totally loving, then we are free to leave this earthly school having passed our examinations. We will then be allowed to move on to higher universities, where we are taught greater wisdom and deeper love.

11 I know that whenever I violate love I myself will one day be the one who is treated unlovingly. It is only

through this that I learn to be more loving with my thoughts, words and deeds. Everything I do to hurt others will one day hurt me. The Laws of Karma that govern this learning process are always just. Unfairness does not exist for me. This is why I don't put blame onto other people or situations; instead I ask myself what it is I need to learn from a situation in order to balance things out from an earlier life. Nothing happens by chance.

12 I know that everything in life has a purpose. Nothing is senseless. Everything that comes my way has some kind of meaning for me. This is why I will endeavour to find the purpose behind everything that happens to me.

13 I know that it is entirely down to me how quickly I evolve spiritually. I myself am responsible for whatever happens to me, since all these things are born out of the thoughts I held, words I spoke or deeds I acted out in my past lives. In order to live another life on earth in joy and love I will use my present life to give others much joy and love. I alone am the architect of my fortunes. I can hold no one else responsible since I am, was and will be responsible for everything that happens to me whatever that may be.

14 I see life as a gift, in which each life on earth is an opportunity to develop myself more and more in love and understanding. It pleases me to help others in

their development and to allow them to help me on my journey. Therefore I am grateful for each day I am given to learn and discover more about love. I am grateful to be given the chance to turn my consciousness more and more towards the laws of life and God's love.

THE INFLUENCE OF
REINCARNATION ON SOCIETY AS A WHOLE

1 Awareness of reincarnation as a fact, being part of everyday life, we will see every person as having equal rights. Discrimination of any type or manner will be a thing of the past. Intentional dishonesty or victimisation, even when following orders, will be seen to create personal karma.

2 The Law of Karma becomes common knowledge when stating: 'What you consciously do to another you will one day experience yourself, either in this life or another.' The Law of Karma is always just. Every atrocity carries a karmic debt. The Law of Karma serves the learning process.

3 When everyone knows that it is possible to have lived in any country or with any race, or members of a certain religion, or could do so at some time in the future, we develop a sense of belonging together. When this occurs there will be no more competitive thinking between the different states of this world, no

more working against each other, but rather with each other. It will be a one-world community in which we will treat each other with respect, tolerance and understanding.

4 In emergency situations we will be more willing to help each other, knowing that among the people of some distant part of this planet who are suffering starvation or some other major catastrophe there may be among them some of our relatives and friends from a past life. If particular nations ignore the needs of others this will again create karma for them. Therefore we will be offering our help more readily to those in need. There will be a general increase in the involvement in the well-being of other nations and that of individual countries.

5 Everyone will develop a totally different awareness of belonging and will accept responsibility as being part of the state. If, for instance, I deceive the state by withholding taxes, something will one day be taken from me for karmic reasons. What I do to the state or to another individual one day will be done to me. This is why honesty is the best insurance policy for your future life.

6 Before becoming a globally responsible citizen, each person will feel the need to share all the responsibilities as a citizen of his particular state. If he continues to live just for his own interests and is using the state to his benefit he will one day find

himself in situations where he is used. Egocentric attitudes and actions are a guarantee for experiencing unfairness and lovelessness in a later life.

7 Religious communities and world religions will integrate reincarnation into their belief systems in order to have a chance of survival when this knowledge becomes widely accepted. There is no such thing as a single life, only a cycle of single lives. With every lifetime, the soul evolves to greater perfection. Reincarnation is the most just religion, giving everyone the chance, when once again incarnated on earth, to make up for what he violated against: namely loving his fellow man. God is no longer the villain who allows crippled babies to be born or millions of people to starve to death or die in wars.

8 Regression therapy will have a major, important role to play in the future. In social services for instance, drug addicts and alcoholics might be led back to the cause of their addiction in order to delete the programming that caused their addiction in the first place. Psychiatry will no longer be imaginable without regression therapy. Unnatural behaviour to the detriment of oneself or others may have past-life origins, which must be uncovered, treated and healed. The National Health Service will pay for training regression therapists and will happily take on board the cost of this therapy. This will save on other

extremely high costs for existing therapies that are usually slow to work and sometimes even ineffective. Regression therapy by contrast will frequently prove successful in a very short space of time.

9   In the field of psychology many old and cherished theories will need to be replaced with new ones, which grant much space for reincarnation. Universities will establish faculties of reincarnation psychology.

10 The medical profession will have to do much rethinking. Through the discoveries made by Professor Stevenson we now know that birth deformities may not be genetic, nor caused by viruses, but in most cases can be traced back to previous lives, and in particular to past causes of death. Reincarnation will also play a large part in surgery. In many cases, before conducting an operation that is not entirely necessary, the doctor or surgeon will refer the patient to a regression therapist. Here will be decided, for example in the case of a vagotomy, whether or not a wound received in a previous life had already weakened the stomach area. If this is the case then it is advisable to treat it with regression therapy. Failing this, symptoms of some kind or other are likely to continue to manifest in that area. For example, if a person was killed in a previous life by a spear wound to the kidney area, he will often experience chronic pain in this region, even if

doctors cannot find anything wrong with him. The co-operation between the medical profession and the regression therapists will become an obvious necessity.

11 Once we know that we will almost definitely be reborn on this earth, keeping the planet clean and healthy will become an obvious thing to do. This will enable us to return to a healthy planet where we will be able to continue our spiritual journey. We will care more about our surroundings and will not allow the earth to become polluted.

12 Philosophy will praise those great philosophers who have already been advocating this knowledge of reincarnation. The acceptance of reincarnation creates a whole new way of thinking, and will create new philosophical schools of thought and working models, which will rely less on abstract thinking. Instead they will catch up on, consolidate and integrate the 'empirical' general data deducible from all the knowledge uncovered through regressions into past lives. The afterlife, or intermediate realm, will also be thoroughly investigated. This is where we exist as souls before being reincarnated on earth. Philosophy will pose the question: Who or what created this system of reincarnation and the afterlife, for what reason and why? Ontology will gain a completely new perspective as we endeavour to connect to our centre of being via personal trance

experiences, journeying to our centre or possible initiations to get in touch with the basic truth of creation itself.

13 The arts will gain tremendous momentum, since a new creative theme will be opened up to them in which public demand could become huge for anything related to the theme of reincarnation. Film, television, theatre and especially literature will no doubt adopt this theme. The representations of people and their motives for certain behaviour will be reflected against a background of their past lives in which the Law of Karma will play an important part.

14 We will concern ourselves less with reputation, power or ownership, since we will know that it is more important to nurture the love inside ourselves. This is why we will be more inclined to collect inner riches instead of outer ones. We will treat life with more respect and will view being able to spend time on this earth as a valuable gift, the opportunity to learn more and more about love and God's laws. Reincarnation will contribute immensely towards making this world more beautiful and loving and one in which it is a blessing to be allowed to live, love and learn.

References

1 Carol Bowman *Children's Past Lives*, Chapter 7.
2 Barbro Karlén *Und die Wölfe heulten – Fragmente eines Lebens*, Basel 1997.
3 Sybil Leek *Reincarnation – The Second Chance*, pp. 36+.
4 Jenny Cockell *Yesterday's Children*, London 1992.
5 Peter and Mary Harrison *Life Before Birth*, pp. 11+.
6 This account is taken from Christopher M. Bache's book *Lifecycles – Reincarnation and the Web of Life*, Chapter 1.
7 Carol Bowman *Children's Past Lives*; this account can be read in Chapter 6 and in the notes at the back of the book.
8 Eli Lasch *Das Licht kam über mich*, Freiburg 1998.
9 This account by Ian Stevenson can be read in his book *Twenty Cases Suggestive of Reincarnation*, Chapter 6.
10 H. N. Banerjee and Will Orsler in *Lives Unlimited – Reincarnation East and West*, pp. 26+.
11 H. N. Banerjee and Will Orsler in *Lives Unlimited – Reincarnation East and West*, pp. 13+ and pp. 184+.
12 Ian Stevenson *Twenty Cases Suggestive of Reincarnation*, Chapter 2.
13 This detailed account can be read in *Twenty Cases Suggestive of Reincarnation*, Chapter 3, and in *Reincarnation and Biology*, pp. 1366–73.
14 For anyone interested in finding out more about this subject, I suggest reading the book by Dr Edith Fiore: *The Unquiet Dead*, New York 1987.
15 This case can be read in Brad Steiger's book *Returning from the Light*, pp. 267+. An even more detailed account can be read in Stevenson's

book *Reincarnation and Biology*, pp. 1579–89, and an abbreviated
version in *Where Reincarnation and Biology Intersect*, pp. 139–40.

16 This account is retold in Sybil Leek's book *The Second Chance*,
pp. 37+.

17 Stevenson *Where Reincarnation and Biology Intersect*, p. 161.

18 Carol Bowman *Children's Past Lives*, Chapter 15.

19 H. N. Banerjee and Will Orsler in *Lives Unlimited – Reincarnation East
and West*, pp. 46+. Also in Stevenson's *Twenty Cases Suggestive of
Reincarnation*, Chapter 5.

20 Peter and Mary Harrison *Life Before Birth*, London 1983, pp. 47+.

21 For more information on regression therapy I suggest Winifred
Blake Lucas's *Regression Therapy – A Handbook for Professionals*, in two
volumes, Crest Park 1993, or books by Roger J. Woolger, Brian L.
Weiss, Karl Schlotterbeck and Garrett Oppenheim.

22 Ian Stevenson *Reincarnation and Biology*, pp. 987–97 and in Stevenson's
Where Reincarnation and Biology Intersect, pp. 92+.

23 Stevenson in *Where Reincarnation and Biology Intersect*, p. 9 and p. 183.

24 Stevenson *Where Reincarnation and Biology Intersect*, pp. 140+.

25 Stevenson in *Reincarnation and Biology*, pp. 1940–70 and abridged in
Where Reincarnation and Biology Intersect, pp. 172+.

26 Stevenson *Reincarnation and Biology*, pp. 1875–81 and abridged in
Where Reincarnation and Biology Intersect, pp. 162+.

27 I advise anyone wanting to know more about it to check the index in
Reincarnation and Biology for the word 'albinos'.

28 Should anyone wish to read more about the consequences of karma,
I suggest reading my novel *Molar* which is written in seven colours
and has so far only been published in German with an English
summary. The first volume can be read in full length at
www.trutzhardo.com (also search the keywords: Trutz Hardo or
Molar).

29 Stevenson in *Reincarnation and Biology*, pp. 1295–1304 and abridged in
Where Reincarnation and Biology Intersect, pp. 123+.

30 The ritual proceedings of dissolving unpleasant symptoms are
described in my book *Das Grosse Handbuch der Reinkarnation* (*The Great
Handbook of Reincarnation*), available in German only.

31 Carol Bowman, Chapter 1.

32 Carol Bowman, Chapter 7.

33 The detailed accounts of Chase and Sarah's regressions can be read about in Carol Bowman's book *Children's Past Lives*, Chapter 1.

34 Adrian Finkelstein 1, *Your Past Lives and the Healing Process*, pp. 36+.

35 Frederick Lenz in *Lifetimes*, pp. 35+.

36 Stevenson in *Children Who Remember Previous Lives*, Chapter 4.

37 Sybil Leek, pp. 33+.

38 Stevenson in *Reincarnation and Biology*, pp. 300–23, and abridged in *Where Reincarnation and Biology Intersect*, pp. 38–41.

39 Stevenson in *Reincarnation and Biology*, pp. 468–9, and abridged in *Where Reincarnation and Biology Intersect*, pp. 51+.

40 Stevenson in *Reincarnation and Biology*, pp. 728–45, and abridged in *Where Reincarnation and Biology Intersect*, pp. 74+.

41 Stevenson in *Reincarnation and Biology*, pp. 973–80, and abridged in *Where Reincarnation and Biology Intersect*, pp. 89+.

42 The photograph of these hands can be seen in Stevenson's *Reincarnation and Biology* on p. 1201.

43 Stevenson in *Reincarnation and Biology*, pp. 1200–15, and abridged in *Where Reincarnation and Biology Intersect*, pp. 120+.

44 To anyone wanting to read more about this subject I suggest reading the book *When a Child Dies*, by Silvia Barbanell, London 1984.

45 Stevenson in *Reincarnation and Biology*, pp. 1186–99. Pictures included of Lekh's hands. This account is abridged in *Where Reincarnation and Biology Intersect*, pp. 119+.

46 Stevenson in *Reincarnation and Biology*, pp. 1466–75, and abridged in *Where Reincarnation and Biology Intersect*, pp. 134+.

47 Stevenson in *Reincarnation and Biology*, pp. 1429–42. Three pictures of his head are included. This account is also abridged in *Where Reincarnation and Biology Intersect*, pp. 131+.

48 I have written about the importance of the findings of this great research scientist in my book *Rebirth – The Hard Evidence*. I truly believe that Ian Stevenson deserves the Nobel Prize for Physiology or Medicine for proving that most birth defects are relics from former lives.

49 Best described in her book *On Life After Death*, Berkeley 1991.

Bibliography

Christopher M. Bache: *Lifecycles*, America 1994.

H. N. Banerjee and Will Orsler: *Lives Unlimited – Reincarnation East and West*, New York 1974.

H. N. Banerjee: *Americans Who Have Been Reincarnated*, New York 1980.

Carol Bowman: *Children's Past Lives*, New York 1997.

Adrian Finkelstein: *Your Past Lives and the Healing Process – A Psychiatrist Looks at Reincarnation and Spirituality*, Malibu 1996.

Edith Fiore: *The Unquiet Dead*, New York 1987.

Trutz Hardo: *Wiedergeburt – Die Beweise*, Munich 1998.

Trutz Hardo: *Das Grosse Handbuch der Reinkarnation – Heilung durch Rückführung*, Munich 1998.

Peter and Mary Harrison: *Life Before Birth*, London 1983.

Sybil Leek: *Reincarnation – The Second Chance*, New York 1974.

Brad Steiger: *Returning from the Light*, New York 1996.

Ian Stevenson: *Twenty Cases Suggestive of Reincarnation*, Charlottesville 1986.

Ian Stevenson: *Reincarnation and Biology – A Contribution to the Etiology of Birthmarks and Birth Defects*, Westport, Connecticut 1997.

Ian Stevenson: *Where Reincarnation and Biology Intersect*, Westport, Connecticut 1997.

Index

page numbers in *italics* refer to illustrations

Also available from Rider . . .

Exploring Reincarnation

THE CLASSIC GUIDE TO THE EVIDENCE FOR PAST-LIFE
EXPERIENCES

Hans TenDam

Exploring Reincarnation is the classic guide to past-life recall,
written by one of the world's leading experts. Hans TenDam's
definitive study includes fascinating stories and case histories
from around the world, as well as intriguing theories about the
relationship between body and soul.

This ground-breaking work looks at all the issues
concerning reincarnation, including:

- the most recent research
- the relationship between past-life memories and
  paranormal abilities
- cases of sudden recall of past lives
- karma
- events prior to birth and beyond death
- counselling techniques for past-life therapy

On the strength of the evidence in this fascinating book, it
becomes clear that the subject of reincarnation holds great
implications for us all today.

Life After Life

Raymond A. Moody

First published in 1975 this classic book about living after
bodily death remains a worldwide bestseller. Fascinating and
eminently readable it is a ground-breaking study of more than
100 people who have experienced clinical 'death' and survived.

Their extraordinary descriptions of near death experiences
are strikingly similar and so overwhelmingly positive that they
can change the way we view life, death and the spiritual
hereafter.

*'I had a floating sensation . . . and I looked back and I could see myself
on a bed below.'*

'There was no pain, and I've never felt so relaxed – it was all good.'

*'There was a feeling of utter peace and quiet
and I found myself in a tunnel.'*

'All I felt was warmth and the most extreme comfort I have ever had.'

For all those who have lost a loved one or are simply interested
in the phenomenon of death, *Life After Life* offers insight and
firm reassurance.

'It is research like Dr Moody presents in his book that will
enlighten many and will confirm what we have been taught for
two thousand years – that there is life after death.'
Elisabeth Kübler-Ross M.D.

The Light Beyond

Raymond A. Moody

In his ground-breaking work, *Life After Life*, Dr Raymond Moody pioneered research into the 'near-death experience' or NDE. In this, his stunning sequel, he explores how many NDE survivors have uncannily similar stories to tell, and considers what their extraordinary stories can teach us.

As Dr Moody reveals, those who return from an NDE invariably talk of incredible out-of-body travel, of meeting heavenly beings or deceased loved ones, and of returning to consciousness with a greater appreciation of life. NDEs appear to inspire permanent change, a thirst for knowledge and a willingness to love. Dr Moody examines the moving experiences of children as well as adults, and shows how recent scientific findings seem to confirm rather than refute their stories.

Engaging with the expert witnesses from medicine, psychiatry and sociology, Dr Moody asks challenging questions and provides intriguing answers to those who wonder about dying. His message is provocative yet offers a reassuring glimpse of hope from the frontier between life and death.

HOW ... CK

COUNTRY

Living

FOR SALE

it's about so much
more than an
old house and a pin
on a map

A Season-by-Season
Pandemic ∧ Survival Guide
(and post-pandemic)

 it's about reconnecting with the natural world

Jacob Chalfin and Jesse Liebman

Jake

I would like to dedicate this book to Pickering Creek,
the creek I grew up on, for nurturing the
Tom Sawyer spirit of my youth;

Nature enriches all our lives in so many wonderful ways.
May this book help promote the idea that we all have a duty to
leave this place better than we found it.

Jesse

I would like to dedicate this book to the town of Roxbury, CT
— a paradise and, even better, a home.

TABLE OF CONTENTS

INTRODUCTION

So, you're moving to the country! Maybe this has always been your dream, and the Coronavirus pushed up your timeline a little. Or maybe this was never your plan, and you're just dodging life's big curve ball. Either way, you're in for quite a ride! Living in the country can be wonderful and romantic (the clean fresh air; chirping birds and rustling grass; the freedom of open space; the tactile, visceral experience of the changing seasons; living soil instead of lifeless concrete; and the unobstructed view of the sky and stars from horizon to horizon)... or perhaps you might find it a bit isolating, full of daunting challenges in an unfamiliar environment (grappling with the weather from season to season, doing yard work on a whole new scale, and vigilantly maintaining your house to make sure that it is not reclaimed by the very nature that surrounds it).

No less important than mastering rural home ownership will be integrating into the new rural community you are joining: learning a new way of life, observing country etiquette, meeting new neighbors, developing friendships, and forming new bonds.

This fun little guidebook aims to provide you with the basic knowledge to make your first year go as smoothly as possible. Take it from us: we're first cousins who come from completely different backgrounds, but, because of the pandemic, have found a new common bond over our shared love of country living. Our experiences center on the east coast, but the principles in this book are relevant nationwide, from whichever city center you are trying to escape to whatever rural hamlet you are now considering.

Jake grew up in rural Pennsylvania, rode horses, and worked on farms his whole life. He and his family live in Chester County, Pennsylvania, in a home he recently renovated, with a stream running through the backyard. When not tending to his yard, flower beds and vegetable gardens, home maintenance projects, and children, Jake's job is selling dirt (ahem: horticultural soils). He makes premium composts and specialty engineered soils for residential and commercial applications all across the Mid-Atlantic States. He also brings a unique "insider" perspective from his role as one of his township's joint supervisors.

Jesse grew up in New York City, the quintessential "city kid" who never owned a car until age 37. With limited experience of rural life from a childhood weekend/summer country house, Jesse is otherwise a blank slate when it comes to the rhythms of life outside a big city (he's one of those people who finds riding the subways, packed together with total strangers, to be entirely normal). With the theme song from the early video game, *The Oregon*

Trail, playing in his head, Jesse and his family packed up all of their belongings in the summer of 2020, piled into their Prius, and struck out from Brooklyn. Avoiding cholera and dysentery, they forded rivers, dodged roving bands of marauders, and landed safely in Litchfield County, Connecticut. After a steep learning curve, "frontiersman" Jesse now happily spends his time dealing with roofs, gutters, basements, underground springs, dead trees, chain saws, lawn care, wild animals... and everything else one encounters in an old house in the country.

Both Jake and Jesse agree that living in the country is fantastic. It does wonders for both the mind and body and can help provide a sense of grounding in the chaotic and tumultuous world we currently find ourselves living in. But like anything, living in the country needs to be done the right way in order to get the most enjoyment and fulfilment from it.

We will cover many practical and philosophical ideas aimed at improving and expanding your rural living experience. We begin with some social advice, so you can fit more smoothly and comfortably into the fabric of the community you are joining. We then walk you through the house hunting and purchasing process — or should we say gauntlet? — including some of our own recent, real-life experiences. In the middle of our handbook, we provide you with the key to unlock the door to rural living. Peruse our reference guide for home and property maintenance, fold the page corners, and take notes. This step-by-step, season-by-season "survival" guide provides critical "how to" information not easily found in Google searches or instruction manuals. For those of you who are now living out in the country, this section will provide you with between-the-lines information — the "hows," "whys," "whens" and "wheres" — for equipment and tools, tasks and strategies, and fun, leisure activities. This is the kind of information passed down from generation to generation by folks who have spent their whole lives living outside the city limits.

Since living in the country is as much a mental state as it is a physical one, we also provide some true-life anecdotes that illustrate our personal journeys and the philosophies we have developed along the way. We round out the book by exploring how best to cohabitate with the natural world, and the wild critters who share it with us.

So, welcome! We hope reading this book provides a few chuckles, some new perspectives, and, most important, helps make your transition a little smoother and a lot more fun...

CHANNELING YOUR INNER CHAMELEON

If ever there were a sore thumb to stick out, you're it. It's very hard to hide out in the country (think *My Blue Heaven*). You can't retreat behind your newspaper on the subway or vanish into a crowd of thousands, and let's hope that by the time you read this, the days of wearing masks are winding down. Like a chameleon, you have to find a way to blend into your new surroundings.

It's not just Emily Post and aristocrats who have a claim to manners. There are ways of behaving in the country, too, that require careful attention. Country folk might live *near* barns, but they weren't raised in 'em, as the saying goes. The key is to learn how to recalibrate your "limbic system" in a way that will help you achieve balance and harmony in your new environment. If you happen to inquire as to where one might find the local Apple store, don't be surprised when the directions lead you to an orchard. And if you find yourself at a cozy general store, you might want to refrain from commenting out loud, "Hey, this is just like that Netflix show *Schitt's Creek!*"

You and your family are the big city outsiders moving into the neighborhood, so you'll want to leave behind some of those cityfied habits and adopt something more laid-back and, well, rural. It's a matter of culture, and your urban mores are going to stand out like a hybrid-electric smart car at a monster truck rally.[1] After all, moving to the country isn't like spending a weekend at an AirBnB in the Catskills. That's like going to a hotel with everything prepared for you in advance. Real country living means you are responsible for the outcomes and have to manage the work yourself — and there's no packing up early if it starts raining or if a bear comes knocking at your front door. You'll want to take an interest in the local culture and cultivate practices that will endear yourselves to your new neighbors.

Keep in mind that there is a difference between how one should behave in a quaint rural community that caters to seasonal vacationers and what folks will tolerate in an "all four seasons," non-tourist community. The locals will at first see you as an uninvited guest, a stranger in their community. It's not that country folk aren't friendly — quite the opposite — but consider how it looks from their perspective: It's disconcerting to see city folks coming out from Covid-19 hot spots and renting or buying up homes – and even if you buy your own house, you're still perceived

---

1 Kris Frieswick, "So You've Bought a House in the 'Burbs. Here's How to Make Good With Your Neighbors," published February 18, 2021, https://www.wsj.com/articles/how-to-be-a-good-neighbor-11613663031?mod=re_lead_pos5.

as a visitor. It will help to understand their perspective and make a strong effort to respect the local culture and earn their friendship. Once you get on the right side of your neighbors, you will find that they'll give you the shirt off their back. Country folks are generous and welcoming, but it's important to consider that your "Plan B" is likely their first choice — and their entire existence. Many of your new neighbors' families have lived here for generations.

The common expression, "It takes a village," is grounded in the idea that living in the country is a group effort. Imagine arriving home late in the day only to find that a tree has fallen across your driveway, and, while you do theoretically own a chainsaw and can cut up most of the sprawling limbs, what really saves the day is your neighbor, who stops by just before dark and offers to drag the heavy trunk section off to the side of your driveway with his tractor. Yeah, that's how life unfolds in a village, and it is a testament to small-town life that such generosity and thinking about the needs of others still persist. These days, it's refreshing to be able to experience firsthand that kind of humanity.

Villages are made up of many different kinds of people, all working together towards a common good. You yourself will come to play a vital role in your new community (even if you don't yet know what that will be), so here are some ways to think about where you're coming from… and where you've landed. It's okay to be different (no judgements); it's just the reality of the situation, and this book will offer you a few rules of the country road (so to speak) in order to help you steer clear of the ditches. For starters:

Yes, there are certified organic vegetables and fresh baked goods to be had.

No, not all local stores are part of Seamless, GrubHub, or UberEats.

Yes, in many places you can actually find some pretty awesome kombucha.

No, you shouldn't try to order a double pumpkin spice latte with extra soy milk foam at the local diner.

Yes, the local school has internet and wifi, with remote learning capabilities.

No, there probably isn't a local WeWork space (but who needs one, anyway?).

No, there's no dedicated bike lane.

Yes, the cars will go around you.

No, don't ride three-across on small country roads.

Yes, you should wave at every person or car that you pass on the road (even if you have no idea who it is). While in town, making eye contact and saying a cordial "hello" to passers-by is a normal thing that happens out here.

Also, be mindful of your running commentary and try to avoid catching foot-in-mouth disease. There's a good chance that the person you're making small talk with at the gas station is related to one of your neighbors — or was formerly married to one. It might not be *Sex and the City*, but the country does provide its own interconnected web of affairs and family intrigue.

Hot Tip 1: Don't be hyperactive about waving. Just a quick wave will do. You can practice at home by looking in the mirror. If your hand gets blurry in the mirror when you wave, you're doing it wrong. Back and forth once. That's all you need.

Hot Tip 2: Consider practising patience and tolerance as you begin to settle into your new community and try to be open-minded about local traditions and possibly different political and religious viewpoints. You might not be in Kansas, Toto, but you sure aren't in the big city any longer. One sad outcome of the last two presidential elections is the fact that America feels so polarized, a reality that is most pronounced along an urban/rural divide. We'd like to think that it doesn't have to be this way. In fact, this Covid-fueled migration and subsequent blending of people from different backgrounds might actually help folks see one another, not as left and right, blue or red, but as fellow Americans. Ironically, perhaps one silver lining of the pandemic is that the people moving out from cities are leaving their entrenched "media bubbles" and actually getting a chance to interact more fully with people in other communities. You may likely have different life perspectives than your neighbors, and you don't have to agree with them about everything. But it will help if you avoid engaging in the culture wars that really just tear everyone apart. There is a different context in the country. Give yourself some time to get to know your community and try to "walk in their shoes" a while before jumping to conclusions. Keep the conversations to the business at hand. You can share tools, advice, a good laugh, and enjoy a barbecue without talking about social welfare programs or pipelines. Sports banter is usually safe ground, so talk football and baseball all you'd like. When in doubt, there's always the weather...

THE MONEY POT VS.
THE MONEY PIT

BUYER BEWARE

This may sound odd, but houses are living beings. They eat, they breathe, they pump, they get tired, they get sick, they break, they require love and attention. If you've only ever rented a home — or even if you've owned an apartment in a city — you most likely have yet to feel the sense of connection that comes from figuring out the little quirks of home ownership: from searching for and buying a home, through lovingly repairing and maintaining it, to the sense of pride that comes from extending its life for many future generations. And if you're looking for an older home (an *antique* home, as they say in the biz), like from around the time of the American Revolution, then get ready to fall in love with its charm and for a few... um... problems you'll have to solve.

If a house is alive, then you might rightly think of all the parts and systems in the house (the furnace/boiler, the basement, the electrical system, the plumbing, the septic system, the duct work, the floorboards, the windows, the air-conditioner, etc.) as a body's organs. Each system performs its own specific task, but all the systems are connected. Heart and lungs. Shower and water heater. You get the point. Like humans, houses require constant care, and while they can be frustrating and expensive at times, they also give back, providing us with shelter, the feeling of warmth and safety, the sanctity of family and communal gathering (whenever not forced to socially distance). A house is literally the framing that supports you and your family as you live and grow, forging indelible memories through the seasons and years.

As with everything else in this era of viral contagion, it has become standard in house hunting to conduct a "virtual tour" of the property. Doing so is truly a waste of time. Yes, a virtual tour can show you the general layout and give you a sense of colors and sizes and some design features. But it doesn't tell you *anything* about how it feels to really live there. Have you ever tried to smell anything through a computer screen? Yeah, it doesn't work. Or what about the surrounding properties? What does your neighbor's house across the road look like? What other potential, unanticipated eyesores await you when you actually start moving in? Sure, take the virtual tour to get a very general sense, but don't skip the visit. Take a day off from work and drive up to see the real thing. It's a completely different experience.

In addition, as has been well documented by numerous

media outlets, pandemic home-buying has led to a shortage of single-family homes on the market.[2] As more homes get snapped up, the second wave, or "Class B inventory," coming onto the market definitely requires more careful scrutiny. Many of these homes may not have been designed or intended to be used year-round. Instead, these seasonal vacation homes pose their own set of unique challenges, specifically related to insulation and energy efficiency, and they may lack decent HVAC systems to handle the coldest or hottest months of the year. They may even lack basements or attics, making them hard to retrofit with new or upgraded HVAC systems. Some houses have wells and septic systems that may work well for occasional use, but could quickly fail when used consistently. Point being: all homes are unique, built for the original owner's needs, but not necessarily yours.

In the pandemic, decisions to move out of the city are probably driven by emotions and most likely not part of a previously considered plan. But emotions need to be carefully evaluated, for they can cloud one's better judgment and lead to unintended consequences. Gut-check yourself: Why are you doing this? What is your end goal? Where do you see yourself a year from now, two years from now, five or more? Your pandemic solution might

---

2 Emily Badger and Quoctrung Bui, "Where Have All the Houses Gone?," published February 26, 2021, https://www.nytimes.com/2021/02/26/upshot/where-have-all-the-houses-gone.html?referringSource=articleShare.

be right for the short term, but will it be right in post-pandemic times?

We want to make sure our readers are thinking clearly and critically about this huge life decision and not falling victim to a herd mentality. If you're just looking for a safer spot to hunker down until the vaccine calvary rides in to save you, consider renting (though rental prices aren't exactly cheap). But if you can see yourself living in the country for at least a few years, if not longer, then purchasing a home would make sense. Buying a home will be a good investment for your lifestyle and may even pay off over time. But if you buy a home in a panicked rush at the peak of the housing market and later decide to bail out and head back to the city, then that could be both bad for your wallet and cause you additional stress. The fluctuating housing market will undoubtedly swing the other way at some point.

Important factors to consider when selecting a home is the location, specifically the proximity from your current social and employment nexus. Avoid the awkward mistake those desperate people made when they bought homes out of state without telling their employers.[3] Just how far outside of the city limits can you go without jeopardising your career, social life and family relations? How many ties are you willing to cut? How much of a

---

3 Laurel Wamsley, "Workers Are Moving First, Asking Questions Later. What Happens When Offices Reopen?," heard March 9, 2021, https://www.npr.org/2021/03/09/974862254/workers-are-moving-first-asking-questions-later-what-happens-when-offices-reopen.

fresh start do you really want? The best deal for your dream house with views of forested hills and rolling pastures amid a natural wonderland may be located more hours than you'd want to commute on a daily basis. If you plan to work remotely for the foreseeable future, fine, head out to the frontier, but if you are still going to be dependent on commuter rail or if you plan to drive, you probably won't want to look for a home beyond a two-hour radius from the big city.

As you stare down one of the biggest moves of your life, here's everything you need to know about buying your home.

Hot Tip: Research your property on Google Earth. Zoom in and out and look for farms or industrial businesses nearby that may generate sounds and smells or traffic. Maybe the sounds and smells won't be a bother to you, but if it is a concern, ask around about these operations and find out if it will affect your quality of life. Do this *before* putting in a bid. Don't put yourself in a position in which you find yourself at odds with a long-time local business that provides an important service to the community and whose zoning and operations are permitted by the municipality.

Jesse _____

My wife knew she wanted an older home, but neither of us imagined we would end up in one that was built in 1790, a time just barely removed from colonial America and from that little Revolution that changed the course of our nation. If you can remember your US History course from high school, you'll recall that in 1790, there were only thirteen states, and it was the year that President George Washington gave the first "State of the Union Address." It was the year of the first US census, counting 3,929,214 people living in America at the time.

Well, since then, America's population has increased almost one hundred times over. You can imagine how many more homes there are now than used to be back then. So stepping into a house from 1790 feels a bit like time-traveling.

We fell in love with the house — and its three fireplaces — on our first visit. The property is bounded by low stone walls, there's a barn perched in the distance on the crest of the hill, and sometime in the 80's a previous owner had installed a pool. Additionally an old shed/small barn had been moved from another location on the property and attached to the side of the house and refashioned into a first floor master suite. On our inspection we went into the attic and found what looked like original signatures of the men who had built the house. In the basement, we found a wet and dirty trench around the perimeter (more on that later). But when my wife saw the charming exposed beams throughout the house, she was sold and we signed on the dotted line.

If you're an attentive reader, then you probably know that in the list of things we observed on our first visit, it wasn't the exposed beams or fireplaces that caused us weeks of repairs and cost us a pile of money. (That's right: it was the basement!)

We don't regret moving into our beautiful old house, but we do wish we had kept our eyes open to more of the flaws, defects, oddities, deficiencies, failures, and money-pits that might have been staring us right in the face. We were just too blinded by those exposed beams...

SELLER'S MARKET

Chances are, if you're reading this book, you were forced out of your long-time metropolitan urban center by the Covid-19 pandemic. You — along with thousands of others — decided that being crammed together in a subway and in high-rise elevators with infectious neighbors just wasn't the right choice for you and your family right now — and you were probably right. Congratulations!

But that also means that you're now in competition with many thousands of people for the home of your dreams: a three-bedroom, two-and-a-half bath, two-fireplace, creek-running-through-the-backyard, converted attic office/guest bedroom, four-acre rural paradise. Which means: it's a seller's market.

This probably isn't news to you. After all, most of the time, in competitive urban environments, it can often feel like a seller's market. But as we write these words, it *really is* a seller's market. Newspaper articles have breathlessly covered the plight of homebuyers who no sooner saw a property pop up on Zillow and tried to arrange a virtual tour, only to find that there were already over one hundred inquiries and fourteen sight-unseen offers. It's insane. The urban exodus, coupled with the historically low interest rate environment, has been like throwing gasoline on a fire.[4]

All-cash deals go more smoothly, but if you do need a mortgage, make sure you have a pre-approval letter in hand from your lender. It's not quite as good as cash, but it will help make you more competitive.

So: if you're serious about buying a home outside the city, clear the calendar, sharpen your elbows, and get ready to be aggressive (but know your limits, so you don't get pushed around). Also, get to know a good real estate agent.

REAL ESTATE AGENTS

Why do you need a real estate agent? Good question.

Theoretically, you don't. You are free to email the agent

---

4 Kenneth R. Gosselin, "Connecticut home sales heat up as New Yorkers flee and at-home workers look for more space; this summer's real estate boom may just be the beginning," published September 4, 2020, https://www.courant.com/business/hc-biz-connecticut-home-sale-boom-20200904-gdwejd3eafhotfajaj74pdydku-story.html.

for the sale and arrange your own tour and make an offer accordingly. But having your own representation obviously avoids any potential conflict of interest with the seller's agent, whose interests don't necessarily line up with yours. Your own agent can also provide you with so much more unbiased background about the area, the roads, the school system, future development trends, negotiating strategy, and particulars on the property than you would ever know on your own. This information will be critical for you before you waste your time possibly overpaying, buying the town dump, or, say, selecting a great house in a bad school district.

A good agent is like a coach, team captain, and quarterback, all rolled into one. Their strategic playbook/game plan will seriously elevate your success. The energy level, breadth of experience, and talent of agents can vary. Buying a home is obviously one of the biggest decisions you will ever make for yourself and your family, so it makes sense that the search process is such a personal one. For this reason, it is also critical to find an agent whose personality and style meshes with yours. However, it may also be beneficial to find an agent who will challenge you to expand your thinking or tell you what you might not want to hear. *This is a good thing.* So once you have selected an agent whom you trust and with whom you work well, be prepared to accept some advice that is unpleasant to hear, but may prove invaluable.

Sometimes, it's the things we don't want to hear or confront that are critical pivot points along the journey. Don't get stuck with an agent whose personality, methods or ability does not work well for you. First, do your homework, solicit recommendations, and conduct a few interviews. With a little legwork, chances are you can find a great agent from the start. However, if after a little while you don't feel like your agent is right for you, and you can't seem to catch that fish, then by all means, it's time to "cut bait."

Hot Tip: If you haven't narrowed your search down to one particular county or even to one state, it would not be unreasonable to enlist a team of agents who will work separately on different areas of interest. You're leveraging their knowledge of specific geographic regions, so it's not a one-size-fits-all situation. Be upfront about this strategy and there shouldn't be any hard feelings.

Jesse _____

My wife and I benefited greatly from meeting a few good agents over the course of our search. The first agent we met was very helpful in coaxing a pandemic-phobic seller to the table to allow an on-site tour, then was helpful in getting a response about doing an inspection, then was a very nimble go-between when we put in our offer. Though we ended up not moving forward with that property, the agent's advice about old homes still rings in our ears: "When buying an old home, it's easy to know where to start fixing things; it's hard to know when to stop." Even though our involvement with him didn't make it to a closing, it proved to be a very insightful little piece of wisdom from an experienced agent (though it would take us some time before we learned how to apply it).

We eventually stumbled onto an agent for the property we eventually purchased in Connecticut. This agent was responsive and active in chasing down listings that fit the "antique home" description and were also located in good school districts. It didn't hurt that his background as a contractor gave him a good eye for which old homes (charm be damned) were clearly not worth the hassle. When the 1790 listing came around, it was a particular selling point that there was a brand-new standing seam metal roof protecting the old structure. We learned another piece of home-ownership wisdom from him: "Houses are basically roofs and basements. If you've got a good roof and a good basement, your home is safe."

BIDDING (AND BIDDING WARS)

Home prices have been going steadily up during the pandemic, particularly in exurban areas where people have fled in order to shelter in place more comfortably.[5] The competition is stiff, so remember to keep a cool head and not let your emotions get the better of you. Better to lose

---

5 Nicole Friedman, "Surging U.S. Home Prices Gain Momentum as Rally Intensifies," updated February 11, 2021,
https://www.wsj.com/articles/surging-u-s-home-prices-gaining-momentum-as-rally-intensifies-11613062810?mod=article_inline.

on your seventh offer than to overpay for something that turns out to be a lemon.

There's no such thing as an asking price any more. There's just the highest amount that some desperate person is willing to pay. Don't be that desperate person who bids a ridiculously high amount over the asking price. And please don't submit offers to properties sight unseen. You might think it gives you a leg up on the competition, but it doesn't serve your interests or anyone else's, and it really just wastes everyone's time. Know your budget and don't get pushed around, but plan for a 10-15% reserve as dry powder, just in case things get really competitive. Some more advanced tactics include offering a large deposit of "earnest money" in order to demonstrate that you have the cash to close a deal, as well as to show that you are intensely motivated to follow through with the purchase. You can also try to insert a sneaky thing called an "escalator clause." What? You never heard of an escalator clause? Neither had Jesse…

Jesse _____

When we put in our offer for the home we eventually bought, we were told that there was another couple interested in the property and that we would have to put in another higher offer to try to beat them. So we did, but it turned out that the other couple put in a higher offer that matched ours exactly, so we got into the worst of all positions for a buyer: the "highest and best offer" round.

Honestly, I don't know how "highest and best" is even legal. It gives the seller all the power as the two bidding parties blow the roof off the purchase price. Someone might end up paying a lot more than the asking price just to win the war! We felt so dispirited that our months-long, dedicated, and very methodical search was going to evaporate into nothingness — and our budget didn't allow us simply to offer a lot more in order to win.

After some frantic Googling, we came upon something called an "escalator clause." In essence, you put in your offer, then you add a sentence: "And I will pay XXX more than any other competing offer." It's kind of ridiculous how easy it is, and it prevents your bid from wildly exceeding what the market will bear, though of course, if your competitor bids $100,000 over the asking price, then you either take out a larger mortgage or you smile and slowly back up toward the car and skip town, never to be seen or heard from again.

Not everyone will accept an "escalation clause" — and in fact, our seller didn't — but it doesn't hurt to try. Even though we couldn't use one, simply asking about it did spark a conversation that gleaned some more information about how much higher we would have to go to win the bid. And then we won!

Another way of standing out in a seller's market includes writing a love letter to the sellers, explaining how they will be handing off their baby to a loving family that will care for and treasure it forever. Truly, no hyperbole is too much. Include the phrases "dream home" and "change our lives" as much as you can. Send pictures of your beautiful children. If you don't have children, send pictures of your pets. If you don't have pets, go get some pets. The point is: It's a personal process. A human being is selling to another human being, so get ready to play the saddest violin in order to pull on their heartstrings. There's an instructive expression used by agents: "Happy mail, happy sale."

If you win the bidding war, you'll sign the contract for the agreed-upon amount. Remember: signing the contract doesn't lock you into completing the purchase when you include standard contingency clauses, such as potential issues discovered in the home inspection process, or the delivery of a clean title unencumbered of mortgage liens, tax liens or zoning problems. Definitely make sure you and your agent insist upon whatever contingencies you need to feel totally secure about following through with your purchase.

Hot Tip: Don't blow your whole budget on the purchase price. If it's an old, historic home you're buying, or even just a regular home in the country, you will be smart to hold some cash in reserve for any unforeseen problems you will inevitably encounter... which usually happens about a day and a half after you've moved in.

APPRAISALS AND
HOME INSPECTIONS

If you're financing your purchase, the bank or mortgage lender will require a third-party home appraisal. If you have ever attempted to purchase a home before, you will be familiar with this provision. This appraisal, however, only provides current market comparable price information. An appraisal should not be confused with a home inspection.

We strongly recommend that you get a home inspection. Many inspection companies will offer standard inspection packages covering basic things like the house's structure and mechanical systems, but they might also offer elective items, like septic and well inspections, radon gas testing and thermal scanning for moisture issues. Generally speaking, the older the house, the more extra tests you should choose. It's so easy to get wrapped up in your home-buying fantasy that you might not be looking at the house with enough of a critical eye — many pandemic home-buyers rushed to purchase properties that ended up having significant defects.[6] When you're imagining all the home's potential, it's easy to overlook little details that actually might turn out to be not so little. Your home inspector will help provide you with some good perspective and a healthy dose of reality. Ask him or her every tough question you can think of!

Inspecting the Structure

A home inspector is not an engineer, so don't expect deep,

---

6 Candace Taylor, "These People Rushed to Buy Homes During Covid. Now They Regret It," published February 11, 2021, https://www.wsj.com/articles/these-people-rushed-to-buy-homes-during-covid-now-they-regret-it-11613062856?page=1.

technical insights. But they do have practiced eyes (and maybe a background in construction that can really come in handy). They know how to spot defects in the foundation, or the roof, or the siding. They can size up where the HVAC (heating, ventilation, air conditioning) mechanicals stand in their life cycles. Their trained eyes are like X-ray vision, helping you see through the aura of your potential home in order to find the problems lurking underneath.

Like real estate agents, not all inspectors have the same experience level or skill sets. Ask around and get a referral for a well-regarded local company. Then, before you attend your first home inspection, try to learn as much as you can about what to look for. Learn enough to be dangerous, but then trust your "pre-qualified" inspector to do their work unencumbered. If you are looking at a unique property, such as a 200-year-old colonial or a modern home made up of cantilevered concrete, steel and glass, try to find an inspector that has special experience with those types of structures.

As part of the inspection, you may see a variety of odd-looking contraptions in the basement that comprise the water purification system and even a water treatment system. There's a good chance the house is on a well, and you can no longer rely on the public water utility to manage the water quality. It's *critical* that you test the water. Test it for everything (nitrates, bacteria, lead, arsenic, radon, pesticides, chlorides and chemicals, such as MTBE). Back in the day, some folks would bury abandoned fuel oil tanks rather than spend the money to remove them and remediate the soil properly, and some of these tanks leaked petroleum into the groundwater. It's a simple test for MTBE, so make sure to be aware of this potential problem to be able to feel confident in your water quality if it passes inspection. Water purification systems often include, but are not limited to, a series of filters that remove sediment, odor, and taste, and should also have a UV light that kills bacteria.

If it's an old house, make sure that there are no remaining lead pipes in your plumbing system as lead will contaminate the water. Ask if the water is hard, soft, or is heavy in iron. While these are  not usually harmful issues for humans, some water types, such as hard water, can potentially be harmful on the plumbing system. The good news is that there are ways to neutralize these effects with water treatment systems that are different from the purification systems previously mentioned. These systems can help remove iron, and help soften hard water. If your house has an existing system, learn how it works and how to maintain it. Some water-softening systems require regular attention, such as literally adding bags of salt to a part of the system called a brine tank. If you need to replace a system or install one for the first time, make sure you have a clear understanding of what is the best system for your particular water issue. Hard water, which indicates extra mineral load, such as calcium, can cause scaly buildup that can clog shower heads and wreak havoc on dishwashers and the insides of hot water heaters, greatly reducing their normal functional lifespan.

Also, have the well checked out to make sure it's up to code, that all the components are working properly, and that the pressure is strong. If there is any question about the integrity of the well or if it looks like it might not last much longer, it would be wise to get a specialist to give you a more in-depth evaluation. A specialist will be able to tell you how all the components of your particular water system fit together and if you are likely to need any new or upgraded equipment.

If you don't have public water, you probably don't have public sewer. This means you have a septic system, and they are definitely a big-ticket item! All septic systems need to be thoroughly checked for proper function and future capacity. You want to be very thorough as you have someone inspect the septic system (and if you're in tow, be ready to hold your nose if fumes escape). Many homes more than thirty years old may have systems that no longer meet new updated health codes. If you're purchasing with a mortgage, chances are the mortgage company will require the system to be upgraded, and if you're purchasing with cash, you should also want to know that the system has been vetted, is in good, working order, and has been pumped out by the previous owner. There are many different types of systems depending on available land area and type of soil. Whatever type you have, make sure you learn as much about it as possible, including exactly what design it is, its current capacity and functionality, and the amount and type of annual maintenance it will require.

Test the air in the basement and first floor for radon, which is the second leading cause of lung cancer.[7] Getting the results for all of these tests will help you put your mind at ease or will at least help you budget for the repairs and improvements that need to be made prior to moving in. And remember, awareness of problems can also be an important part of your final price negotiation, as we will discuss later. In older houses, have your inspector check for lead paint or asbestos insulation. If any is found, it needs to be remediated. Also, check for termites and other WDO's (wood destroying organisms), such as powder post beetles. If you see fine wood powder anywhere below wood, that is a strong hint that there is a problem.

Finally, make sure you evaluate the condition of the windows. Beautiful old windows with wavy glass (or any single-pane window, for that matter) are likely to be quite drafty and have low "R value" (the measure of the quality of the insulating capacity), whereas new windows with double paned glass are much more energy efficient. Replacing windows is a big-ticket item so they are worth extra consideration, but the good news is that money spent on window upgrades does improve a house's value.

---

7 "Health Risk of Radon," United States Environmental Protection Agency, accessed April 5, 2021, https://www.epa.gov/radon/health-risk-radon.

. . .

It might not be convenient, but make it your number-one priority to be present for the home inspection. When the home inspector is going through the property, follow closely to see what he is inspecting, but do not distract him. Take notes and save your questions for when he is in between sections of the inspection. The inspector may break down the inspection into sections (roof, exterior, interior, plumbing, mechanicals, and so forth). Ask for a quick summary of each section after they have finished logging their notes while the visuals are still fresh and before they start the next section.

If the inspector tells you the furnace is old, ask how old and how many years of useful life it has left. Ask if it's oil or propane fueled. Write down how many amps the electrical service is set up to provide. Ask about the insulation. Ask about the roof, the gutters, and drainage. Ask them to look into their crystal ball five years, ten years, and fifteen years from now to see what the house will look like in the future. They will probably demur and give you a non-answer answer, but keep pushing. Try: "If you were buying this house, what would you be wary of?"

The truth is, you won't know all the right questions to ask, but your presence itself will spark conversation and maybe even a closer look at a few questionable issues that may be discovered. Just like a good agent, a good home inspector can help get you to some important details quickly, so make sure you ask around and get a highly recommended home inspector.

Hot Tip: For older houses, definitely get a chimney inspection. Chimneys are potentially an existential threat to your home. A bad chimney can lead to some sooty smoke belching into your living room or, even worse, a devastating fire. There are lots of things to know about the state of your chimney. Does it have broken or cracked mortar? Is the damper working properly? Is there a chimney liner? How many flues do you have? Does the heating unit vent into its own flue or into the same flue as the fireplace? If necessary, you may need to have a professional service do a more detailed inspection by sending a camera down the chimney from the roof.

Inspecting the Landscape

Depending on how large the property is that you're preparing to buy, or how heavily it is landscaped or wooded, you should evaluate the grounds just as you would the house itself. Maybe it's pretty straightforward and you can get a decent condition assessment on your own, but for larger, more complex landscapes, consider hiring a professional landscaper to walk around the grounds with you.

Perhaps the most obvious potential risk in your landscape (both to your body and to the structures) are large trees. Large trees are majestic and beautiful, providing shade and comfort from the summer sun. Older homes, in particular, may have beautiful legacy trees that can be over a hundred years old (or more) and have borne witness to the birth and evolution of the nation. You might not know it, but much of the original forests of the Northeast United States were completely cleared as America built the foundational infrastructure of the nation during its initial settlement and then during the industrial revolution. The "New World" even exported wood back to Europe because the "Old World" had already depleted its forests. The trees you see today are part of the landscapes and forests that have been re-planted since then.

It's good to first assess if the trees are healthy or not. This can be trickier in the winter when the leaves are down, but a good landscaper should be able to tell, no matter the season. Dead or dying trees can pose near or longer term threats, so getting a pruning/limbing "take down" estimate would be wise. Trees overhanging the driveway, electric lines, or the house should also be scrutinized. Do they need to come down, or perhaps just trimmed back? Maybe they are perfectly fine as they are. Remember that healthy trees can provide energy-saving shade and pleasant ambiance in the summer, not to mention great habitat for squirrels, chipmunks and birds. So don't be too quick to remove what can be a really great asset in your landscape. Pay special attention to trees and large shrubs that might have root systems that could pose a threat to the foundation, or even to the septic system, or to pipes that run in and out of your basement.

Have the landscaper evaluate the integrity of any

retaining walls that might be on the property. Retaining walls provide important structural ground support and help stabilize different elevations in the landscape. In addition, check to see if the landscape surrounding the house is properly graded to ensure storm water will run away from the house and not flow or leach into your basement. Check the condition of any fencing, stone walls (which are more ornamental than structural), or paver, slate, or brick patios. While you have the landscaper checking on the major risk issues, take the opportunity to get an estimate for what kind of annual maintenance and associated cost will be required to keep the property looking sharp. If you haven't had to maintain a landscape before, it might surprise you how much time, effort and money is involved — as the saying goes, "buying the boat is the cheap part…" The good news however, is that unlike a boat, the landscape will provide you daily pleasure all year round.

Leveraging the Inspection Findings

If you find things during the inspection process (and you will) which have not been disclosed by the seller or already factored into the negotiated price, then this is the time to bring it to the seller's attention. If the issue is significant enough, you may ask them to correct it or take an equivalent price reduction (which would then mean that you would do the work on your own after you closed). It is not uncommon for big-ticket items, such as septic systems, to fail inspection and need replacement. Don't panic; it's all part of the process.

Hot Tip 1: Ask the seller to provide a few recent utility bills, so you can see what the electricity/gas/propane/heating oil are likely to cost you every month. In addition, high costs of heating and cooling usually point to inadequate insulation, so at least you'll know about potential future projects, such as window replacement or insulating ceilings/walls/crawl spaces.

Hot Tip 2: It's also savvy to ask for a renovation work schedule and a list of major appliance installation dates. This information will provide you with some general idea about the remaining life expectancy of these improvements. Even better, ask the seller for a list of names and numbers for all contractors and service providers — from handymen to landscapers and electricians, heating fuel and trash companies. Getting that list gives you a leg up when something breaks because you will know immediately whom to contact. These service providers probably even know your house better than you will and can be great sources of information as you learn the ropes.

Jesse

Luckily for us, we didn't have many health/sanitary issues when our water and air were tested. Our home inspection revealed that the air radon level slightly exceeded the limit of what was considered safe, and the septic inspection revealed that it hadn't been pumped in more than three years. As part of our agreement to move forward with the purchase, we asked the seller to pump the septic tank and to install a radon mitigation system. They agreed, and those two services more than covered the total cost of the home inspection.

However, we do wish we had been more aware of potential issues when the inspection occurred. For example, who would have known to follow the gutter down the leader pipe to see where all the rainwater ended up after it ran down from the roof? Well, it turns out that the water from the roof was deposited right at the corner of the house, where it promptly soaked into the ground and then into the basement through the old field stone foundation. We didn't really know anything about drainage, nor how the roof structures were connected to the basement, but we did end up with a costly education via a steep repair bill when we regraded (i.e. pulled back the dirt that was pushed up against our house and buried a pipe to carry the roof water away from the house).

While we were doing that drainage work, we also discovered that the conduit leading from the house to the well wasn't buried as deep as it should have been and that the head of the pump was actually six feet below the ground level, which isn't sanitary or up to code. So, yeah, that cost some more money, too... remember when we said how everything in a house was connected?

As it turns out, we were moving so quickly, we didn't have time for a dedicated chimney inspection. Months later, when it got colder and we wanted to start lighting fires, we were told that because our furnace didn't have a dedicated flue, we needed to install chimney liners both for the furnace and for one of the fireplaces. What's more... we couldn't use the other fireplace. Major frowny face.

I should add that none of these issues — even if we had known about them before purchasing — would have stopped us from buying our house. We love where we are, and every house, even newly constructed houses, will have its own set of issues to address in the short and long terms. Still, I wish that we'd had a leg up in terms of what to look for, if only to know how to budget and plan for the years ahead.

CONTRACTS AND CLOSING

If you've made it through the initial price negotiation (and bidding war), signed the contract, and conducted a thorough inspection without encountering any deal-breakers, then you're ready for the final stage: closing.

If any serious issues of deficiency or disrepair are discovered during the inspection, then now is the time to utilize the inspection contingency clause you wisely put into the contract. If it turns out that behind the attractive facade, the house truly is a rotting pile of bricks/wood/ stone, then you can cancel the contract and get back your deposit. But it is more likely that you will find a few minor or major issues that, if resolved, are not going to deter you from buying the house. Work with your agent to come up with a list of reasonable requests for the seller to review. For example, if you discovered that a radon reduction system needs to be installed, you can ask the seller to have this done or take the equivalent cost of the system off the price. Similarly, if the roof, say, is in need of replacement, or if the furnace is over thirty years old, now is your chance to try to do some horse trading, so to speak. Keep in mind that the seller isn't likely to agree to everything on your list, but you might be able to strike a compromise on several items, ensuring your newly negotiated price reflects the house's "fair value."

The other important thing to figure out is the timeline for the closing. This is where your own personal situation comes into play. Maybe you're locked into a lease that doesn't expire for another four months, and you don't want to walk away and lose a month or two of rent. In certain instances, it may be possible to agree to an elongated closing timeline, giving you extra time to wrap up your affairs and move within a more civilized time frame. Some purchase contracts can provide flexibility in the closing schedule, such as optional extensions built into the timeline, just in case something comes up, such as your job taking you out of town or… you need to get a haircut… or the dog ate your homework. Such wiggle room is quite standard and, if you've gotten to this point in the purchase process, chances are the seller will be amenable to a few, slight delays.

Conversely, if you're desperate and need to move in before the start of school, you can try to speed up the closing process and maybe also entice the seller to take a small discount if, say, you pay all-cash and agree to close quickly. (If you were already paying all-cash, maybe you can get them to reduce the price if you move quickly and take over the electricity, gas, and tax pro-rations sooner rather than later).

Keep in mind that now is your last chance to back out of the deal entirely. If the inspection yielded major issues and the seller is unwilling to make any adjustments to the purchase price, it is always within your power — and perhaps your strongest negotiating tactic — to simply walk away.

But let's say you hammer out the last few arrangements and agree to move forward with the purchase. Chances are, some time within the next three months, you'll be ready to close.

Closing is not just about signing the paperwork and collecting the keys. Before the closing, you'll be allowed to do a final walkthrough to make sure everything in the house is as negotiated. This can either be a pro forma kind of stroll or very frustrating. Most likely, it will be smooth sailing, but just remember that the war is not over, so if there were things agreed upon that the seller failed to address, you don't have to proceed with the closing until you come to a new arrangement. Also, make sure you get a copy of your closing documents and your settlement sheet well in advance of the day of closing. This will give you a chance to look it over carefully (with your attorney assisting you) and understand all the built-in closing costs, from pro-rated real estate taxes, sales tax, transfer tax, and other recording and legal fees. If you're buying with a mortgage, these fees will generally be incorporated into the loan, but if you're buying all-cash, these will all be out of pocket. It's critical to review these costs ahead of closing day so you know what to budget for.

Hot Tip 1: Do purchase a title insurance policy, which is a guarantee that the deed to the property will be correctly put in your name and that you own it, no matter what. It also means a title company has fully researched the history of the title guaranteeing that it is free and clear of any liabilities against the title. In the event the title company has missed anything the insurance also protects you in that scenario as well. It may be a little more than you'd budgeted for, but it's a one-time fee, and it's worth it, just in case some crazy people come out of the woodwork after you purchase it, claiming that it's actually their property. (If you're purchasing with a mortgage, the mortgage company will require this automatically.)

Hot Tip 2: If you're embarking on this adventure with someone you're not legally married to, it would be wise to put the mortgage and property deed into only one person's name. The financial reimbursements can be arranged between you and your partner, so that the financial burden is considered fair, but in the unfortunate circumstance that the house outlives your relationship, separation is a whole lot cleaner when you're not jointly tangled up in a mortgage.

DEFERRED MAINTENANCE
(All That Glitters is not Gold)

The moment you execute your purchase, the rose-colored glasses come off. It's not buyer's remorse or anything, but as you move into your new home, box by box, you will start to notice little deficiencies that you just didn't pick up on during the walkthrough. Hopefully, none of these will add up to too much trouble. But it's the bigger stuff that will sneak up on you over the next few months. So hold your breath because something is coming…

Sorry, we're not trying to sound pessimistic. You just have to be realistic that houses are like icebergs: there's only so much you can see until you get beneath the surface. But don't sweat it too much. If you've followed our advice, undertaken thorough inspections, and set aside money for these potential issues, then you will be a-ok.

Hot Tip: Many states offer free home energy audits, which are a great way to better understand your home's total consumption and to provide solutions for making your home more energy efficient. They're also a great way to get *free* swag: free LED lightbulbs, *free* foam insulation applications and sealing of ductwork, *free* water-efficient shower heads. Once you've gotten the paperwork from the audit, you may be eligible for a range of rebates from your electric utility company on major equipment (say, hot water heaters) and services (insulating ceilings and walls). Rebates and incentives will vary state by state.

Jesse

My iceberg was mostly water-related. You'll recall that expensive basement drainage system we had to install and how the water run-off from the roof needed to be drained into a pipe that ran away from the house… which led to the work on the well pump. Well… later we discovered an underground spring running down the hill from our neighbor's property into our yard, turning that corner of the yard into mush and weakening the foundations of four ill-placed pine trees.

A storm with strong winds rumbled through one night, and we woke up to find one of the pine trees had blown down. As I cut up the mess with my newly purchased chain saw, I realized that it was the mushy ground that had destabilized the tree's root system. It wouldn't be long, perhaps, until the three remaining trees would topple, potentially hitting the house.

So, we started investigating the source of the water and found an old, collapsed drain pipe buried in the ground. Because of the failed pipe, the spring water wasn't running down to its drain and had instead been slowly seeping subterraneously toward our house's foundation.

We hired one of our neighbors (remember how important it is to build relationships within your new community?) who had extensive experience with the area from having grown up nearby and who just happened to own a property management company. He dug a trench from the corner of our yard (where the spring water was running under the stone wall) to the old pit-drain. The trench was then backfilled with gravel which surrounded a perforated pipe. This system is known as a french drain, which collects and directs both subsurface and surface water. For good measure, we had him take down the three remaining trees and dig out the stumps. By the time the work was all done, we had not only solved the drainage issue, we had also opened up our lawn quite a bit. Two days later, when another thunderous storm rumbled through and knocked out the power, we were so glad we had done all that drainage work and no longer had the stress (or risk) of the trees falling on the house. We considered it money well spent.

With our limited experience, it would have been impossible to know about all of this just by visiting the property a couple of times or even by doing a thorough inspection. Luckily, the water issues were all solvable, but they were only possible because we set aside money for such work in advance. When buying an old home, we learned, it's good to be prepared for the unexpected.

NO PAIN, NO GAIN

Houses are transgenerational and even transfamilial; we are merely caretakers along the way. But even so, there is a sense of pride and stewardship one can get through the trials and tribulations of caring for a home.

As was once infamously said: "There are known knowns. There are things we know we know. We also know there are known unknowns. That is to say, we know there are some things we do not know. But there are also unknown unknowns, the ones we don't know we don't know."[8] It sounds pretty convoluted, but after your first year of homeownership, you'll be able to relate to this piece of wisdom. Sure, things will break at the most inopportune times. You'll spend money you don't have (and didn't budget for) for things that will provide you with absolutely no pleasure. But the rewards will come.

Maybe you renovate a bathroom, or expand the garage, or put an island and a gas range in the kitchen. Maybe you build a garden, or plant an orchard, or tap your maple trees, or decide to raise chickens. These are the things that will not only bring you real pleasure, but also give you a sense of pride, knowing that some of these are legacy improvements for future families to enjoy. (And, hey, they'll add to the resale value years down the line!)

Not only will you get a crash course in home maintenance, the things you learn to fix and maintain will, over time, give you a sense of confidence. You were once a flat-footed urbanite waiting for the super or specialty repair man, but soon you'll be using tools whose names are actually part of your vocabulary and fixing parts of your house you once didn't know even existed.

What you're really taking part in is the process of renewal. Houses change, just like the seasons, in cycles of growth and decay. Fixing what's broken and planning for the future will make for a strong, healthy, vibrant home.

8 Michael Shermer, "Rumsfeld's Wisdom," published September 1, 2005, https://www.scientificamerican.com/article/rumsfelds-wisdom/.

ADJUSTING TO YOUR NEW SURROUNDINGS

WORK LIFE

Lucky you! You didn't lose your job in the Coronavirus Pandemic Recession! Your company changed its policies to permanently allow working from home. You can leave your 600-square foot Upper West Side studio for a three bedroom in the woods, instantly improving your quality of life without any loss of income. If anything, by refreshing your company portal at just the right times, you've gotten better at making yourself look just as busy, while taking mornings and Friday afternoons off.

But you probably do still have to be productive occasionally, and that will require video conferencing and submitting your spreadsheets via Google Docs by certain deadlines for whatever kind of marketing/accounting/tech start-up/digital ad agency/remote teaching/finance job you still have. So here's some advice: keep it to yourself!

Like to multi-task? Great, but keep that indoors. Don't

go strolling through the woods while talking on speaker-phone. Maybe it's par for the course to video-conference on the subway platform, but don't do it while you're pumping gas or at the supermarket. Don't do a "walk-and-talk" Zoom call down your country lane. It will look like you're deranged and talking to yourself, and your neighbors will think you're crazy as you spread your business all around the neighborhood. Please chill out with all those FaceTimes and duck-lip selfies, and don't group-text your friends and family while recreating outdoors. Remember: the country is a noise-pollution-free zone, so let the birds and animals do the chirping, not your smartphone.

These unwritten rules are also applicable for exercising outdoors, or for talking to your therapist or life coach. If you are used to jogging with headphones or Airpods as you listen to the latest podcast or book on tape, remember that doing so may be dangerous because there are no dedicated pedestrian lanes, and you can't hear the cars around you. Whereas audio in your local gym was crucial for breaking up the monotony, try to make a conscious effort to notice the local flora and fauna; allow your observation of the changing seasons to be your entertainment. Be present in the moment and enjoy the natural sounds around you, or maybe just be grateful that you can hear the pickup truck racing around the bend. We all have screensavers with dreamy images of places like the Grand Tetons... well, now you're actually lucky enough to be out in your local version of it. So our advice: do your work in the quiet of your spacious new home, but when you're outdoors, put down the tech and embrace the countryside with all of your senses.

PLAY GROUNDS

Jesse ————————————————————————

One of the main reasons my wife and I decided to move out of the city was our kids, who, in addition to benefiting greatly from not being stuck in a Brooklyn apartment with us 24/7 during a raging pandemic — and vice versa — were starting to need more space to run around. For six months, when the Coronavirus turned New York into the country's first and worst hot spot, we pulled ourselves back from going out anywhere unnecessary. When the playground closed, it was a dark day.

We had been used to playing "Playground Roulette," choosing which local spot to go to with the kids based on the weather, the proximity, and the type of equipment (swings, slides, sandbox, sprinklers, etc.). I admit that I could be quite the snob about the quality of the local playgrounds, making a particular effort to search out some of the awesome new ones on the Brooklyn waterfront. (I could also be quite critical about the old, dirty, and decrepit ones.) So when we started looking for a house outside the city, we definitely made sure that proximity to playgrounds was part of our search criteria.

Lucky for us, we ended up buying right near the town

playground (it's about half a mile away, close enough to walk to). During the summer, it was great to be able to go there, and we soon met many of the other NYC transplants, who, like us, were reveling in the open space, the quality of the equipment, and the cleanliness of the bathrooms. This town clearly knew how to maintain its playground. Other great playgrounds in neighboring towns featured brand new "spider's web" climbing ropes and something I had never seen before in a playground: a zip line.

After a few months of going to the playground, I had the realization one day that the families at the playground were all basically NYC transplants. However, whenever we made plans to meet up with local families, we never went to the playground. Why? Because, unlike the New York City crowd, all the locals knew how to find fun and recreation out in the surrounding landscape... They were all taking advantage of nature: the original "play ground!"

After I realized this, my wife and I began to make more of an effort to find the local nature preserves, hiking trails, and outdoor spots for the kids to explore. Once we knew what to look for, it really opened up our horizons.

Jake _____

Growing up in the countryside is a wholesome experience for children; it certainly was for me. There are so many wonderful benefits to being able to run about carefree in the outdoors, experiencing all of nature's wonders: soil, moss, worms, beetles, birds, fish, fungus, turtles, trees, water, fire, ice, air, death and life. There wasn't a day I didn't come in for dinner covered in dirt, scratched up, exhausted, and happy.

Our planet's ecosystem is very delicate and, when children are young and full of wonder, it is a great time for them to develop an understanding of how it all works. They can see firsthand how interconnected the plant and animal kingdoms really are, feeling it, seeing it, smelling it, tasting it, and learning to love it in their own way through their own discoveries.

This is our opportunity as parents to teach our children about the symbiotic relationship humans have with the natural world. Walking in the woods, running in the meadows, and splashing in the creeks, all of these natural adventures help foster appreciation. Children will learn to value nature by catching fish, raising chickens, hunting, hiking, camping, cultivating vegetables, shoveling snow, and ice-skating on ponds, observing up close both the power and at the same time the fragility of nature through the passing of the seasons.

DRESSING FOR THE SEASONS

Guys, if you're over thirty-five and have at least one child it may be time to ditch the skinny jeans. In the country, you will find that they are just not as warm as regular fit, nor can you bend over safely while doing yard work.

Also, if you have a penchant for dressing in all black, consider adding a little color to your wardrobe and, glamorous celebrity imitations notwithstanding, it is courteous to remove your sunglasses when indoors. Think practical when pulling on your duds in the morning, but we're not suggesting that you look like you just came from a photo shoot for the L.L. Bean Christmas catalogue, either. Most important, dress according to the seasons. There are no fashion shows, so dressing in something expensive and/ or exotic won't earn you style points. Out here, clothes are worn to serve a purpose, like, say, keeping you warm or dry... we know! Crazy, right!?

There are many smart choices to make, especially when you plan to live in the country through all four seasons. You know the old saying, "There's no such thing as bad weather, just bad clothing." Yeah. And we don't mean bad fashion; we mean bad function. So take a look at what other folks are wearing. Most people have their waterproof rain gear, plus some all-purpose outdoor shoes, *plus* heavy duty snow boots for the blizzards. If you're going to be getting muddy working in the yard (and you will), you might consider some taller Muck Boots or equivalent, but don't forget that an all-purpose house shoe, like a pair of Crocs, allows you to go indoors and outdoors easily when the weather is nice.

In the city, maybe you're used to your season-round, lightweight, thermal puffy coat, but country living requires a little more variation. For yard work, consider a heavy duty coat made by such well-known brands as

Carhartt (or a similar generic brand). These are good because they are rugged and won't get snagged or torn on branches or brambles. They also cost a lot less than a Canada Goose, Coach or a Michael Kors, so let them get dirty (that's what they're intended for). And, as your grandmother used to remind you, layering is always a good idea. You can layer up or down wherever you are in the middle of a project without having to stop what you're doing and go back into the house. For those really cold winter days when it's so cold and dry that your breath catches in your throat, a good set of moisture-wicking, breathable thermals (top and bottom) are always clutch.

Hot Tip 1: Tufted sheeps wool and furry footwear are okay, but wear them where it will serve you best: in the form of slippers/moccasins around the house and in the living room in front of a roaring fire.

Hot Tip 2: When you're volunteering for a tree planting day at your local nature preserve, don't show up sporting brand-new shiny leather work gloves. Scuff 'em up and get those puppies broken in before taking them out in public. And if you don't have time to actually break them in, just rub them in the dirt a little so it looks like you did. Same goes for your boots. Also, only use the gloves for the roughest tasks where you actually need some protection; for the rest of the work it's time to toughen up and get those hands dirty — literally.

Hot Tip 3: As you are learning, country living is not a beauty pageant, and you'll rarely if ever describe your neighbor's outfit as "trendy," but don't forget that important life lesson: "Don't judge a book by its cover." Appearances can be deceiving, so don't be surprised if you find out later that the kind, unassuming, slightly disheveled man with the dirty jeans with whom you just made small talk at the hardware store is actually the billionaire founder of a company that is a household name… or maybe he's the local school principal… or maybe he lives in a van down by the river. Either way, clothes don't make great people; good intentions, generosity, and kindness do!

LIVING UNLOCKED

One of the nice things about living in a more sparsely populated place is that you don't have to worry so much about a burglar breaking into your home and making off with your electronics. City living is filled with locks and keys and security cameras. If the front and back wheels of your bicycle aren't chained up, you're likely to lose one of them. Same thing with your stroller: chain up everything that can be easily detached and pilfered. Your car, too, is easy to steal if you leave the key fob in the cup holder!

Out in the country, crime rates are much lower, and you and your personal property are generally much safer. That doesn't mean you shouldn't lock your doors and take precautions with your belongings; but you can rest easier about heading out of the house and leaving the door unlatched. You will come to know who your neighbors are and who the delivery people coming and going are. You — and they — will know when someone unknown is prowling around. And, of course, you'll find a great spot to hide the spare key in case you do get locked out.

One major reason that crime is low is that most people know each other from their children's school, or from their involvement with various local groups, extended family, or other community affiliations. In the city (or even the suburbs), people can live their whole lives in the same building (or on the same cul-de-sac) with their neighbors and never get to know them. But out in the country, it's not uncommon for whole communities covering thirty square miles to know each other right down to whose children belong to whom (and even the names of each other's dogs).

You will likely get to know the police officer who is employed by your town, which is quite a different experience than strolling by the nameless NYPD cops on patrol in their squad cars. In Jesse's town, the police officer mans the crosswalk at the local elementary school during drop-offs and pick-ups, often wearing silly costumes to entertain the kids. He raises horses and gives the kids carriage rides in the fall. Oh yeah, he also chases down vigilantes who have crossed the state border with a stash of stolen weapons

— yeah, it really happened. We said crime rates are lower, but we didn't say there isn't any crime at all!

Jesse

When I was a kid, my parents bought a country house in upstate New York, and we got to enjoy weekends and summers up there, out of the city and in nature. It was the site of many, very happy memories of family times together — and also some strange surprises.

One weekend, my dad went up to the country with a colleague of his and when he opened the door, he noticed that something seemed a little different. The house didn't look exactly like he had left it the time before. So he started poking around. Nothing in the kitchen. Nothing in the living room. So he went upstairs to the bedrooms. Upon opening his bedroom door, he happened to come upon a naked woman who had invited herself in and even eaten all his ice cream. (!)

My Dad called the police and eventually discovered that the woman was a Harvard graduate who had a history of mental illness and that she had found where the spare key was hidden and had decided to vacation in our country house, uninvited. No harm done, I suppose, but a little more excitement than one bargained for in one's private, peaceful retreat.

Moral of the story: if you're not going to live in your country home full time, invest in some readily available, wifi-connected security apps that will alert you to any unwanted intrusions. And hide your spare key in a safe spot!

THE LAY OF THE LAND

DRIVING

Jake _____

As a township supervisor, one of my tasks is to review the monthly state police report. My township is a low-population, rural splotch on a map, but we do have one main curvy transecting route that commuters from outside our township speed across everyday at rush hour. On average there are about twenty-six single-car accidents per month. These are folks that hit trees or skid into drainage ditches for no reason at all, completely unprovoked (our trees are quite polite and generally mind their own business). Whether it's raining, snowing, or even if it's a perfectly dry and clear day, these commuters never run out of finding creative ways to crash. 100% of our accidents _do not involve our township residents._ You can connect the dots, so...

Do please drive slowly. **Don't text.** Yield to tractors, trucks pulling livestock trailers, and farm animals. Don't race past your neighbors while they're out for a walk or even when you're just passing by their front yard. Remember that in low-population centers, people will recognize your vehicle and remember if you were the one speeding past their front yard or impatiently tailgating them on their way into town. Keep an eye out for dogs too; many folks let their dogs run free. Watch out for deer, especially in the fall at dusk when mating season clouds their judgment.

Also, take care when driving over wet leaves, which can be as slick as ice. If you find a branch across the road, don't just drive around it; put your flashers on, get out of the car, and move it off the road (the same goes for turtles).

Do be aware of black ice in the winter. As you drive down a road in the middle of an open field, the road might be entirely clear, but the minute you pass into the shade of the woods, invisible black ice will be lurking.

Also note that in winter at the break of dawn, there is always a temperature inversion, and ice can skim coat the road for a critical thirty minutes and then disappear. Don't be that person who has to figure out how to crawl out of an upside-down car or call the tow truck because you've just skidded through the fence and found yourself in the middle of cow pasture. While there are plenty of weather and navigation apps that can help you predict driving conditions, we suggest you look up from the phone and evaluate for yourself the weather conditions that are all around you.

As you drive around, you will become painfully aware

that many of the street signs are either hidden in over-growth, or completely missing; many of the ones you can still see have probably been used for target practice. If you're using Waze, or Google Maps, or some other GPS-based navigation app, you might find that as you get further out your cell signal begins to fail you. At some point, you may find yourself completely turned around and hopelessly lost, with a few bored cows staring at you blankly, unconcerned with your misfortune.

If you see a local and you're lucky enough to flag him down for directions, don't get too excited; you are about to be taken to a whole new level of confusion. For the local will give you directions based on landmarks and the names of people and properties that may or may not still exist in real life. It might sound something like this:

"So, turn around and go past the Kennels and the Hundred Acre Field. After the old Wickersham Farm, turn right. Then at the great Penn's Wood Oak, turn left. Go about three miles and look for the third long driveway on the right with the rusty gate and the mean-looking dog. Don't worry; he's a pussy cat."

Translation: Pass random landmarks that hopefully, but might not actually, help you recognize where you are. Any time you hear "old" in the description, be aware that it might not exist anymore. Trees referenced by name may or may not still be standing, so keep your eyes open for towering giants or rotten stumps.

So we say good luck to you and suggest that you start to figure out your own landmarks. Look for a big hill that you can see from far away and use that to orient yourself or a creek that you know which side home is on.

Hot Tip: In the fall, don't park under the black walnut trees. They will drop their nuts and dent your car like dimples on a golf ball.

CATCHING THE WORM

Country living rewards those who plan ahead. (And believe us: you don't want to get caught short.) This means building extra flex time into your schedule, whether that's running an errand or doing some yard-work. In the country, places are farther away, on average, than you're used to, and the scale of tasks is bigger and can take longer. So bake some extra time into your schedule, which should help you avoid feeling rushed. Planning ahead is one important way of putting the stress of the "rat race" behind you.

Remember how you always used to complain about Daylight Savings time and not understand the importance of why your sleep schedule was disrupted twice a year? Well, the whole point of DST is to maximize daylight — not exactly a primary concern when the work you do depends on office lighting or when your outdoor activities are illuminated by street lamps. But for life in the country, daylight is essential, which means that work and chores start at daybreak, and driveway basketball ends at dusk.

At the risk of sounding trite, out in the country, the early bird really does catch the worm.

Do stock up your pantry wisely for the inevitable event when the power goes out for a day… or five. And, yes, the power will go out. And, no, you can't expect ConEd to come and fix it "right away." Big storms will knock out your power, and, as the universe is prone to doing, it will happen in direct proportion to your level of preparedness. Don't worry: it's not going to be Armageddon and you don't need a fallout shelter, MREs, and a cache of weapons. But be sensible and make sure you have candles, batteries and flashlights, and maybe a few jugs of water at the ready. It's also a good idea to keep some canned soup and other non-perishables you can easily prepare without the aid of electrical appliances. Gas grills (outside use only) or cast iron wood-burning stoves are really useful when the power is out and the oven won't turn on. You can use them to cook your perishable items before they spoil or to boil water and heat up soup. If you have the cash and you're really risk-averse, buy a whole home generator and have it professionally installed.

Hot Tip 1: Unlike living in a home supported by a public water utility, your new country home likely comes with its own well. Make no mistake: this is very different from the charming caricature you're used to encountering on a putt-putt mini golf course. When the power goes out, get ready for no water in the sink, no showers or baths, and no water to flush your toilet. Why? Because your well is powered by… an *electric* well pump.

So unless you have a generator, you'd better start planning for one flush per toilet… "if it's yellow, let it mellow; if it's brown, flush it down." (Power hack: Since most toilets are gravity-fed, you can always pour water into the top of your toilet reservoir if you have it to spare. Some folks will fill up a bathtub with water ahead of a severe weather event (a hurricane or ice storm) and then use the tub water for various purposes (washing, flushing). For drinking and cooking, pre-fill some clean five-gallon water jugs.

Hot Tip 2: Keep the liquor cabinet well stocked. When Netflix is out, a couple of stiff drinks will definitely help you pass the time until the power comes back on.

THE DUMP

First thing first, don't call it a dump. It's a "Transfer Station," where old, dead garbage shuffles off its mortal coil and moves on to a better place. If you've only lived in a city, you really have no idea what to expect. But out in the country, unless you pay for a private company to collect your garbage from the large bins you wheel out to the road, you may have to purchase a sticker from the town clerk authorizing your vehicle to dump household garbage, recyclables, paper products and cardboard, scrap metal, bulky trash items, and electronics at the transfer station. In some towns, you pay à la carte to use the dump… er, transfer station... whenever you have an item that isn't acceptable for the regular trash service. (For information about composting, see Chapter 6: Playing with Fire... and Soil... and Water.)

Getting rid of trash in a safe and environmentally friendly way is more important — and more expensive — than ever. That's because so many towns are seeing surges in packages and deliveries because of the pandemic, and because, for geopolitical reasons, China is no longer willing to accept the millions of tons of garbage that the US has shipped overseas for decades.[9] As the endpoint of global trash changes, all cities and towns in America are going to have to come up with new ways to pay for and manage their garbage. For the moment, it is simultaneously important to adhere to town policies and to find new ways to foster sustainable lifestyles.

Jesse

I've been used to being awakened at 6 AM by trash collectors my whole life. The large trucks make a racket as they work their way up the block, and most of the time, meticulously organized garbage cans end up strewn across the street. I get it. It's not a fun job, but it always seemed to me to create more of a mess than it should have.

Ever since my family has moved out into the country, we've had to adjust to hauling away our own garbage two

---

9 Saabira Chaudhuri, "Recycling Rethink: What to Do With Trash Now That China Won't Take It," published December 19, 2019, https://www. wsj.com/articles/recycling-rethink-what-to-do-with-trash-now-china-wont-take-it-11576776536.

or three times per week. After some initial confusion, it's become a seamless affair. It's nice to be able to easily dispose of old wires, bulky junk, and metal (which actually earns the town money when sold for scrap). It's also useful to physically handle our own garbage and to see how much waste we generate and how many boxes we receive for all sorts of deliveries. It has definitely made us conscious to make sure all Amazon deliveries are grouped together into as few packages as possible. We're searching out local places to buy in bulk and to preserve our used cartons and plastics for eco-friendly refills.

PRIVATE PROPERTY, SHARED SPACES

The country doesn't have any sidewalks or bike lanes. If you're out pushing your fancy UPPAbaby Vista stroller down the road, make sure you're ready to jump out of the way of traffic. So if you plan to go out for a walk, make sure you pick a quiet road or find a park. Apart from land trusts, nature preserves, and maybe some US Forest Service tracts, all the land around you is private, so ask for permission if you would like to walk across your neighbor's field or through their woods. That pond that you want to dive in or cast a line in is probably owned by someone.

At the same time, when you're living out in God's country, the unwritten code is that it's everyone's responsibility to keep the community safe and clean. In the city, chances are you don't spend much time picking up the trash you see collecting at the curb. That's because the municipal authorities employ people to do it (whether they do it well or not is another question). But if you're out walking in the country and see trash, pick it up. Even if it's not yours or not on your land. Nobody will think it's weird, and the more trash you collect, the more respect folks will have for you.

Jesse

Although it might seem like a negative to pick up other people's trash at the side of the road, it's a small price to pay for no longer having to do the weekly (or even twice-weekly) alternate side of the street parking sweepstakes. Every Monday, at 9:05 AM, I would curse under my breath and rush out to the street to move my car from the Monday side of the block and double-park it on the Tuesday side, waiting for the street sweeper to chug its way up the block and sweep up all the accumulated debris.

The real menace were the traffic cops, who marched up the block and ticketed anyone who hadn't moved out of their Monday spot. If you weren't sitting in your car, they'd slap a ticket on your windshield and, no matter how you'd protest (even if you were standing ten feet away chatting with your neighbor), they wouldn't relent.

Then, once the cops and the street sweeper had left, everyone would drag-race to get their cars into an open spot on the Monday side. I don't miss the stress of "The Alternate Side of the Street Parking Wars." My fenders and bumpers still carry several dents from hard-fought parallel parking battles. Not having to move my car and not getting a ticket feel like wonderful luxuries. I'll gladly pick up someone else's trash every once in a while.

FARMER HEROES

It's not just roosters who announce the crack of dawn. In general, the work day on a farm starts before sunrise, so you can expect trucks, tractors, and other big machines to rumble down the road before you've brewed the coffee. And if you live near a farm, you're sometimes going to have to get used to many "interesting" smells that waft your way, too.

Please don't be annoyed by early morning noises and occasional smells. Learn to embrace them and even grow to love the smell of freshly spread manure. Remember: as long as you can still smell manure, then you know the strip malls haven't overtaken your rural paradise.

Beyond not finding yourself at odds with farmers who might seem unrelatable, look a little tired and worn, and maybe smell a bit funny to your cityfied nose, try to actively support them by buying their eggs, milk, cheeses, veggies and other delicious fare from your local co-op, farmer's market, or farm stand. The food will be tasty and fresh, and you'll be helping to reduce the carbon footprint of your food consumption by buying locally. Another major benefit is that you will be strengthening the bonds with your neighbors while participating in securing the financial viability of their agricultural enterprises, ensuring that you are giving farmers every opportunity to continue to cultivate and care for the farmland that you love to look at as you drive around your new rural landscape.

Farming is one of the most difficult businesses out there. Many farmers are land-rich and cash-poor. They farm out of love for the land and their livestock, out of a fierce sense of independence, and in keeping with generations of family tradition. No independent farmer is in it for the fame, healthy work/life balance, compensation package, vacation time, or pension (there is none). Farmers have no safety net. They can do everything right, only to have their crops destroyed just before harvest by a devastating weather event. Or they can do everything right, like, say, investing in the latest milking technology, only to have their legs cut out from under them when political winds shift, causing milk prices to plummet. If you think the cut-throat world of corporate law is stressful, just imagine the stress you would feel if you were responsible for feeding and milking 300 cows a day, knowing that in any given year a new Farm Bill could change policies — upending in an instant the whole cost structure of your business. Or maybe Congress signs a new trade deal — in the '90s, NAFTA, now the USMCA — thoroughly altering the global grain market. Yeah, it's a tough business.

Yet farmers soldier on. The truth about food prices is that what we pay in the grocery store doesn't accurately reflect what it really costs to produce the food. This is because there is no margin built in for the farmer's risk exposure. This is a harsh reality, and it is the reason why so many farmers are tempted or forced to sell out to big agribusiness companies or to land developers. How farmers make their money likely has little to do with your ability to survive your recent move to the country, but this illustration may help you understand your neighbor a little better. And maybe, oddly enough, you might find that you have more in common with farmers than you think.

Grease stains and muddy boots aside, you should think of farmers as entrepreneurs. A typical single-family, independent commercial farm is actually a multimillion dollar business. In addition, while it may not be obvious, farmers are actually using cutting-edge technology, including satellite imaging and weather mapping, GPS-guided planters, soil moisture and nutrient probes and monitors, and they even perform sophisticated livestock breeding techniques. On paper, their business might not look a whole lot different from your new tech firm or the business concept percolating at the incubator hub. Farm folks are really dialed in.

If you're still trying to figure out how to think about farmers you can put them into one of two boxes. First, you can think they're crazy for working so hard in a business with such a tough chance of success; or second, you can think of them as heroes.

Lastly, and most importantly, the success of farmers and farming as a viable way of life is delicately intertwined with open space preservation. Not all the local farm crops will end up in your nearby farmers' market, but, whether the fruits of their labors are sold locally or through a regional grain exchange, farmers and their land still play an important part in shaping the community. Farming and land conservation/open space preservation go hand-in-glove, and farmers can take some tax advantages by trading development rights for conservation easements, which protects the land from future development. Large tract public nature preserves can offset management expenses by keeping the land in sustainable agricultural production. Farming-friendly public policy and community support of farms are also critical. The easier it is for farms to operate (in a sustainable way), the more likely farmland will remain intact.

So when you see mud on the road from tractor tires, know that those tracks represent the efforts to protect and preserve the business of farming, farmland, and open spaces — all of which make possible the rural lifestyle and picturesque views that we all love.

PATIENCE AND BALANCE

You are no longer in the land of 24-7 instant gratification. There are no fluorescent-lit Duane Reade superstores or ATMs on every corner. It won't be possible to walk half a block to the corner bodega at midnight when you have the munchies, and Uber Eats isn't a thing out in the country... yet.

You can probably get most of the essentials from a local general store, or, if you go farther afield, a supermarket chain. But they won't be open 24 hours a day and probably not on Sundays, so make sure you stock up on groceries so you're not left hanging for any last-minute eventualities.

Most important, learn to love what a three-day Amazon delivery window really means. Anything that arrives faster than three days means you haven't gotten far enough away from the pandemic/job/relationship/insert-personal-crisis-here that you were trying to escape when you fled the city. Life is just a little bit slower in the country, and that's a good thing. Our overfilled schedules, 50-plus-hour work weeks, and near constant screen time have become insidious features of our everyday lives. It takes vigilance to strike an intentional balance between our careers, our personal relationships and families, and our leisure activities. Many Europeans enjoy a healthier balance than Americans, but in many ways, a country lifestyle makes possible what city living all too often does not.

Hot Tip 1: If you're like Jesse, then you've never heard of "Blue Laws" until you moved out of NYC. In New York, you can buy alcohol wherever and whenever you wish. But "Blue Laws," which are arcane Quaker, Prohibition-era, liquor sale restrictions, vary by state and county, so make sure to double check what prohibitions exist in your new neck of the woods, or you may be the only person showing up for Super Bowl Sunday empty-handed.

Hot Tip 2: When you are lucky enough to cross paths with an "old timer," stop and take a moment. Respect what these folks have to say and your patience will be rewarded with a wealth of wisdom, a few great stories, and perhaps some local history, too. These folks may move a little slowly and take their time getting to the point, but they are the fabric of this new community you chose to call home. When they are generous enough to share their lifetime of experience, consider it a gift.

HUNTER GATHERERS

Chances are, you've never owned a gun before, and you probably haven't fired one, either. Back in the city, you probably associated guns with cops and robbers, but out in the country, guns are a normal feature of life. Guns are used for hunting and target sport; children are brought up from a young age learning how to safely use and behave around firearms.

First things first, don't go into the grocery store and say, "What's up with the Second Amendment, anyway?" Second, don't go diving behind your car when you hear gunshots — and please don't call 911. It's either somebody out hunting in the nearby woods, or a few friends just down the road shooting clay pigeons and throwing back some cold ones.

Whether you agree with hunting or not, it does play a vital role in animal population control. The locally hunted animals are not endangered species. No morally corrupt trophy hunter is going to shoot a white rhino crossing through your backyard. The truth is that deer, for example, no longer have any major predators to keep their populations in check. Deer populations have soared thanks to an abundant supply of food from lawns and crop fields. The loss of woodland habitat from development has also led to larger, more concentrated herds in the remaining open spaces and in people's backyards. Controlling populations through seasonal hunting helps prevent collisions with cars, which can be quite deadly for both parties involved.

So before you start eulogizing Bambi's mother, just remember that deer will wage war on your shrubbery and vegetable gardens. You will have to select your landscape plantings by knowing and avoiding a deer's dietary pleasures. You might even need to fence in your vegetable garden and grow a little extra to set aside for wildlife's tithe. Even the most staunch vegans might feel the rise of militant feelings when it comes to defending their butter crunch lettuce and kale crops.

There are a few different hunting seasons to be aware of, mostly during the Fall and Winter months. This is not only because folks have more free time and the visibility is better when the leaves are down, but more importantly it does not disrupt birthing season and the raising of young ones in the spring and summer. There are several regulated time frames for different kinds of deer hunting, using a rifle or a bow, for example. There are also goose, duck, pheasant, turkey and bear seasons, just to name a few.

Hot Tip 1: It would be wise to learn when your local hunting seasons are and even smarter to take a hiatus from your nature walks during such time. Hunters are smart and careful, but it is always a good habit to wear brightly colored clothes when you're out exercising, even if you're just strolling down a quiet country road. You should stick to the road, both for your own safety and because you don't want to spook the prey.

Hot Tip 2: Venison is delicious. Definitely figure out how to purchase some locally hunted meat and make it a part of your cuisine. Once again, you'll also be supporting your neighbors.

5

SURVIVAL STRATEGIES

A PLAYBOOK FOR LIVING
SEASON BY SEASON

When should you clean your gutters and have your chimney swept? How do you know if you should have your lawn seeded and aerated or when to plant your vegetable garden? When should you strap on that tool belt someone bought you as a gag gift and attempt a home repair, or when would it be smart to call a professional? What kind of power equipment should you buy (lawn mowers, chain saws, etc.) and which type is most suitable for your property?

The answers to these questions — and to so many more — lie in knowing how to manage the unique tasks and challenges each season presents.

TRUSTED SOURCES

In the city, you're probably used to owning a small tool kit, a snow shovel, and a toilet plunger. Maybe you know something about changing a fuse or resetting your circuit breaker that controls the electricity, too. You've probably painted an accent wall in your apartment and hung up some pictures. But in the country, that's just the beginning of the gear you'll need.

When it's time to invest in property maintenance equipment, the smartest thing you can do is buy local. When it comes to making big purchases, such as riding mowers and snow blowers, you will be a fish out of water. We strongly suggest you avoid the big box stores. Lowe's and Home Depot might be oases in the urban desert, but out in the country, there are better options.

Buying at your local store might mean you spend a few extra bucks, but it will pay you back in spades when you need your equipment serviced or later, when you need advice from a trusted source. Building a relationship with the nice folks at your local store (Ace Hardware, Agway, or a one-off independent hardware and garden center) is critical. You will get fast and experienced service. Unlike at a big box store, you won't find yourself lost, walking through canyonesque aisles, stuck in plumbing supplies when you're just trying to find two-cycle engine oil and grass seed. The nice folks at a local store will take the time to talk with you and guide you to the appropriately sized equipment, best brands, and essential accessories. You can be confident that you will get the right gear at a fair price and that you will know how to use it and care for it before you receive the delivery or carry (or push) it out the front door.

Your friendly associate can also be a great referral source for local handymen, who are people you will inevitably need when your rain gutter detaches from your second-story roof, or when the heavy, old wooden shed door rots off its hinges, or if you need help figuring out where the water in your basement is coming from. They might even offer you one of their high schoolers to help you out on the weekends to do yard work from time to time.

Perhaps even before you head off to your local store you can check in with your neighbor for advice. If they've lived there for a while, they can be like a real-life Farmers Almanac, and generally an all-around reference guide. Heck, they might even know more about your property than you do at this point; weird, but true. Take their advice on any given topic, from gardening to when to open and close the pool if you have one, or when your porch is showing signs it needs to be stained again. If they ever volunteer advice, they aren't being know-it-alls; they just have a lifetime of experience that they want to share.

Hot Tip 1: Don't go around asking for a super. Upscale city condos have supers; country houses need handymen.

Hot Tip 2: You will have a lot of recurring tasks that are easy to forget, so consider setting reminders in your phone for things like changing water and air filters (quarterly or semi-annually), or having the septic system, furnace/boiler, and generator serviced annually — just to mention a few examples.

SPRING

"Nothing is so beautiful as Spring –
When weeds, in wheels, shoot long and lovely
   and lush;
… What is all this juice and all this joy?"
      —"Spring," by Gerard Manley Hopkins

The world thaws, melts, and washes the ground. What was cold and frozen becomes mush. The grass pushes up through the warming soil, the flowers open. Color returns. The air is filled with chirping and buzzing. Everything is so happy to be alive. No, this is not David Attenborough narrating *Planet Earth*. This is your backyard.

The poets make it sound so beautiful… but for you, it's time to get to work. Here's a breakdown of the type of preparation you'll need to do to be ready for the season.

A. Equipment

a. If your lawn is at least an acre, consider getting a zero-turn ride-on mower. They are easy (and fun!) to operate, and their turning efficiency will significantly cut down on your mowing time. When selecting a weed wacker/weed eater, we suggest following the advice from your local hardware store. If you have a third of an acre or less, you might be able to get away with an electric model, but for a backyard larger than that, you really do want to get one that is gas-powered.

b. If you already have a mower, make sure you have it serviced (oil, spark plug, and filter changes, and blade sharpening). Do this early — before the spring rush. Don't be that person who waits too long and then demands a quick turn-around. That'll probably put you at the end of the line.

c. If your dreams for a vegetable garden are finally getting realized, then you're probably encountering the need for several essential tools: a hoe, a mid-length handle gardening spade, a shovel, a hand trowel, a long handled three-claw scratcher for weeds — and a kneeling pad is also helpful to protect your knees. One of the tools we use the most is a high quality hand pruner. Watering cans, hoses, and sprinklers are always helpful, as are snug-fitting, stretchy, mesh gardening gloves with rubberized fingers and palms. Buy them by the pack and have plenty extra lying around. (For more on gardening, see Chapter 6: Playing with Fire… and Soil… and Water.)

B. Landscaping Tasks

a. Have your kids pick up sticks around the lawn *before* you mow. Country living is a family affair, so this is a great way to teach the kids how to do their part. Save the twigs for kindling, make a bonfire, or throw them in the woods.

b. Don't buy into the chemical craze and, please, ignore the bombardment of lawn care commercials; you probably don't need to fertilize your grass and, no, dandelions will not ruin your life. They are actually quite beautiful, and pollinators need them. It's unfortunate that certain lawn care companies have worked so hard to demonize dandelions, which can be quite fun to pick and play with. Your kids can make dandelion chain necklaces; they can "paint" their skin with the easily-rubbed-off yellow tint. Dandelions have a pleasant, subtle smell, and your children can poke them in their hair bands or weave them into braids. When dandelions go to seed, they are fun to pick, blow into the wind, and watch as the puffy seeds float into the air like bubbles. Lastly, not that any of us will ever get around to it, but you can actually make wine out of dandelions — and in our book, anything that can make wine is a good thing!

c. If your lawn is looking thin, you might want to spread grass seed and do a topdressing with a ¼ inch of compost. Cool season grasses, such as bluegrass, fescue and rye, germinate best in spring and fall, but you really can seed anytime, especially if you are reseeding after a renovation project. When watering the grass with a sprinkler in hot weather, it is best to do so in the morning. This will prevent the water from steaming/burning the sensitive seedlings or sod in the midday sun or causing fungus to creep into the wet grass overnight.

Hot Tip: If you're seeding bare ground, rake the seed into the top ¼ inch of soil to insure good "seed-to-soil contact" and spread a thin layer of straw over the area, which creates shade, thereby maintaining moisture through the hottest parts of the day.

d. Set your mowing height at around three inches. Any lower and you may cut the grass so short it could cause it to burn out, especially in the middle of the summer. Do not collect your grass clippings with a bagging attachment on your mower (in fact, avoid the upsell and skip buying the bagger attachment). Instead, leave the grass where it lies. Not only are grass clippings full of nitrogen, which is good for feeding your soil (thereby eliminating your need to pay for fertilizer applications), but it will also save you a ton of work. On some mowers, you can choose between regular blades and mulching blades.

On other mowers, you can get an attachment that covers over the exit shoot, which causes the clippings to get chopped up more. This attachment can also be used in combination with mulching blades. The key is to mow frequently enough that your clippings don't end up so thick and clumpy that they smother and kill the grass. In the spring, when the grass is growing at its fastest rate, you will need to mow more frequently to stay ahead of it and to avoid a build-up of clippings that will smother the grass. If you fall behind because of rain, you may have to go back over your yard with a rake and spread out any clippings in areas that are too thick. If you find yourself mowing so frequently you feel like a hamster trapped in a wheel during April and May, don't worry: the mowing frequency will slow down during the summer. For best results, time your mowing for when your grass is dry.

Hot Tip 1: If you plan to play croquet or want to practice your short game on a home-grown putting green, you can drop your mower height in a particular area so the balls will roll better. But if your ground is bumpy, be careful not to scalp the high spots in the process.

Hot Tip 2: If possible, alternate your mowing pattern each time you cut. Not only will the diamond-shape cutting pattern look cool, it helps prevent over-compaction of the soil from repeatedly tracking over the same ground and will reduce burn-out marks from your zero-turn pivots.

Hot Tip 3: Always clean wet clippings off your mower deck top and undercarriage before putting the mower away. This will prevent possible fires and rusting. Also, get your blades sharpened once or twice a season. Dull blades cause plant tissue stress and can invite turf disease.

e. Early spring is a good time for mulching gardens or trees before the weeds come up. Make sure you don't pile the mulch up against the tree or shrub trunks or flower stems. Avoid what is called a mulch "volcano" as it creates a moisture zone that will cause potential molds or rot and creates habitat that harbors destructive pests that could bore into your plantings. Make sure you can still see the "root flair" at the base of your plantings. And, please, keep it natural; only McDonald's should be using red-dyed mulch... and even that is questionable. We recommend triple-ground and *well aged* natural mulch, or even compost.

C. Leisure Activities

a. In April, create your own Easter egg hunt by hiding homemade-dyed eggs (or the plastic kind filled with treats) in your backyard, a field, or the woods. (Better yet, if you decide to acquire some chickens, they will lay the eggs for you to use!)

b. Go watch a steeplechase horse race, or participate in a charity trail run.

c. Grab a pair of binoculars and an Audubon Society guidebook; birding can be fun. Learn who your migrational neighbors are as they begin their mating rituals and nest-building.

d. On May Day, see if you can find a local Maypole dance.

e. Visit a public garden for inspiration on what types of flowers and shrubs you might want to plant at your home.

f. Buy a half-share or full-share at your local CSA Farm (Community Supported Agriculture). One of the great things about CSAs is that when you buy a share, it's up to the farmer to choose the vegetables, so every week becomes a fun surprise. Put your trust in the farmer's hands, and you will love the haul of weekly, ever-changing fresh veggies — and cooking with vegetables you've never heard of before will be a fun way to expand your palate.

g. Do a little research into the history of your

town or region; there are likely structures and monuments from Revolutionary-era America nearby and maybe even from pre-colonial times, too. See if you can find out more about the American Indian tribes that roamed your land for centuries before Europeans arrived in the "New World." Lots of towns have museums that not only explain who these people were, but also run workshops on weaving, planting, and building in Native American and colonial ways. Some might also offer camps for kids.

h. Find a quiet road or a county park or a local nature preserve. Ride bikes or just take a stroll as the world comes alive again, awakening from its winter slumber.

i. If you have a pool and you will be opening it up for your first season, now is the time to find a pool maintenance company and a source of water if you need to have it trucked in.

SUMMER

"   ...Season of
joy for the bee. The green will never
again be so green, so purely and lushly

new, grass lifting its wheaty seedheads
into the wind. Rich fresh wine
of June, we stagger into you smeared
with pollen..."

—"More Than Enough," by Marge Piercy

A. Equipment

a. Summer is the easy season, so just make sure you have enough water guns to fight back the heat.

b. Old houses don't have the best ventilation/air circulation, so if you don't have central air, make sure you have some energy efficient A/C window units and oscillating fans to dispel the heat.

c. To avoid mold, be prepared to have a dehumidifier ready for when the humidity sets in. You should definitely have at least one running in the basement at all times. Set it up so that it automatically drains into a sump pump well (if you have one), or into the drain of a slop sink.

d. Now might be a good time to learn how a chainsaw works. Ask your local hardware store salesman for advice, but a medium to medium-small saw is probably a good size to safely learn on and should be just enough power and bar length to cut through your average tree limb clean-up project (while not being so bulky that your arms get tired after twenty minutes). If you're buying the saw, then also go for the protective helmet/visor/earphones and the cut-proof chaps. (No need to cut an artery while you're having fun with your new power toy.) Just like weed whackers, chain saws have two-cycle engines and burn a fuel mixture of gasoline and oil. For simplicity, consider buying premixed fuel instead of making your own mixture using gasoline from the pump, which has ethanol and can corrode the engine.

Hot Tip 1: When sawing, don't force the saw; let the chain pull the saw through the wood, *and always keep your chain out of the dirt.* For maximum safety and performance, make sure to use a freshly sharpened chain that has the right tension adjustment.

Hot Tip 2: It's always a good idea to have a backup chain, so you can do a fast swap-out if you dull your chain in the middle of a project. Using the chainsaw will be the single most dangerous activity you do, so please pay close attention when your sales person runs through the operating procedures.

Hot Tip 3: If you're cutting a limb that is suspended off the ground, first make a cut ⅓ the depth of the limb from the bottom and then finish your cut coming down from the top. This will help you avoid getting the bar pinched in the limb as it begins to sag.

Jake

A landscaper friend of mine cut a gash in his leg one day while working for me. Fortunately, my neighbor (who is a horse veterinarian) was home at the time, and we were able to kindly coerce her into sewing him up on the spot so he wouldn't have to lose the rest of his day stuck in the emergency waiting room. We were lucky that it wasn't such a deep cut and that she was able to patch him up. It was quite the scene, if you can imagine a vet sewing up my friend's bloody flesh wound while he sat on the tailgate of his pickup truck parked in my driveway. Chainsaws are no joke, even for professionals! While it looked ugly, the wound luckily did not put my friend out of commision.

B. Landscaping Tasks

a. If you have to cut down any dangerous-looking trees, or if a storm took the initiative and knocked them down for you, then this is a great time to stockpile firewood. Once you have cut your wood into rounds, it's time to split. But unless you have a hydraulic splitter, you will want to make sure that your rounds are dry/seasoned and showing cracks in the ends, which is when you can most easily split the wood by hand with a maul. If your rounds are still "green," go ahead and stack them as they are and give them a few months to dry out. To be clear: mauls are for splitting and axes are for chopping. With the right maul and a properly seasoned round, you will shatter that wood with one godlike swing. (It's a lot of fun and it feels like a true-life Hollywood moment when the wood just shatters under the force of your blow.) You will find that this new chore is actually one of the most satisfying experiences. It's also good for the ego if you can position the work area so that your spouse can catch a glimpse of your newfound prowess. In addition, if you're looking to take out some stress from your job, family life, the American political system, or this blasted global pandemic, splitting rounds can be much better than psychotherapy — and cheaper, too!

i. Cut an 18-24-inch, perfectly level round out of the thickest part of your log and use that as your splitting base. Then set your other rounds on top of that base, one by one, to split. This will save your back and also keep your maul out of the dirt.

ii. If you don't have any firewood of your own, make sure to order wood early from a trusted supplier who comes well recommended. Jake likes to buy his wood as early as possible just in case it's not perfectly seasoned, giving it more time to dry out.

iii. Some suppliers will offer cuts of different lengths, a good thing to be aware of, depending on the size of your fireplace or wood stove.

iv. Don't be cheap when it comes to firewood. The quality can vary greatly and you will get what you pay for.

v. Whether you are buying wood or supplying your own, remember that poorly seasoned wood is not just annoying and difficult to burn, but is also bad for your chimney. (For more on wood and fire management, see Chapter 6: Playing with Fire... and Soil... and Water.)

b. If you haven't done so already, now is a good time to make sure your heating fuel contracts are set up for the Fall and Winter. If you use propane for your oven/stove, or for your water heater, or for your furnace or boiler (or for all three), then contact your local propane company to learn about their fuel pricing plans. Similarly, if your furnace/boiler uses oil, then contact your heating oil company. In either case, sign up for automatic delivery and have an emergency service plan set up. Also, see if they offer a pre-buy fuel price special. If you suspect your heating unit is on its last legs, consider switching to propane, if it isn't already. Propane units are cleaner, better for the environment, and require less maintenance than oil.

C. Leisure Activities

a. Find a swimming hole at a local creek or pond.

b. Go tubing or canoeing down the local creek or river.

c. Go fishing.

d. Set up a sprinkler in your yard; if your yard is sloped, bust out the Slip 'n Slide.

e. Invite your neighbors over for a BBQ.

f. Make a bonfire and cook smores. (Just make sure you're not in a drought year or a wildfire-sensitive area.)

g. Find a local brewery and sample their full slate of beers.

h. If you plan to set off fireworks on the Fourth of July (or any day), make sure you check if there are any local municipal ordinances regulating their use. Please consider your neighbors when planning to set off fireworks. Give them a friendly "heads up" (pun intended). Lastly, it is very important that you make sure there isn't any livestock too close by. Fireworks can startle livestock, and if they panic, they could run through their fencing and get hurt... or worse.

i. Keep riding those bikes and taking long walks.

j. Return to that public garden to see how the seasonal flowers have changed. Go early and beat the heat.

FALL

"Season of mists and mellow fruitfulness,
Close bosom-friend of the maturing sun;
Conspiring with him how to load and bless
With fruit the vines that round the thatch-eves run;
To bend with apples the moss'd cottage-trees,
And fill all fruit with ripeness to the core…"

— "To Autumn," by John Keats

A. Equipment

Aren't those fall colors so beautiful? The leaves burn orange, red, yellow, and purple. But then they fall, so…

    a. It's leaf-blowing time! For anything larger than half an acre, go with a gas- powered unit. For anything less than half an acre, an electric cord or battery powered one should do fine. Of course, you can always try to do it the old-fashioned way (with a rake).

Hot Tip: After your last mow of the season (and after the leaves have been fully removed), remember to gas up and add fuel stabilizer to your mower, weed whacker, leaf blower, and chainsaw. Fuel stabilizer prevents water vapor and corrosive build-up in the engines. Without this preventative step, your equipment might not start up or run well the next time you need it. If you have a snow blower, you would want to do this step in the early spring after the last time you use it.

b. If you have a decent sized driveway and walkways, consider buying a gas-powered walk-behind snow blower. Do this early in preparation for one of those sneaky early fall snow storms. These machines are really worth it if you live in an area that tends to get a lot of snow. Consider the cost of having your driveway plowed for a whole winter; the snow blower will pay for itself after a few years, and you won't be left guessing as to when the busy plow guy will show up.

c. If you have a long, winding driveway, purchase some snow stakes and make sure you hammer in enough of them to map the outline of your driveway. That way, you'll know where everything is when it's under a blanket of white.

B.   Landscaping Tasks

a. Have the chimney inspected and cleaned. Sure, you did it last year, but it's worth it for the peace of mind, ensuring you don't burn the house down. While a cozy wood fire might not be top of mind in September, now is a good time to get this task checked off as these types of appointments can get booked up far in advance.

b. Rake/blow/mulch leaves. Do not wait for them all to drop. Keep your workload light and in manageable increments. Do it once per week for the three or so weeks while the leaves drop. The best and easiest way to handle the volume of leaves is to put a mulching attachment and mulching blades on your mower deck. The mower will then chop/mulch up the leaves fine enough that they will not smother the grass and will end up feeding the soil as they decompose.

  i. If your property is surrounded by woods, there will probably be too many leaves for you to clear just by mulching. In this case, you will probably need to haul a good portion of them off the lawn. Use a large tarp and make a dump pile at the edge of your property. After a few years, this pile will provide great compost. If you don't have a good spot for a leaf pile, you can always haul them to the local municipal recycling/compost center or pay a landscaper to do it. You can also burn them; it's fun and smells good, but it's not the best thing for air quality, and your town may also have restrictions on burning leaves for exactly that reason. Much better to recycle them into compost (see Chapter 6: Playing with Fire... and Soil... and Water for more on composting).

 Hot Tip: If possible, don't try to do any of this in windy or wet conditions.

c. Drain, roll up and bring your garden hoses inside.

d. Bring in or turn over your flower pots so they don't freeze and crack.

e. Bring your patio furniture inside the garage or put it down in the basement for storage.

f. Clean your gutters after the leaves are down, which will prevent clogging and overflowing while the weather is still cool, and also icing over (ice damming) when it's below freezing. Ice build-up can weigh gutters down and cause them to pull off the eaves. If you have a lot of trees near your house, you may well have to clear the gutters several times as the leaves come down, but if you install leaf gutter guards, you can skip this cleaning hassle in the future.

g. Bleed the radiators (if you have the old-fashioned kind). This removes any air pockets that would inhibit the smooth flow of the cycling hot water. Look for the little air valve on the side of the radiator, and if you have any problems, call a plumber.

h. Stack a small "feeder pile" of firewood close to the house (on your porch or in your garage). This way it's readily accessible and you don't have to go for a frosty hike when you need to feed the fire.

C. Leisure Activities

a. In early fall, make a plan to visit a local farm or orchard and...

   i. ...Go apple picking. We're sure you already know this one, but at least now you don't have to drive two hours to do it. Even better, go apple picking twice!

   ii. ...Pick your pumpkin from a real pumpkin patch instead of from the Whole Foods parking lot.

   iii. ...Go for a hayride, ride a pony, and get lost in a corn maze. Make a huge leaf pile and let the kids and dogs jump into it and have a good wrestle. Take slow-motion videos of the leaves being tossed in the air and raining down.

b. Fall is also a good time to plant bulbs, trees and shrubs.

Hot Tip: If you plant trees and shrubs in the fall, you won't need to water them as frequently as you would have if you had planted them in the spring. When they wake up out of dormancy the following spring, they will be much more hardy because their fresh root growth will not have been disturbed.

c. If you're not too worn out from raking all those leaves and splitting wood, keep riding those bikes, taking family walks, and competing in charity runs.

d. Bring the kids on a turkey feather hunt. After a flock of wild turkeys has moseyed through your yard, follow in their footsteps and see if you can find a long, beautiful tail feather.

e. Make a bonfire and drink apple cider. Correction: make a bonfire and drink *spiked* apple cider.

WINTER

"They are a gift I have wanted again.
Wanted: One moment in mountains
when winter got so cold
the oil froze before it could burn.
I chopped ferns of hoarfrost from all the windows
and peered up at pines, a wedding cake
by a baker gone mad. Swirls by the thousand
shimmered above me until a cloud
lumbered over a ridge,
bringing the heavier white of more flurries…"
— "Horses in Snow," by Roberta Hill Whiteman

You're so full of summer sun, it's hard to believe that the heat won't last forever. But when the weather finally begins to change in the fall, it's a good time to start planning for colder climes, when you'll be figuring out what to do with all the snow when it arrives.

A. Equipment

a. Make sure you have a good snow shovel with a scoop that isn't too big for you when loaded down with snow. If you plan to use your snow blower, double check that it's gassed up and easily starts. Do this in mid-September as this will give you time to fix any possible issues you might discover.

b. Always make sure you're well stocked with a topped off gas can, salt and also cinders/fine gravel/grit if you have a steep driveway.

c. Depending on how far north you have fled, you might want to consider a set of snow tires for the car that you can swap out seasonally. If you have flown very, very far north, you might even consider snow tires with studs (small, dull, metal spikes that give your tires extra grip on ice). Obviously, all-wheel-drive vehicles will handle adverse conditions best, followed by front-wheel drive. Rear-wheel drive cars are the least useful. Just remember, however, that all-wheel drive does not mean all-wheel stop. Also, consider always carrying a short-handled shovel, jumper cables, and an emergency bag filled with things like a blanket, flashlight, ice scraper, extra jacket, winter boots, and maybe an energy bar. You never know what might happen if you get stranded, so be prepared to self-rescue...

B. Landscaping Tasks

a. When at all possible, clear snow from the driveway and foot paths *before* driving or walking on them. Once driven or trodden upon, the compacted snow will be very hard to scrape off and may end up turning into ice.

b. With deep snow falls, get out and clear the snow several times while it is actively snowing. This will make it easier and more manageable than waiting until the snowfall is finished. If you have a wet, heavy snow, wait until it's finished falling, but then clear it right away. Even if it's only a few inches, wet snow can lock up and become very difficult to move if left on the ground too long. You might have a sense of this already from clearing city sidewalks, but don't underestimate the new size of the area you will be clearing. It's not just a curbside parking spot anymore.

c. If your driveway is bigger than what you are comfortable handling, you can of course always get the local plow guy to put you on his route. Just make sure you set that up in the early fall. Snow plowers will be in demand, and they may not have enough time to add you to their routes, so don't be that person calling around in a panic during the first big snow of the season when you can't get in or out of your own driveway.

d. If you have leaky windows and can feel cold drafts of air, you can buy a plastic shrink wrap kit. It's an easy, cheap, temporary solution that really does make a big difference. Maybe next season you can save up and install quality replacement windows. (Jake used this plastic wrap every year when he was a frugal bachelor, but after he took his future in-laws out for dinner and asked for their daughter's hand in marriage, the next purchase he made — right after the ring — was a set of replacement windows for the entire house…)

C. Leisure Activities

   a. Find a local cut-your-own-Christmas tree farm, then go… cut your own Christmas tree.

   b. Go ice skating on a local pond or stream, or find a pick-up hockey game. Try your hand at ice-fishing.

   c. Buy a family ski pass at the local town hill.

   d. Snow can be glorious fun. Grab a sled or snow tube and find a hill; build a snowman or fort; and definitely have a snowball fight.

   e. Buy a pair of snowshoes and/or cross country skis and trek through the fields or deep into the woods. Listen carefully: a fresh snowfall brings a special kind of magical silence that can feel restorative.

   f. Now that it's cold, you have permission to go full L.L. Bean. Put on your hat, scarf, coat, and felt-lined boots and go for a crisp, refreshing walk in the snow. The fire will feel twice as nice when you come back inside.

   g. Clip some greens from your spruce tree, yew

shrub or holly tree, then forage some bitter-sweet vines at the edge of the woods and collect some pinecones. Now you can make a home-made wreath for your front door, one that you can be proud of (you can purchase a wire wreath backer from your local garden store).

h. Tap a maple tree! It's easy to learn how!

PLAYING WITH FIRE...
AND SOIL... AND WATER

If you're looking to take a deeper dive into some of the topics discussed in the previous chapter, here are several key aspects of country life: fire management, wood storage, composting, and planting a garden.

UP IN SMOKE

Only use "well seasoned" wood, which means that the wood is dry from being split, stacked, and aged for about a year. Poorly seasoned wood holds moisture and will not only be harder to burn (you will hear hissing and possibly see water bubbling/boiling out of the ends of the wood), but the smoke from that wet wood will also contain moisture vapor. This moisture bonds to the creosote in the smoke and causes it to stick to the inside of your chimney. Bad news. Conversely, when burning dry wood, which gives off drier smoke, the creosote does not stick to the chimney as much. In the normal course of burning fires, creosote, which comprises tars and resin, will build up in your chimney slowly over a season, depending on how many fires you burn. This is normal, but in order to make sure the creosote build-up isn't dangerous, you should always have your chimney inspected and cleaned annually. Burning wet wood will increase the amount of creosote over what is normal for a season, thus causing higher risk of a chimney fire.

KNOCK ON WOOD

Hardwood is the best wood for burning because the harder and denser the wood, the more BTUs (British Thermal Units) it contains. Not all hardwood contains the same BTU's. For example, maple and poplar don't burn as hot or as long as oak, elm or hickory, just to name a few. You can really understand the differences in wood density when you pick up a split log. An oak log will be almost twice as heavy as maple. When sourcing firewood to purchase, know that you'll pay a higher price for firewood with a better mixture of the higher BTU woods.

Never burn pine/evergreen wood — soft woods or, more technically, coniferous resinous trees — indoors. When burned, the sap and resin in these woods will create lots of creosote and tars that will stick to the sides of your chimney and build up quickly in dangerous quantities. As the logs burn, the resins and tars will create superheated, fiery flare-ups and also make loud popping noises as little explosions of fiery embers scatter. (Embers from hardwood can also pop and scatter, so it's always a good idea to have a fire screen.) Reserve any softwood you collect on your property for use in outdoor fires only. (One bonus for burning softwoods outdoors is that pine smells great and the flare-ups and sparks are fun to watch!)

For all you climate scientists out there… one thing to keep in mind when lighting fires or burning leaves is that you are releasing carbon into the atmosphere. Your individual actions will not be greatly exacerbating global warming, but it is something to be aware of. We think it's always good to consider how our own actions and lifestyles affect the planet. But there is a loophole for having guilt-free fires: see "Composting" below for a "*Cool* Tip."

WOOD STORAGE

 When storing your wood, it's a good idea not only to cover it with a tarp, but also to keep it elevated so it doesn't soak up ground moisture. You can elevate your stack on two parallel long skinny limbs, or you can stack it on shipping pallets. You can generally get pallets free from a hardware/garden center store, especially if you've been building a good relationship with them (ahem!). Wood is sold by the cord or half cord. A cord is a stack of wood that is 4' wide by 4' tall by 8' long. So two pallets generally hold a cord of wood. You can leave the sides of your stack open to let air pass through.

It is a good practice to stack your wood away from

your house, since wood piles are notorious for harboring mice, squirrels and bugs that you don't want inside of your house.

BUILDING A FIRE

Everyone has his or her own preferred way of building a fire, and even two Boy Scouts might disagree on what the "correct" way is. There are basically two options: the "tepee" design and the "log cabin" design.

For the "log cabin" design, lay a bed of crumpled paper on the fire grate, then place kindling over that, and then make a two-level, criss-cross stack of small rounds or skinny split wood. You don't need to go overboard. Save the towering paper fire inferno for the outdoor bonfire — your insurance company will thank you! Once your original stack burns down a little and you can see some red embers glowing, add the larger pieces of firewood as needed. For your outdoor fires try the "tepee" design: crumple up newspaper in the center of the grate, then lean small sticks together until they make a circular tepee structure over the paper, with smaller sticks on the inside and larger sticks on the outside.

If you're having trouble getting your fires going, remember three things: 1. Kindling is really important to allow time for the larger logs to ignite; 2. Fire feeds off of oxygen, so don't just pile wood up in a heap; leave room for air flow; and 3. Make sure your wood isn't wet.

Hot Tip 1: To make sure the smoke draws nicely up the chimney and doesn't smoke out your living room, light a long piece of twisted paper and hold it high up directly under the open flue, letting it burn until you can't hold it anymore. Your chimney will be full of cold, stationary air that can sometimes prevent a newly lit fire from drafting up the chimney properly. Priming the chimney with the lit paper will create an up-draft that clears out the stationary air from the chimney before you start your fire. Now, when you light the fire, the smoke will be pulled right up and out.

Hot Tip 2: Indoors or out, you will live longer if you avoid using gasoline or other similar type accelerants for starting fires. Stay safe and use paper and dry kindling.

Hot Tip 3: After a few fires, the ash will build up, and you will need to remove most of it. Leave a little bed of ash behind; it will help insulate the next fire, thereby making it easier to start. Discard the ash in your compost pile, or some folks like to put it on icy parts of their driveways.

Hot Tip 4: Wood Pellet Stoves. If you've bought a house with a wood pellet stove, avoid the novice mistake of buying the wrong kind of wood pellets and starting a chimney fire. There are pellets made specifically for stoves and there are different wood pellets produced for animal bedding... Who would have known? Check the label!

COMPOSTING

Jake _____

I am in the business of commercial composting, so it is a subject that is near and dear to my heart. Composting at home can be just as important and rewarding as on the commercial level.

First of all, don't worry about making the perfect compost or getting too technical about it. Keep it simple. Find a con-venient — but out-of-the-way — spot and simply make a pile on the ground or build a three-sided bin (you could use repurposed shipping pallets). Your compost bin will become a catch-all for food scraps, extra grass clippings, livestock manure and bedding, mulched leaves, garden prunings, etc. Try and keep a good balance of green and brown inputs, also known as carbon and nitrogen sources. Think of food scraps, manure, and grass clippings as "nitrogen/green" and prunings, animal bedding, and leaves as "carbon/brown."

If your compost is very dry, add some water, but be careful not to make it too soggy, either. You probably won't achieve the seed-killing temperatures that commercial composters reach, so keep anything that could add weed seeds out of your compost. Simply add your inputs as they are generated and stir the pile with a pitchfork or shovel from time to time. Eventually, it will begin to break down and you can start to use it as a source of organic humus and fertilizer for your lawn or garden.

This is a great activity for the kids, both a practical chore and a science lesson all in one. You could possibly appoint the most willing and engaged child as "Compost Manager," which simply means that it's his or her daily task to take out the kitchen scraps…

You can put bones and meat scraps in your compost, but before you put anything too savory into the mix, consider whether or not your own pets will try to scavenge your pile or if you are in an area that might attract bears. Using an enclosed barrel design composter could help you avoid these issues.

Hot Tip: Keep a compost pail with a filtered lid in your kitchen for convenience, and then empty it into your compost pile once or twice a week.

Cool Tip: The process of making compost and then using that compost to enhance the soil around your property is actually one method of doing what is known as "carbon sequestration." Yes, that's right: composting organic refuse can actually prevent carbon from being released into the atmosphere. Putting carbon back into the soil is a practice that can help decrease your carbon footprint. So maybe now you can feel a little better about building that cozy fire knowing that you have a way to offset your carbon emissions. By composting regularly, you can come closer to being carbon-neutral.

GARDENING

Over the last few years, there has been a renewed desire across the country both for transparency in food production and supporting sustainable local food sources. There seems to be new national awareness of how impor-

tant it is to secure and provide access to fresh healthy, nutrient-dense vegetables for everyone from urban food deserts to rural communities. Now, as a result of the pandemic, with families spending more time at home or in new homes that now have room to garden, this trend has led to a huge surge in home gardening.[10]

There are many gardening philosophies out there, and many books for you to read, but our advice once again is to keep things simple.

The first principle of gardening is: healthy soil equals

10 Christopher Walljasper and Tom Polansek, "Home gardening blooms around the world during coronavirus lockdowns," published April 20, 2020, https://www.reuters.com/article/us-health-coronavirus-gardens/home-gardening-blooms-around-the-world-during-coronavirus-lockdowns-idUSKBN2220D3.

healthy plants. You can make an in-ground garden by removing sod and roto-tilling compost into your existing soil, or you can build a raised bed and fill it with compost-amended soil. With a little research, you should be able to find and purchase high quality compost or pre-mixed, compost-amended soil at your local garden center.

Locate your garden in full sun and make sure you have a water source nearby. In some situations, it might be helpful to fence in your garden to keep out deer, groundhogs, rabbits and other creatures that still believe in a free lunch.

Plant your crops so that you have a constant supply of harvest-ready veggies throughout the whole season. Below is by no means a comprehensive list, but it includes most popular crops.

In April, you can plant early-season crops, such as radishes, spinach, onions, leeks, lettuce, cabbage, beets, peas, brussel sprouts, and carrots.

In May, you can plant tomatoes, squash, melons, eggplants, peppers, sweet corn, cucumbers, potatoes, and herbs.

By May, you can start picking asparagus, peas, lettuce, kale and spinach; by June, you can pick more peas, beans, and herbs.

In July, you can plant another round of cool season crops for a fall harvest. In July, August, and September, the majority of your crops (tomatoes, peppers, broccoli, cauliflower, and corn, just to name a few) will be ready to pick.

By September and October, you can harvest potatoes, squash, pumpkins, beets, cabbage, and carrots just to name a few.[11]

Keep in mind that starting from seed or starter plants makes a difference in the number of growing days. Some plants, such as corn and tomatoes, even have different varieties that mature faster or slower. For example, "Early Girl" tomatoes will be ready to harvest faster than, say, the "Mortgage Lifter" variety. Planting both kinds can extend your harvest.

Often, a particular crop can ripen and be ready to pick all at once, and you might end up with more than you can consume. Plan ahead and have recipes at hand to help inspire ways to cook or incorporate these abundant veggies into your diet. (As you research which crops are best for your regional growing zone, keep track of the recommended planting times and know that some veggies, such as asparagus and rhubarb, come back every year, while others need to be planted annually.)

Planting a vegetable garden is fun, but sometimes enthusiasm can fade as time passes and one gets bored waiting for crops to ripen. Gardens take work, preparation, planning, constant monitoring, diligent watering, weeding, and fending off intruders, so be sure you're ready for a whole season of cultivating. When harvest time comes, one can't help but reflect on the magic of how a little seed has become a huge pumpkin or how a once-small tomato seedling is now yielding fifty juicy tomatoes. As you bite into your home-grown veggies and taste the freshness, there will be no doubt it will have been worth all the effort.

Frosty Tip: It's easy to get excited about starting your garden on an unseasonably warm late March or early April day. But unless you're planting lettuce, kale, or another cool-season veggie, resist this temptation to plant. In the Mid-Atlantic, for example, the rule of thumb is to wait until Mother's Day. This will ensure that your garden does not get zapped by a late spring frost.

Hot Tip 1: If you're going to plant tomatoes, buy the extra large heavy duty cages; it's amazing how big these plants will grow.

Hot Tip 2: When your tomatoes finally ripen, the output will probably overwhelm you. (There are only so many tomato sandwiches one can eat at lunch.) So consider freezing some in large ziploc freezer bags, then over the winter you can pull a bag out now and again and make delicious pasta sauces. And also: start slow. Consider limiting your first year's planting to no more than four to six plants. Those little starters might not look like much, but if given the right amount of love, they will love you back and then some! Down the road, you could even start experimenting with canning, which can be useful for a whole variety of veggies and fruits.

Hot Tip 3: Veggie gardens can be pretty, too, so don't forget to sow in some flowers that you can cut later and put in a vase to brighten up your kitchen or dining room. Also some flowers, such as marigolds, not only make your garden look nice, but also attract important pollinators and repel while also being unpleasant to some certain animals that would otherwise try to eat your veggies.

7

PERSPECTIVES
AND ANECDOTES

MINDFUL GRATITUDE

If you're going to live in a rural community, it's important to demonstrate that you truly and sincerely care about and enjoy your surroundings with all five of your senses. You might perceive the country views as "natural," but the truth is that a lot of work goes into what you see. Coming into a rural community should be thought of the same way as entering someone's living room. Country folk treat the outside like it's the inside of their home. Not only is the natural world the engine of much of the local economy, it's also a source of great pride. Locals have a staunch passion for the beautiful world they maintain, and they are fiercely protective of it.

Here's the biggie: be present in the moment. This is not just a mantra from your yoga class, and you don't have to go full hippie in order to practice it in your daily life. The natural world is something to savor, not something to treat like a backdrop for a selfie you are dying to post on Facebook or Instagram. When you're out in the country, put your cell phone on silent, take a deep breath, exhale, smell the scent of the pine trees, and listen to the crispy fallen leaves under your feet. Slow down.

Believe it or not, slowing down to smell the roses (as goes the saying) and resisting the urge to check the nearly nonstop phone notifications we are all bombarded with demonstrates your respect for and interest in your local abode. It can be an expression of gratitude, living in the moment and absorbing your surroundings with all five senses. Local folks will notice this and appreciate the appreciation you're giving to your surroundings.

Hot Tip: Avoid falling back on old habits. From time to time, check in with yourself. You know your body lives in a rural postal code now, but where is your mind?

PACING YOURSELF

Jesse
Subway Story _____

City life can be overwhelming. I was born and raised in NYC, and I never quite realized how frenetic the place is until I left for college. When I came back after a few months and then again at the end of freshman year, I could feel how my body began to tense up again after having been in a more suburban, spacious environment. Don't get me wrong: city energy is great. There's a lot of passion, a lot of youthfulness, a lot of surprises (some good, some bad). But fighting through crowds and using public transportation is stressful. It's very hard to avoid the constant friction of living so close to so many people, and many New Yorkers frequently talk about finding a way to "escape."

If you live in the city long enough, you develop excellent survival strategies. My favorite way to deal with the crowds was knowing at exactly what door of the subway to stand so that I could jump off the train, sail through the turnstiles, and leap up the stairs to the street without getting caught behind the slow-moving herd. I honed this strategy carefully, and it came to be automatic for me to take a certain set of stairs to enter and exit the trains, and to know at what steel column to stand to ensure I found my way onto and off of the train at the right place. This was especially necessary at rush hour, when being at the back of the line could block me from transferring to another train for my last leg home. I probably saved twenty minutes every day when I executed these maneuvers properly. There's nothing like the feeling of racing down that last flight of subway steps, screaming "Hold the doors!" and squeezing your body through them without getting your hands, coat, or backpack caught. (And nothing worse than when your backpack gets caught in the closing doors, and the train won't move because the conductor refuses to release the doors and let you in, and everyone in the car glares at you, cursing you, your children, and all of your descendants for at least nine generations.)

Another favorite tactic of mine was walking in the street instead of the sidewalk. One of my first jobs was in Times Square, and I had to walk in the street if I had any hope of getting to and from the office in a reasonable amount of time. Times Square is filled with tourists (or it was, at least, before the pandemic), and most of them are looking up at the shiny signs and flashing lights – which means that they're not moving forward. So I took to walking in the gutter of the street, letting yellow cabs (and Ubers and Lyfts and Vias) swoosh by me. It was probably very dangerous, but in my head, as a lifelong New Yorker, I felt I owned all of the pavement, anyway. (As Ratso Rizzo, Dustin Hoffman's character, says in *Midnight Cowboy*: "I'm walkin' here! I'm walkin' here!")

Now that I live in the country, I'm finally letting go of these urban survivalist behaviors. I've gotten used to driving my car to get wherever I need to go, and I find that it's much less of a struggle to get places than it used to be. I actually enjoy driving to our local general store to buy some staples or grab a sandwich for lunch. But I do still sometimes choose to walk on the side of the road (it's only a mile to the store), which I'm sure is a little odd for my neighbors to see. I enjoy the exercise, fresh air and additional exposure to nature. What does it matter if I can drive there in three minutes, but it takes me twenty to walk? It's not like I'm going to miss my train or anything.

Jake
Alaska Kayak Story——————————————————

Several years ago, my wife and I were on vacation in Alaska. We had booked a guided two-hour kayak trip out of Whittier and as we were getting ready to launch, I saw a jet-ski tour group zoom past us and disappear across the water. I remember thinking, "Darn, that looks like a whole lot of fun." I was jealous that they would get to see so much more cool stuff since they could cover so much more distance than we could in our kayaks.

As it turned out, our slow, little paddle that barely amounted to much more than a few nautical miles was bursting at the seams with incredible experiences — none of which we would have had a prayer at seeing had we been moving faster.

What looked like it was going to be a boring paddle seemed to be over in the blink of an eye. I was so amazed by and engrossed in the new world around me that the time just evaporated. We saw spawning salmon on their death swim entering a small rocky tributary from the ocean. Porpoises swam under our kayaks, while sea otters and sea lions popped up to investigate us. We passed an important bird-nesting cliff site and, while our guide described what we were looking at, we watched a hawk swoop in and snatch an awkward fledgling and fly off, causing the whole colony of birds to erupt into a crescendo of alarm and swirl through the air with frantic angry cries. Our little paddle turned out to be an intense, raw, and deeply elemental experience, one which I will never forget.

In our fast-paced, modern lives, it is all too easy to be blind to the world around us. This was an important lesson for me, learning that slowing down can open our eyes and be the best way to see more of the everyday beauty and mystery around us. If I had been going faster, I would have missed all of it.

LIFE LESSONS COURTESY OF MOTHER NATURE

Jake

Brain Freeze _____

One of my favorite tactile pleasures is when I'm either doing physical work or exercising outside when it's cold. My body is warm, maybe a little sweaty, and when a sharp breeze buffets my face with biting, frosty air and I draw a breath into my lungs, it feels, raw and rejuvenating. It awakens all my senses and breathes energy into my soul. I feel intensely alive, present in that moment, as if I could conquer anything.

Another great sensory gift is the rhythmic, pulsating peeping of the baby frogs in the marshes, which call out in a soothing and enchanting chorus. It's the official announcement that spring has sprung. In the low light of the misty dawn or in the dusky evening, this reverberating sound is ripe with the anticipation and excitement that the awakening of spring signals for the warm seasons ahead.

These wonderful gifts of the country are so easy to miss

in our distracted world, when we're more used to the vibrations and dings of a text message or the fake cricket sounds of a ringtone. Believe me: it's not the same thing.

I consider myself especially well attuned to hearing mother nature's orchestra, but even I can fall deaf to it sometimes. On a beautiful day this past summer, I took a video of my son riding his glider bike. Later that evening, when I played the video back on my phone, I was shocked at how loud the birds and the crickets were in the background. I was so focused on my son that I had tuned everything else out completely. It's a forgivable offense, but it made me wonder how many other times I had subconsciously tuned out mother nature.

Jesse
The Circle of Life —————————————————————

One of the best experiences I've had actually started off as a terrifying and expensive problem. Our new country home came with two enormous Ash trees on the property, overhanging an area where my daughters liked to play. Unfortunately for us, the trees had been infested by the Emerald Ash Borer, a non-native invasive beetle that burrows under the bark and lays its larvae in the tree. When the larvae hatch, they eat their way out of the tree, feeding on the tissues beneath the bark and cutting off the flow of fluids up and down the tree. To make things worse, woodpeckers then come and peck through the bark to eat the larvae. All of this slowly kills the tree, a process that is called blonding.

One of the dead limbs fell off one day, which was how we discovered that we had a major problem. The trees needed to be cut down by professional arborists. I was astonished that it cost thousands of dollars to cut down the two trees, so rather than pay the company to haul away the wood (which would have cost an additional grand!), I had them leave the trunk in sections for us. Little did I know that they would leave pieces that weighed more than 2,500 pounds.

I decided to borrow a chainsaw from a neighbor and began to cut up the manageable sections for firewood – and a good thing, too. Around this same time, we had our fireplace and chimney inspected by a professional chimney sweep, and he said we had a dangerous amount of creosote build-up in the chimney. He sprayed some chemicals on the back wall of the fireplace and as high up the chimney as he could and told us to burn ten hot fires. I asked him how to make a hot fire, and they suggested I use ash wood. Bingo! Things were beginning to fall into place.

I made it through most of the smaller trunk pieces with my borrowed chain saw, but then I reached the end of my abilities. Luckily, a neighbor down the road had a great idea: stand the bigger sections up vertically in a row so that the kids could jump from piece to piece. I remembered that this was what the Prospect Park Alliance back in Brooklyn had called a "natural playground." Lucky me. I had a natural playground in the middle of... nature. Even better, the neighbor down the road had a tractor, and he came over and hoisted up the enormous pieces, positioning them in just the right spots. After a few days of planning and executing, we had created four thrones, one "Flintstone" car, a huge table for tea parties, and an elaborate eighteen-step playground rising up into the sky.

As the weather grew colder that winter, I burned a hot fire with ash wood every night, and I thought of all the warmth and enjoyment we got out of two old, dead trees. It took a lot of time and effort, but it was a rewarding experience. Now, as I set up the dried rounds and split the logs with my maul, I have Elton John's "Circle of Life" playing in my head.

8

CREATURES GREAT, NOT SO GREAT, AND SMALL

WILDLIFE

When you're out in the country, your fellow homo sapiens are not the only neighbors you have to learn to get along with. Everywhere — in the trees, in the skies, under your front porch, in your attic — are critters, some more lovable than others. So embrace the wildlife!

But let's be real: for better or for worse, your country retreat is probably not that wild. You're not living in Alaska, and the East Coast is just not as rugged as it used to be. Nonetheless, you must recognize that you have moved onto *their* turf and that living together successfully requires that you adhere to a symbiotic code.

For the most part, wild animals mind their own business, and it should be with great pleasure that you get to spot them from time to time. Remember: if you have a problem with the wildlife, you probably caused it. So be smart about your small dogs, but don't worry about your pet cats (they are actually quite lethal and can hold their own just fine outdoors). Be mindful of your food storage, trash, and compost pile and all should be fine.

Bobcats and bears may sound scary, but are not prevalent in many places. However, if there are any where you live, they most likely want nothing at all to do with you. Honestly, they think you smell really bad, they don't love your scented shower gel, and unless you've got food in your pocket, they're really not interested in striking up a friendship.

It may go without saying, but it's never a good idea to feed the wildlife, aside from perhaps a bird feeder in your yard; however, bird feeders can attract other critters, some as innocuous as squirrels, but also possibly bears, so do some inquiring before you end up with your own personal zoo.

In general, American black bears are lovers, not fighters, and much prefer eating berries, rather than humans. Coyotes, if you're lucky enough to hear them cry out at dusk, generally mind their own business, and raccoons are only dangerous when they are drunk on fermented berries (just kidding: they are not mean drunks) or have a rare case of rabies. The only life-or-death situation that exists relates to your chickens (should you choose to get some; see below) — or your rescue chihuahua who was let out for a bedtime tinkle and left outside for five minutes too long...

Yes, you might get some field mice trying to sneak into your house when the temperatures dip in the fall, but at least they're not hardened sewer rats with criminal records, immune to poison, like the ones you are used to seeing scurrying between the subway rails. Field mice are not that hard to trap and relocate or dispose of. If you get a raccoon, fox, opossum or groundhog in your garage or shed, maybe store whatever they're looking for somewhere else and then plug the hole they created during their break-in. If you see a skunk, well that's cool, too; just back away slowly.

Please refrain from leaving poison bait out for animals. Once ingested, the poison will get transferred up the food chain. Don't be that person who poisoned the mouse, who poisoned the fox cub, who poisoned the bald eagle…

Snakes may invoke the most terrifying thoughts in your mind, but they are certainly more afraid of you and more likely to slither away quickly than to bite. You will find them in creepy places, such as the outside stairwell to the basement, coiled in a bucket in the corner of your garage or sunning on a warm rock in the garden. The truth is that these critters — along with hawks and other birds of prey — are very helpful at keeping your local mouse population under control. So, the next time you are down in your basement gagging because you just walked into a spider's web, only to turn and be startled by a snake skin dangling inches from your face from the electrical conduit between the floor joists, don't jump out of your own skin…

Enjoy sharing space with your new co-habitants! After a while, you might even be able to differentiate individual animals from their herds or flocks. You might notice that one humming bird has a ruby throat, while his girlfriend has green plumage. You will start to notice migration patterns as the Canadian Geese form their v-shaped flight patterns, honking across the sky. You will recognize the swirling smoke-like plumes of starlings as they spin low overhead or as they descend to rest in the trees with a cacophony of chirping. Maybe you will even get used to the sight of black vultures, perched ominously in dead trees. Maybe you'll even catch a glimpse of a mysterious owl.

Most joyously, you will even bear witness to new families arriving each spring, each one caring for their baby ducklings, fox cubs, or spotted fawns. Many animal couples will claim a spot on your land and come back every season to berth/hatch and raise the next generation. After a while, it might feel like you are all part of a big mixed-species extended family. The best part is that, with these family members, there are no creepy uncles — and nobody talks politics on Thanksgiving.

Hot Tip: When you and your family go to bed, a whole world wakes up outside your door. In the morning, you might see the signs of their through traffic criss-crossing your yard: paw prints, nibbled shrubs, animal droppings left as souvenirs. Some carefully placed and fairly inexpensive "trail cams" can capture these nighttime festivities. They only start filming when they detect motion, and many of them send the footage right to an app on your phone. You can watch your own personal CritterTube in the morning.

Jake

It gives me and my young children great pleasure to watch the seasonal migration of our local wildlife. I love watching my son run to the window every morning to see if he can spot any deer or fox in the meadow. I personally enjoy drinking an afternoon cup of tea while looking out on my stream at the great blue herons who take turns regally stalking through the dark pools and shallow rapids hunting for their dinners of fish. Who needs a zoo when you have this kind of activity all around you?

Jesse

On our property we have an upper field and a lower wetland meadow. Shortly after moving in, one of my first and most intrepid feats of country living was to take my newly purchased zero-turn mower and attack the overgrown meadow while it was dry and the ground was firm in mid-summer. No sooner had I started across the field when a red-tailed hawk flew in low right behind me and perched on a branch overlooking the field. I admit that I was a little terrified at being so close to a bird whose talons were plainly visible to me, a mere twenty feet away. It was even more unsettling when the hawk swooped down at the mower... in order to grab a little field mouse who, unlucky for him, had just been exposed in my wake.

Over the course of the next hour, while I systematically reduced the overgrowth into chopped stubble, I watched the hawk catch four more mice and fly off to devour them. An hour earlier, I could have sworn I had met a mortal enemy, but after mowing the field with the hawk right near me, I felt that I had made a new friend. And, I realize, that hawk is pretty smart. Every time the sound of my mower reaches his ears, he glides over right away and perches on a branch, waiting for lunch.

Hot Tip 1: If you do have some hungry and unwelcome visitors in your garage or shed, store your dog food, bird seed, grass seed and organic fertilizer in galvanized metal trash cans with snug-fitting lids. Avoid using plastic containers; the mice will just see them as a challenge and happily chew through the plastic with ease. If you're keeping your trash cans outside and you've got bears nearby, there are special bins that are resistant to bears.

Hot Tip 2: Always check yourself, the kids and the pets for ticks, even in the winter. When we were all kids, we didn't have to worry about ticks so much when we were playing out in the fields or woods, but, sadly, it is the reality now. Lyme disease is no fun at all. Make sure you give your cats and dogs anti-tick and flea medicine all year round.

Hot Tip 3: Consider putting up bluebird houses, martin houses, and hummingbird feeders. This will definitely bring some color to your backyard. Install a bat house on the gable of your garage. Bats are harmless and eat a ton of bugs, including mosquitos.

PETS...

As you settle into your new country home, you might one day wake up and say, "Hey, why don't we raise some chickens?" And then a few months later, you might murmur, "I've always wanted to own a horse." Another morning, while standing at the kitchen sink gazing out on your land, you might think to yourself, "Oh, wouldn't it be nice to see a few cows tranquilly grazing in the meadow?" Who knows, one day, you might even have the epiphany that you simply must have a potbelly pig as a house pet. Totally normal. Happens to everyone.

Potbelly pig?! Whoa! Pump the brakes! We know there is nothing cuter in the world than a baby potbelly pig. They might look like a ton of adorable, quirky, cuddly fun in your friend of a friend's Instagram post, but trust us: that is not the reality of the situation.

Potbelly pigs grow to be much bigger than you would ever expect, and their scratchy, wiry hair loses cuddleability quite quickly. But that's not all. They are way too smart and way too hungry to be a good house pet. They will destroy your house (and your soul), rummaging and pilfering through every room, closet, and couch cushion. So our advice is to take baby steps and keep it simple. Start with a dog or a cat, preferably one who loves the outdoors and will help get you outside and enjoying nature together. Pets will be much happier (and less neurotic... and thus much more fun to live with) when they are allowed free rein to roam outdoors. You can either fence in a section of your yard with a physical fence or you can go with wireless electric fencing and a shock collar.

Hot Tip: For the physical fence, don't go cheap (Jake learned this the hard way). Get good advice from your local fence company and follow it. If you cut corners, your dog will take great delight, wagging tail and all, in showing you every location around your inadequate fence that he or she can slither or dig under or jump over. If you go with the electric wireless fencing, put in the time to do the perimeter training. Give your dog the time to adjust to the perimeter boundary and, please, don't rush the training.

...AND MAYBE A FEW FARM ANIMALS... OR A FLOCK?

Think you're ready to up your game in the animal world? Are you just dying to tell your old friends about how you make omelettes and poached eggs from your own free-range backyard chickens? Well, if you've survived one full year in the country and you're still yearning to have a flock of speckled hens chortling busily in your backyard, take a minute here to learn about all the good things — and all the evil things — you are about to experience.

The first thing to know when considering whether to get chickens is that it will make taking a vacation a lot harder. It's one thing to put your dog in the kennel or find a pet-sitter, but it is much harder to find somebody that can (or is willing to) also take care of your chickens. Still interested? If so...

Your chicken journey will jump off to a fun and exciting start when you head to your local Agway, or Ace hardware, or pet store to pick out your own fluffy, yellow chicks. They'll look so adorable as they hop around in the galvanized feed trough, bedded in shavings and smelling of fresh pine and baby bird, under the warm red glow of the heat lamp. Then you'll take them home and tuck them comfortably into the cozy crate parked in your mudroom to watch them grow.

Once they are big enough, you'll let them out in your backyard and at night you'll tuck them into that cool, Amish-built nesting house you just had delivered. Every morning, you'll let them out, and they will provide you with hours and  hours of entertainment as they go about scratching and pecking in random acts of ridiculous goofiness.

But then one morning, you will experience evil, the likes of which you never expected to see except in a horror film. You will have had the chickens long enough to name them and to learn their different personalities and daily habits. One of them might even like being held or petted. The kids will fight over which ones are "theirs," and you'll be expecting that any day now they will be laying their first eggs. Each morning you will be on pins and needles as you go out and excitedly check for eggs. That is when you will stumble upon the slaughter: the local foxes have not just slyly helped themselves, uninvited, to a "civilized" chicken dinner. They have ruthlessly and demonicly killed every last chicken in the house for sport and left the mangled carnage scattered about for all to see.

 This kind of carnage is hard for even the most seasoned of farmers to witness. That awful feeling in the pit of your stomach is caused by so much more than just the sorrow for the loss of those delicate lives, not to mention all those months of wasted effort. It's the maddening pointlessness of it all, the fact that they couldn't just take one chicken to eat, but felt compelled to terrorize and murder every hen they couldn't take with them. It is truly a devastating thing to experience.

After a period of mourning and then healing, you may decide to rebuild bigger and better, learning from the hard lessons of the past. You might now defiantly assert that "the chicken coop has been fortified like Fort Knox." Even so, for some of you it will be hard to get past the living nightmare you have experienced. Emotionally scarred, you may never recover. You will close this dark chapter with a for sale ad posted to Craigslist: "Amish-built Chicken Coop, good to excellent condition."

Of course, raising chickens can also go smoothly, if you've figured out how to keep them safe from predators. Owning chickens can be rewarding, but don't dismiss the time commitment you will have to make. Having chickens is great for teaching kids responsibility, as well as providing them with the understanding of how complex animals are, how they need to be cared for, how they are part of the cycle of life, how food is produced, and the value and reward of hard work.

So go for it: move that chicken palace into your backyard. It might be hard sometimes to force yourself out into a cold January morning to feed the chickens, clear the ice from the water trough, and clean up all that poop, but the delicious eggs will definitely be worth it. Your chickens will ruin you forever from buying store-bought eggs, and all other yolks will dim in comparison to your incredibly rich, golden ones. This process of raising delicate little chicks into mature, egg-laying mother hens will give you a sense of survivalist independence. The little pioneer woman inside you will swell with pride.

This is a quintessential experience for those living life in the country. Beauty and cruelty dance delicately together across the sharpened edge of a cold steel blade.

Be patient and trust the process. In due time, you will learn the tricks that make it easier and worthwhile. The happy, little "Charlotte's Web" barnyard is within reach.

Hot Tip: Chickens are the new garbage disposal and will love to eat all your kitchen scraps. But you may need to chicken-proof your flower gardens and porch pots, or else get ready for lots of nosey pecking and unwelcome plant dismemberment....

EPILOGUE: RAISING A GLASS TO NEW BEGINNINGS, EXPANDED HORIZONS, AND ELEVATED PERSPECTIVES

GOODBYE, CITY LIGHTS

As we mentioned earlier, crime rates are lower in the country, so outdoor floodlights are just not necessary. You don't need security lighting or ostentatious accent lighting shining on a tree or up at your double-height gabled entryway. You might not be able to see it at night without a light, but trust us: your special feature will still be there when the sun comes up in the morning.

There's something special about gazing out over a valley and not seeing a hazy glow or glinting lights. Dazzling lights may be cool in the Hollywood Hills, but you will come to see that the darkness stretching out like a blank canvas, unblemished and open to imagination and possibilities, is both peaceful and freeing. A few motion-sensored solar lights along the path or a porch light on a timer is fine. But remember that, as with the many other things you are leaving behind, you are also bidding a fond farewell to light pollution. Enjoy the darkness and use it as an opportunity to rest your overworked retinas.

The good news is that, when you look up into the night sky, you will be amazed at how many stars and planets you can see. And if you're really lucky, you should even be able to experience the wondrous and dreamy Milky Way. Invest in a telescope and pick up some celestial maps, and you'll soon be able to name the constellations, too. Even without technology, just experiencing luminous full moons and catching a glimpse of meteor showers, comets, eclipses, and once-a-century cosmic phenomena is truly wondrous.

In your backyard, on a warm summer's evening, nothing is quite as magical as the fireflies rising up from the grass, pushing higher and higher, as dusk blurs into darkness.

THE AGONY AND THE ECSTASY

By now, you've learned that moving to the country is by no means a transition to a bucolic, sleepy, dull life. Leaving the 24/7 energy of the city will lead to a recognizable shift in the delivery of your daily stimulus, but, don't worry, there will be plenty of stimulus.

Living in the country is an invigorating and vivid experience. It is bitter cold and scorching hot; it makes your body ache from head to toe. But it is the pain that brings the pleasure. It is the sense of struggle, survival, and personal triumph that provides the greatest rewards. Out in the country, life is simply bigger and more dynamic, and you experience it more richly as you weave yourself into the fabric of your surroundings.

Life in the country is certainly not clean, quiet, or easy. Many things will happen that are maddening and frustrating, but through these challenges and experiences you will learn more about yourself, and you will find that you become stronger, more grounded, and more confident than you have ever been.

And then, every once in a while, maybe on a day when nothing seems to be going right or you're just feeling low, you will be stunned by an unexpectedly magnificent and touching moment. Maybe it's the innocence of a delicate spotted fawn frolicking in a meadow, or perhaps it's a sunset that is so stunning it fills your soul in a way that may move you to tears... tears of gratitude, wonder, and joy.

A PARTING TOAST

Jake and Jesse would like to raise a glass in toasting you as you head out on this brave and bold new adventure! You might be a million miles out of your comfort zone, but we are confident that you will land on your feet.

Hopefully, this book has given you a leg up on what you are likely to encounter in the country, setting you up for success as you head out into the unknown. Believe it or not, you are well on your way to an enriching life experience.

As with anything else in life, you will find that actually living in the country is not as daunting as *contemplating* living in the country. Some things can only be learned through experience. You will love this adventure and the quirky characters and creatures you meet along the way. Don't be afraid to fail (there will be plenty of opportunities to do so). And when you fail, don't forget to laugh at yourself and to take stock of the rugged and resourceful person you have become.

So relish the wide open spaces, the fresh air, the singing crickets and pulsating peepers, the smell of fresh cut grass, stunning sunsets, bulging full moons, and twinkling stars hanging low overhead on clear, dark, peaceful nights.

In no time at all, you'll stop thinking of it as "country living" and just call it "home."

ACKNOWLEDGEMENTS

Jake

I would like to thank my wife Kate who graciously put our children to bed while I stole time to co-write this book. I am also grateful for her enthusiasm and dedication in providing our children with regular, outside playtime, so they can discover the magic of nature during this innocent time in their lives.

I owe a significant debt of gratitude to the farming and equestrian communities that provide protection and preservation of open space and help maintain the traditions of the rural lifestyle. I wish to thank my neighbors and friends who read early drafts of this book for their wisdom and perspectives: Melissa Marcinowski, Arabella Brockett, and Wendy Walker.

Finally, I am extremely grateful to Jesse whose experiences in writing and publishing made it possible to bring our random thoughts and experiences gracefully together into this fun (and hopefully useful) book. I am so incredibly proud and impressed with how you, Kimiye, Ruby, and Maxine have taken this bold leap of faith moving from Brooklyn to the wilds of the country. I appreciate the love — and the blood, sweat, and tears — that you are pouring into your "new" old home, while joining a new generation of caretakers of the rural community. Jesse, you have shown bravery and focus on your mission to provide your family with the most happy and wholesome life possible. I look forward to sharing your journey and watching your two beautiful daughters blossom in nature.

Jesse

I am grateful to my wife, Kimiye, for her many hours, days, weeks, and months glued to Zillow, searching out the best antique homes, in the best school districts, surrounded by the best nature. You're the best!

I am furthermore grateful for the generous welcome from many people in the Roxbury community, but, in particular, the Martinelli family, from whom it is not possible to borrow more household items than we have borrowed, and whose friendship, generosity, freshly laid eggs, and tractor are the best. We wouldn't have made it without you. And to the Demole, Fenton-Sharpe, Fish, and DeSilva families: we couldn't have asked for better companions on this new adventure.

I am also thankful to Stuart Liebman for his prodigious editing and landscaping skills.

Finally, I am most grateful to Jake for his wisdom, experience, and guidance in helping me stay ahead of the curve balls of country living. Though we grew up knowing that we inhabited two different spaces, I never realized the depth of feeling and authentic joy that being part of nature brought you. You have helped open my eyes to my own ways of living and to the richer life that is possible in harmony with the seasons. It has only taken us forty years, but we have managed to create something useful, fun, and thought-provoking at the same time. I hope that this book honors your persevering spirit, your shrewd intuition, and your dedication to leading the life you have chosen.

AUTHOR BIOGRAPHIES

Jake Chalfin grew up in Chester County, Pennsylvania. His connection to nature began early, as he grew up in an old stone miller's house with a creek wrapping around the property. Complete with the ruins of an old mill, this first home shaped his love of the outdoors and provided a rich environment to explore as fishing, swimming, and ice skating punctuated the seasons.

The most important hours of Jake's formative years were spent in the saddle: endless trail-riding, horse shows, and foxhunting. Jake was consumed with horseback riding, and, at a time when the countryside was a little more free from car traffic and a lot more open, the experience grounded his connection, love, and passion for the natural world. Along with riding, Jake worked on horse and cattle farms, where he enjoyed the rugged labor, which he credits as an early core experience that has shaped him into the person he is today.

Jake attended Colorado State University where he earned a Bachelors of Equine Science degree (while also nurturing his love of skiing). After graduating and working for a few horse racing stables, Jake took a position in 2002 at a newly formed composting company, Laurel Valley Soils, Inc. Twenty years later, Jake loves his work and being a part of the horticultural and agricultural communities his products support.

In 2010, Jake suffered a spinal cord injury while steeplechase racing, which left him paralyzed from the chest down. With the wonderful support of his family, the equestrian community, and his colleagues at work, Jake made adjustments to his new reality, but did not let it slow him down. Now, taking an active role in his recovery, Jake works with the organization Unite 2 Fight Paralysis (u2fp. org) and, with their support, he and a team of advocates successfully persuaded the Pennsylvania legislature to pass a bill that provides funding for research into curative treatments for spinal cord injury.

Today, Jake, happily married, is a smitten father of two young beautiful children and is watched over by the family Border Collie. Jake remains engaged in the equestrian community and also serves as a township supervisor.

Jesse Liebman was born and raised in New York City, where he attended the Collegiate School, fell in love with Latin and Ancient Greek, and went on to major in Classics at Princeton University. After graduating as Salutatorian of his class in 2003 Jesse later attended the New Actors Workshop conservatory, where he trained with George Morrison and Mike Nichols. He continued studying acting with Michael Howard in his private scene study class.

Over the course of a decade, Jesse acted in several films and television shows. He also acted in and directed his own bilingual production of *Waiting for Godot*, which he performed in Paris in 2009, and, in 2014, acted in the second national tour of *Dirty Dancing: The Classic Story On Stage*. In addition, Jesse worked extensively in theater management and production for the hit Broadway musicals *Wicked* and *Beautiful - The Carole King Musical*, as well as for Hang A Tale, a non-profit theater company.

While pursuing work in acting and theater, Jesse also tutored extensively throughout New York City's private schools, specializing in Latin, Ancient Greek, and essay writing. In 2017, Jesse self-published his first book, *How To Write Any High School Essay: The Essential Guide.* The next year, he founded BOOST TUTORS & MENTORS (www.boosttutorsandmentors.com), a tutoring collective that provides creative solutions to academic problems, boosting confidence and guiding students to independence. He is currently working on books about middle school writing and about tutoring in the 21st century.

Jesse lives happily in Roxbury, CT, with his wife, Kimiye, and his two ~~maniacs~~ daughters, Ruby and Maxine.